ommotion

Downstairs and Are Ready for Them.

We call for backup and head downstairs. . . . John and I are on our own.

We get into a huge struggle with these two on the stairs. They are screaming that we're trying to rob them! They call people to help them fight off the robbers—us! At the same time, they are trying to get to their pockets—where we think their guns are. But we haven't actually seen their guns, and you can't exactly say *Time out! Do you have a gun? Oh, okay, I'm going to take my gun out and shoot you, then.*

. . . so I'm wrestling for my life with this guy. . . . It's a big, bloody battle. I'm pounding his head into the concrete, and he's screaming that he's being robbed. I get him in a full nelson, I have my gun in my hand, and finally our backup arrives. They cuff the guys. Both of these idiots do indeed have guns on them, with hollow-point bullets in them, and there was no doubt both were tyring to "do" us. . . . Both guys were picked out of four lineups, were convicted, and sent away for long terms. That was a satisfying arrest.

UNDER COVER
War Stories from the Seamy Side of Law Enforcement

In riveting first-person accounts of real undercover agents and cops, Hans Halberstadt delivers a harrowing behind-the-scenes look at the brave men and women who leave their families, change their identities, and plunge into the criminal underworld to uphold justice.

UNDER COVER

War Stories from the Seamy Side of Law Enforcement

HANS HALBERSTADT

POCKET BOOKS

New York   London   Toronto   Sydney   Tokyo   Singapore

This book is a work of fiction. Names, characters, places and inci-
dents are products of the author's imagination or are used ficti-
tiously. Any resemblance to actual events or locales or persons
living or dead is entirely coincidental.

An *Original* Publication of POCKET BOOKS

POCKET BOOKS, a division of Simon & Schuster Inc.
1230 Avenue of the Americas, New York, NY 10020

Copyright © 1998 by Hans Halberstadt

ISBN: 0-671-01527-3

First Pocket Books printing August 1998

10 9 8 7 6 5 4 3 2 1

POCKET and colophon are registered trademarks of
Simon & Schuster Inc.

Cover photo by Joshua Sheldon/Photonica

Printed in the U.S.A.

To Officer Truman R. "Bud" Boman,
San Jose Police Department, Badge 2767,
a good cop and a good friend

Acknowledgments

This book has been so much fun to write that I am tempted to keep it going until Tris Coburn, my editor, rips the thing out of my hands. Part of the pleasure has been the opportunity to listen to many wonderful stories, skillfully told. And part of the pleasure, too, has been the privilege of meeting and getting to know some of the most charming, friendly—and often heroic—people I have ever worked with.

Among the friendlies is my good buddy, Det. John Buehler of the Modesto, California, Police Department. Jon has been helping me with these books for several years and has been an invaluable contact. Jon's department is a small one, compared to many across the United States, but I have always been impressed with its cheerful competence, energy, and efficiency in serving the needs of its citizens.

And I am likewise indebted to Layne Lathram, Public Affairs Officer for the U.S. Customs Service, and her boss, Bonni Tischler, Commissioner for Investigation. Customs is virtually unique within the federal government by being open and friendly toward authors about its work and its workers, who have some wonderful stories to tell.

I must also salute my fellow unindicted co-conspirator in this business, the legendary Sam Katz, for hooking me up with Pocket Books and with John Politoski and his NYPD "rabbi," Bob Sobocinski. The fraternity of military and law enforcement nonfiction writers is a small one, and Sam is one of its stars. Instead of seeing this project as competition for his own work, Sam graciously and generously helped with numerous contacts and advice.

Another mentor in my foray into law enforcement has been Ron Martinelli, a superb field training officer when he was with the San Jose Police Department and now a superb law enforcement trainer for jurisdictions and agencies across the western United States. Ron has always been an eloquent evangelist for the patrol officer and has generously allowed me to observe and participate in some of his excellent training. Ron introduced me to the wild, wonderful world of undercover operations and is as guilty as anybody for the perpetration of this book.

Thanks also to Lt. Larry "Lumpy" Lundberg, Sgt. Diane Urban, Sgt. Greg Trapp, Bill Mattos, Mike Thompson, David Wysuph, and the many other police and sheriff's personnel who've helped with this book by providing contacts, reading the material, and suggesting changes.

Finally, I would like to salute all the officers and agents who generously decided to share some of their stories with me—despite their misgivings, despite the tradition of keeping these things private. Not all the stories could be included in the book, but I enjoyed hearing them all.

Contents

CONTENTS

Introduction

Law enforcement can be a funny business, but not always in ways that make you laugh. It is a funny business because weird things happen quite often, and it is a business that attracts weird people—on both sides of the badge. An officer or agent routinely deals with people in crisis, one way or another, and with people who aren't willing to accept the limits imposed by society. And cops are allowed to do all sorts of things the rest of society isn't normally allowed to do—carry guns, deprive people of their liberty, drive thirty miles an hour over the speed limit, and park on sidewalks, for example. This mixture makes for good theater.

When cops deal with the public, they often seem cold, remote, humorless; that's because they are society's garbage collectors, routinely picking up all the smelly, broken, corrosive, and morally decaying human beings they can find. While a few of these human discards can be recycled, most can't. Cops take children away from mothers sometimes, and fathers away from children, and husbands from wives. They deal with anger, grief, and denial all day long, and when a cop or agent does a particularly good job, somebody is usually very unhappy and resentful about it.

Sometimes these resentful people attack the officers with knives, guns, blocks of concrete, tree limbs, scissors, and half-empty bottles of Ripple or Mumm's Cordon Rouge; then, sometimes, they have to be shot and killed. Officers and agents deal with people who seem intent on destroying their own lives and the lives of everyone around them, as quickly as possible, if they can. And almost as soon as you get them off the street and into jail, it seems like they're right back out again, turning tricks, doing deals, assaulting anybody in sight, and ripping off everything that isn't nailed down. If you did work like that for forty hours a week, you'd insulate yourself a bit, too.

There's a tradition that cops don't talk much to anybody except cops. But in the privacy of a patrol car on a slow night "in the hole," or at the end of the shift when the uniform gets exchanged for civilian clothes, many cops are friendly, funny people who like to tell stories. Sometimes the stories are grim, or off-color, or politically incorrect . . . but still hilarious. Police work produces lots of stories, and cops collect them the way some people collect stamps. Many of the most amusing and exotic revolve around undercover assignments.

Here in San Jose, California, those stories get told at Bini's Bar and Grill, an ancient working-man's saloon and restaurant up the street from police headquarters and the main jail. Bini's is usually packed to the gills with off-duty cops, parole agents, and probation officers, all swapping lies with each other over a beer or Bini's legendary breakfasts and lunches.

Once a month the Police Benevolent Association, a group of veteran and retired officers (most now safely exempt from the chain of command) gather for drinks, dinner, and storytelling. These stories have a general theme you might call "Incredibly Dumb Things My Partner Has Done to Me Over the Years." Nearly all the stories poke fun at somebody in the room, and virtually all the stories are hilarious.

It turns out that cops all around the country gather to do pretty much the same thing, to make fun of each other and themselves. So do agents of the FBI, DEA, ATF, customs, and all the smaller agencies. Hang around these guys long enough—five minutes with some of them, ten seconds with others—and you'll start hearing about those "memorable moments in law enforcement." The stories are generally light-hearted and self-deprecating, although some describe tragic events and monumental blunders. Even so, they represent lessons learned on the street and on undercover assignments, and they are part of the informal training process that continues for as long as you carry a gun and a badge.

You'll hear stories about the cop who dressed in drag, with short skirt, big wig, and too much makeup, and picked up more men as a prostitution decoy than the female officers working the same sting. You'll hear about the two women who fought each other to get an off-duty New York cab that was actually being used in a surveillance. You'll hear about the amazingly dumb things criminals will do. You'll hear about the officers who do amazingly dumb things, too, like the officer who can't do anything right and gets hurt so often that his sergeant carries injury report forms preprinted with the guy's name.

This book is a collection of these stories. Most are amusing, but some have a dark side. A few aren't amusing at all. The stories come from around the United States, from local police departments, from state and federal agencies. All the stories are from undercover operations of one sort or another, some deeper than others. I've changed a few names here and there, mostly to protect the guilty, and a couple of officers asked to remain anonymous; I don't usually like to do that, but you have to protect your confidential sources in law enforcement, even when the source is a cop.

UNDER
COVER

Undercover Basics

Working undercover is weird. It is the most challenging, most dangerous, most abrasive, most stressful kind of law enforcement assignment. When you go undercover, you leave the safety and security of the law-abiding world—the paragon of which is the uniformed patrol division of any city's police department. As a rookie cop or agent, you take pride in your short, neat hair and spotless uniform; when you go undercover, you let your hair grow long, sometimes wear grimy clothes, and try not to look like a cop at all.

As a rookie cop, you quickly acquire a disdain for crooks and criminals and avoid their society. When you get assigned to an undercover unit, you might start spending a lot of time with crooks, buying them drinks and getting to know them as people. If you work undercover long enough, you may try their dope, pick up a few of their habits, and go over to the dark side. It happens more often than you might think.

Undercover assignments can also be among the most enjoyable, productive, and challenging for an officer or agent. You need to use all your imagination and intellect, you have to be able to think on your feet, make decisions for yourself, and stay on the right side of the law and department policy, all the time. It takes a special kind of officer or agent (a lunatic, according to some) to do the job well and to survive the experience. But for those who fit the role, it can be the most memorable part of a career.

Covert law enforcement operations are a fairly new phenomenon. Until the problem of drug use became a major issue in the 1960s, few departments or federal agencies executed undercover operations. There was active hostility to the very idea of undercover operations within the FBI until the late 1970s. Now, however, virtually all agencies and jurisdictions use covert methods for catching crooks. Undercover operations are a standard part of law enforcement today for several reasons.

The United States has experienced a tremendous drop in the crime rate, across the board, during the 1990s. This drop is the result of many factors but at the bottom of them all is a rising intolerance for bad behavior. Casual drug use, street prostitution, "strong-arm" robberies, petty theft, and all sorts of other crimes were once way down on the enforcement priority list for many law enforcement agencies. That has changed. There is now an understanding that small crimes lead to big ones, and people that are allowed to get away with petty theft may graduate to more serious crimes.

Undercover operations are one part of the campaign against crime, a complement to the uniformed officer on the street. Often, undercover and uniformed officers work together on short-term tactical operations. Together, they've accomplished what was considered impossible just a few years ago—made New York a pleasant and safe city again, for example. The same thing on a smaller scale has happened in many cities and towns across the country.

Undercover operations are used against criminal activities that are generally immune to conventional uniformed operations. At the local level, this usually includes "street crimes" and "vice." Street crimes are purse snatching, strong-arm robbery, assault, and similar activities. Vice crimes typically involve prostitution (both street prostitution and call girls), gambling, and the commission of lewd acts in public. Local law enforcement agencies usually have a drug enforcement unit, too, that functions mostly undercover.

A typical undercover case has three basic phases:

The case begins with the *planning phase* during which a team is recruited, organized, search warrants and wiretap authorization obtained, intelligence gathered, informants debriefed, and funding secured. The planning for an undercover "op" can take weeks or months for a complicated major federal case against, say, an organized crime family, or it might take five minutes for a local department's street crimes team trolling for hookers and strong-arm robbers.

Next comes the *covert phase* during which evidence is collected—drugs bought, incriminating conversations recorded, criminal conduct documented. This is the actual undercover part of the operation, although only one or a few members of the whole operation are likely to actually be operating covertly. The rest will be providing security, surveillance, and keeping up with the inevitable stacks of paper. The covert phase can last minutes or years.

And, finally, the *overt phase* begins when the arrest team pops out of the shrubbery, yells "Surprise! You're under arrest!", charges are filed, and the case prosecuted. Very often the documentation of criminal conduct is so strong in a well-executed undercover operation that the people arrested cut their losses and "cop a plea." Most of the people arrested during undercover operations have long arrest records, and most accept time in prison as a fact of life.

A Case Study

My own local jurisdiction—San Jose, California—is typical of urban police departments. The city has a population of about 850,000, with a police force of about 1,300 sworn officers. That makes San Jose the eleventh largest city in the United States, and with a police department a bit smaller on a per-capita basis than other cities of its size, about as typical an American law enforcement agency as you'll find anywhere.

The San Jose Police Department has been using undercover operations for years, with some dramatic successes. When the downtown area was suddenly invaded by prostitutes in the late 1970s, the Street Crimes unit launched a very successful major campaign against the streetwalkers. The department's burglary detail set up a long-term "sting" operation in a bar that brought in half a million dollars worth of stolen goods, solved three old murders, and recovered tons of stolen property. The drug unit is constantly buying marijuana, coke, crack, LSD, and heroin from small and large dealers within the city, then putting the "habeas grabbus" on the crooks and taking them downtown to the basement of the main jail for booking. When a crook started ripping the gold necklaces off the necks of old ladies downtown, the Street Crimes unit used theatrical makeup to turn three young police women into elderly, frail-looking decoys—and nabbed the "perp" on the first day out.

Like the undercover officers and agents of other jurisdictions around the country, San Jose's covert crew uses imagination and a wicked sense of humor to take care of business and stay sane. Once in a while, to lighten things up, one of the male officers will hit the street in "drag," picking up "johns" looking for prostitution action. One of these guys got more "dates" than the genuine female decoys working with him, around the corner. He's never lived that one down.

Undercover operations come in all sizes and styles. At

4

the most basic level is the plainclothes officer, a guy or gal wearing normal business clothes with a pistol in a shoulder holster and a badge discreetly on the belt. These officers—the only people who drive full-sized Ford Crown Victorias—are pretty obvious to anybody paying attention to what's happening on the street. Normally, a plainclothes officer isn't really trying very hard to fool anybody but just trying to be a bit more inconspicuous on the street. Even so, they make their share of busts.

Vice and street-crime undercover officers go a bit deeper into the role. They might not carry a gun; if they are "carrying," it certainly won't be easily visible in an ankle holster or hidden completely under the waistband. A vice officer's hair will probably get pretty long, and he might grow a beard. Female vice cops tend to wear too much makeup, low-cut blouses, high-cut skirts or shorts, and a *very* inviting smile. Even so, these officers show up for roll call at the beginning of a shift, then go home at night.

The really serious long-term deep-cover work is seldom done by local law enforcement agencies, but by the Federal Bureau of Investigation (FBI), the Drug Enforcement Agency (DEA), the U.S. Customs Service, and other federal and state agencies. These operations often involve long-term placement of individual agents deep within a criminal organization, often at tremendous personal risk. Very seldom will an agent have any kind of weapon to defend against attack—except his or her wits and wisdom, and perhaps some martial-arts skills. One Maryland State Police officer, working a murder-for-hire case, had his "wire" discovered by one of the people he was investigating. His cover team, listening horrified to the radio transmission from the device, recorded the gunshots that killed him.

Undercover operations are dangerous in other ways, too. Deep-cover cases can last for years. During that time the agent will live in an undercover apartment, away from his or her family, completely isolated from them. The agent will associate daily with the worst sort of people—organized crime bosses and their associates, drug kingpins, crooked cops, outlaw gang members—and will almost inevitably become, at some level, friends with some of them. Undercover agents on long-duration operations often fall into an illicit romantic relationship to temporarily take the place of their normal marriage. Sometimes these illicit relationships are sanctioned by the supervising agency, like the FBI.

Agents and Agencies

What does it take to be a successful undercover agent? Quite a lot, actually. It is not a job for which many officers are well suited. You need to be an actor, to start with. You need to have a good deal of self-confidence. An undercover officer needs to be able to act independently, but also follow instructions.

Some cops love undercover work. It can be extremely productive—you can make a dozen arrests in a shift and take a lot of perps off the street. You can, as Ron Martinelli describes later, also get assaulted half a dozen times during a shift, too.

You need to learn to live the role, without crossing over to the dark side. You need to learn to stand like a crook, not a cop. One sure way to get "burned" on the street is to use the posture and mannerisms common to cops—the typical "triangular stance," with feet apart and arms crossed, for example.

You need to learn how to tail somebody in traffic without causing an accident. That's not easy to do when you have to bust red lights in a plainclothes car without light-bar or siren. If you get in a wreck, the liability is all yours. If you don't run the light, you'll never maintain the tail.

Turf Wars

Many agencies and jurisdictions enforce the same laws, and this often creates problems for everybody concerned. The FBI, DEA, and U.S. Customs Service all go after drug traffickers. Sometimes they all gang up on the same people at the same time; sometimes they compete with each other.

The FBI is the most famous and most lavishly funded federal agency, a major component of the Department of Justice, with a broad charter for enforcing laws against organized crime, money laundering, some murders, some kinds of pornography, fraud, and many other crimes. The Drug Enforcement Agency and Department of Alcohol, Tobacco, and Firearms (a component of the Department of the Treasury) are smaller components of the U.S. federal law enforcement effort, with more limited scope and funding.

Although it doesn't get as much attention in the news media, the U.S. Customs Service has a tremendously broad assignment and executes many very effective covert operations. Customs enforces over four hundred laws on everything from drugs to pornography, and it has unique powers. It can, for example, often execute searches and seizures without a warrant. It seizes more drugs, in fact, than the DEA, the FBI, and all other federal and local agencies combined. While the FBI recently made a big deal about the arrests of eighty child-pornography distributors, Customs agents made over three hundred similar arrests during the same period, with fewer agents and a much smaller budget. Customs agents are typically the funniest, craziest, most creative, and innovative federal agents you'll encounter.

Auditioning for the Part

Covert assignments are not for every officer or agent, and many cops simply cannot fit into the role. Some people are very good at it, others can't stop looking like cops no matter what they're wearing. The process of recruiting, training, and managing covert officers and agents is more complex and less formalized than training for the uniformed officer. A lot of it is informal, on-the-job training, although the FBI and other large agencies do have formal programs for apprentice "narklings" (as Anthony Tait calls new covert narcotics agents). For anybody involved in making drug buys, this will involve instruction on accounting for all the money involved, documenting cases, and related clerical work.

The way recruitment works within the San Jose Police Department, the Street Crimes, Narcotics, or Burglary units will advertise a vacancy and accept applications. Anybody who applies is tested primarily on their knowledge of applicable law. Once an individual is accepted, he or she gets a short course on formal procedures and policies of the unit.

"In the Street Crimes unit," retired Sgt. Aubrey Parrot says, "we train by role-playing exercises. We have officers play the role of johns, decoys, cover officers, and show the new undercover officer basic moves that way. You are trained on the basics of "tailing" a vehicle without being "burned," how to pass off a tail to another vehicle, then to pick it up again. The best way to learn this is from other officers who've been successful."

Then it is time to hit the street. The new member of the team is normally assigned to the least critical role—perhaps as a "cover" officer whose primary job is to protect the decoy and who otherwise doesn't have much to do until things go bad. You sit on the corner, looking and smelling like a derelict "wino" and basically wait, watch, and listen. "You bring them along slowly," Aubrey says, "and see who has a knack for it, who enjoys it. Some people really get off on undercover work while others are never comfortable. The suspects on the street are very good at burning cops, and we look for people who can be convincing. Some guys are very good at it, and I had guys on the Street Crimes unit who never made a prostitution "date" in the whole three years they worked for me. On the other hand, I've made four cases *while in uniform!*"

Part of the fun of covert operations can be the competition between officers to make arrests, as Aubrey suggests. It is pretty difficult to convince a hooker that you're seriously interested in a date when you're in uniform, but he and a few other older, veteran officers did it occasionally. "Some of the young guys were *good!*" he says. "Turning them loose on the public was almost entrapment, they were so convincing as street scum."

Law of the Land

One of the major issues in undercover ops is the charge of entrapment. Defendants sometimes claim that the arresting officer talked them into committing a crime the defendant didn't really intend to commit. On rare occasions, it has probably happened, but most departments and agencies take special pains to avoid the charge.

A Count, an Amount, and an Overt Act

In most jurisdictions, drug, prostitution, or similar undercover arrests require documentation of a chain of events. In a burglary sting operation, for example, the person should posses stolen property—and know that it is stolen. That knowledge factor is the part that is hard to prove in court. Perps often help out by saying "Here's something I ripped off from a little old lady down the street." The conversation on tape needs to develop that awareness.

When the San Jose Street Crimes unit goes after "johns" (a prostitute's customers), they are looking for a *count,* an *amount,* and an *overt act.* That means the guy has to first solicit a sexual act for money. He can't just say, "Hey, baby, wanna get laid? Hop in the car" to a female decoy officer. That's consensual sex, and it is legal. As soon as he says, "What's it going to cost? How about 'head' for $20?" you've got the count—soliciting oral sex—and the amount, $20. The law here requires more than that, though; the john has to do something to actively show that he's serious. "Okay," the decoy officer says, "come over to my motel room." She walks down to the Best Western motel on Second Street. When the john drives his car through the "golden arches" over the entrance to the motel parking lot, he's ready to be arrested. "If the john gets cold feet walking up to the door with the girl, we'll normally let him go," one officer says. "Most of them, though, will be staring at the girl's butt so hard that they don't notice anything until the uniformed officer taps him on the shoulder and says, 'You're under arrest.' "

When the Street Crimes unit goes after the muggers and robbers in the downtown area, they station a decoy wino, passed out on the sidewalk or in a doorway, clutching a ghetto-blaster, and with a wallet visible in a pants pocket. The decoy will be covered by a "point" officer observing from a parked van nearby. A cover officer will be within fifty feet or so—a cab driver, perhaps, waiting at the curb. The decoy officer (liberally splashed with half a quart of Night Train or Ripple) will have a radio earpiece plugged into his ear but out of sight.

These operations are especially productive just after the first and fifteenth of the month when Social Security checks have been distributed and cashed by the derelicts in the community, and before the money has all been spent on cigarettes and booze.

It usually doesn't take long for somebody to come along and inspect the body, the radio, and the wallet. If somebody just picks up the radio or wallet from the apparently unconscious decoy, the charge is "grand theft, person;" that can be either a low-grade felony or a misdemeanor. The unit really isn't interested in anything but solid felonies—the kind that will put somebody away for a while, so the decoy holds on to the radio when the suspect tries to take it. If the radio is taken by *force, fear, or threats of violence* ("Gimme that radio or I'm gonna kick your ass!") the charge gets bumped up to "strong-arm robbery," a felony. The decoy releases the radio or wallet, and the guy walks down the street where the arrest team moves in and takes him down, cuffs him, does a preliminary search, and takes him into custody. It is a high-bail felony and qualifies for a "third strike" that, under California law, can put somebody away for life.

Tools of the Trade

Undercover officers invest a tremendous amount of time, energy, imagination, and money into their disguises and personal equipment. For a vice cop working "street crimes" for a major U.S. city, that will involve assembly of a costume of some sort—maybe filthy Levi's, a smelly shirt, a jacket dipped in grease and beer. Or it might mean, for a female decoy officer, a blond wig, a skirt that is too short, a blouse that shows too much cleavage, and six inch spike heels. For an FBI agent like Graham Desvernine, impersonating a Mafia don, this costume will require an expensive suit, a lot of gold chains and jewelry, and a large, expensive car.

Weapons

Nearly every *uniformed* law enforcement officer or agent carries a handgun, primarily for personal protection.

Undercover officers sometimes carry weapons as well, but instead of the full-sized nine-millimeter or forty-caliber autoloaders typically issued to street cops today, the choice is restricted to smaller, more concealable weapons. These range from small forty-five-caliber Colt Commanders and their imitators, down to tiny twenty-two-caliber revolvers and derringers.

The problem of hiding these little pistols is a real challenge. Ankle holsters are one option, as are holsters that hide the gun entirely behind the waistband of the officer's pants. Vice cops normally stash their pistols under the seat, or might sit on them, or build a secret compartment into the vehicle to hold the weapon.

Wires and Recorders

Successful prosecution of a case in court always requires documentation of criminal behavior by the person charged. Getting that kind of documentation for major drug cases and many other major felony crimes can be a real challenge; therefore, a lot of imagination and expense has been invested in developing specialized recording devices just for this application.

The most common way to document criminal behavior is with audio recordings on tape. The officer or agent can carry a recorder—either an off-the-shelf microcassette model commonly used for dictation or a specialized model designed for law enforcement application. These tiny machines will record up to forty-five minutes of conversation on one side of a tape. They are very quiet in operation and can be hidden inside a pack of cigarettes or in a boot.

Much larger but offering hours of recording is the Nagra. This recorder is a version of a machine originally designed for the motion picture industry. It uses reel-to-reel tape and can record up to six hours continuously.

It is a fairly bulky machine, about the size of a book, and much more difficult to conceal. Even so, Anthony Tait, whose stories about his work inside the Hells Angels are included later, wore one in a harness attached to his back. The Nagra nearly proved Tait's undoing when one of the gang greeted him with a slap on the back—and noticed the metallic object under his jacket. "What's that?" the Hells Angel wanted to know. "My gun," Tait said, "don't mess with it or it might go off!" The FBI also supplied Tait with dual Nagras and a sequencer hidden behind the seat in his truck. These machines could record twelve continuous hours of conversation. The FBI tried to get Tait to hide a Nagra in one of his boots, a suggestion that didn't get far—the machine is far too large and bulky to remain unnoticed for long.

Besides the recorders, many undercover operators carry a transmitter—known universally as a "wire." Many makes and models are available, but all have quite limited range, often just a few hundred yards. Somebody, uncomfortably stuffed into a closet, the trunk of a car, or in the rear of some decrepit truck, needs to provide surveillance when wires are used and operate the receiver and recorder.

While early transmitters were fairly bulky, recent models are getting amazingly compact and are becoming virtually undetectable. Tiny television and audio transmitters are now available that are so small that they can fit inside the frame of a pair of glasses. Similar systems are installed in caps, pagers, and all sorts of other common objects. Television cameras and transmitters about the size of a small box of matches can be purchased for only a few hundred dollars and will transmit a signal that can be picked up a half mile away.

Laser beams offer another technique for recording conversations. An invisible laser can be bounced off a window a mile or so distant and its reflection can be used to "read" conversations inside the room. The FBI used this method to record discussions between Anthony Tait and outlaw motorcycle-gang members in Anchorage. The agents monitored the conversations from their own office downtown, over a mile away.

Criminals know very well that undercover agents normally carry recorders or transmitters, and they often frisk people they don't know well on first meeting. Some sophisticated crooks even use RF signal detectors to test for transmitters, but seldom do these devices work on the frequencies used by law enforcement "wires." Developments in covert radio design have made both precautions pretty ineffective.

Search Warrant Etiquette

Sooner or later a covert operation will probably go overt. When it does, the overt phase will likely begin with the service of search warrants on the homes and businesses of suspects. Often, the team executing the warrant will trash the place, leaving it looking like the aftermath of a bad tornado. While it is often legal to empty the contents of all the drawers in the house, to cut holes in walls, and to disassemble the contents of the refrigerator—and then leave the mess—it naturally angers the residents. Some officers enjoy this opportunity for a little revenge on the bad guys, but the technique often results in getting innocent people hurt. What normally happens is that the resident bad guy takes his frustrations out on his wife or girlfriend and beats the hell out of her.

Instead, says FBI Special Agent Tim McKinley, a better method is to do a thorough search, then put everything back nice and neat, leaving the place cleaner than you found it. The resident bad guy will still be mad when he finds out about the warrant, but you haven't made an enemy of his wife. She is, in fact, a potential informant. If you've left your business card with the lady, she might give you a call telling you where to find him the next time he slaps her around before driving off to deliver five pounds of cocaine.

Living Under Cover

Maintaining normal family relationships while working in deep undercover operations is a tremendous challenge. The divorce rate is extremely high, partly because the lifestyle of the "dark side" is often highly attractive.

"The undercover lifestyle was very attractive to me and to most operatives I have known," one undercover agent says. "We enjoy the huge expense accounts and fancy cars. Some get involved with a woman or two, and if you're married, you have the perfect alibi. Instead of having to sneak home at three in the morning, you don't come home at all, for weeks at a time. You have an undercover apartment, stories about who you are, and time and money. You always have to wonder, though, *Is what I am doing going to bite me in the butt later on?* You try to avoid getting involved with the sister of a bad guy, for example.

"But some of us have our horror stories. While working undercover and married, I became involved in a romantic relationship with a woman who was in tight with an organized-crime figure. The relationship was approved by department management as part of the operation—we expected to get useful information from her. We started dating, and it started getting really messy. I thought I had it all under control, then one night she told me that she loved me. I got up out of bed, called another investigator at 3 A.M., and he and I went and had breakfast. We decided that I would never see her again, ever. And I never did, either. When we took the case down a year later, though, one of the district attorneys asked when we were going to debrief this girl. I asked to be present during the interview, to break it to her and let her know that I was a cop to her face. This lawyer interpreted that request as an indication that I had something to hide. I denied that vehemently—a lie, of course, because I was hiding something. But I genuinely liked the girl. And as it turned out, we never interviewed that girl because of their belief that she could be a threat to me and the case. Thank God. To this day, she doesn't know I was a cop and we never developed the information she was supposed to provide. All she knows is that one night, after a several-month relationship, she told me that she loved me—and that I got up, got dressed, left, and she's never heard from me again."

Squeezed
by the Vice

Ron Martinelli is a street cop, criminologist, law enforcement trainer, and author of several law enforcement training manuals on street prostitution, gangs, and unarmed defensive combat. Back in the 1980s his department (San Jose, California) had to deal with a sudden influx of street prostitution in the downtown core area. Along with the prostitutes were many small-time street criminals—strong-arm robbers and muggers—who often preyed upon the homeless street people. Ron was part of the Street Crimes unit responsible for dealing with these kinds of crimes, and here's how they did it.

In the early 1980s, the city of San Jose invested millions of dollars in a downtown redevelopment project. New office buildings, hotels, shops, restaurants, and other business appeared, and a lot of new people started going downtown, too. At the same time, though, the downtown area was heavily populated by a lot of gangsters, parolees, prostitutes, alcoholic transient homeless, and the criminally insane who had been placed in boarding houses by the state in that area. At the same time that downtown business grew, crime grew just as fast.

Customers and business people were being robbed, mugged, and "hit on" by prostitutes. San Jose Police Department started a special undercover plainclothes and uniformed unit for the downtown area, and that's how the Street Crimes unit began.

It was quite a challenge to be assigned to this unit for several reasons. First, when you're a cop, you are a hunter—always alert for problems before they happen, always sensitive to what's going on around you, always watching your back, always keeping an eye on people nearby. You don't look, act, think, or dress like someone who can be victimized! But your job on the Street Crimes unit is to get robbed, to look like someone that a crook can control and exploit. That takes some imagination and some acting.

I found, when I first started on the unit, that I could dress up like a victim and walk down the street—and nobody would bother me at all! It was quite disappointing, so I had to reevaluate what I was doing. What I realized was that I wasn't acting like a victim. I was dressed like one but still doing my "scan," taking aggressive or evasive action, just like I did in uniform on patrol. I'd interviewed hundreds of victims as a patrol officer, and so I mentally went over all those reports. Then I used what I remembered to teach myself to look and act like somebody who could be victimized.

One thing I did was to avoid eye contact with people who were potential threats. I started clutching my briefcase as if it were full of gold bars and diamonds. I acted like somebody on the subway in New York City—very careful to not annoy anybody else.

We had a variety of disguises, and I enjoyed this acting part of the work. One of the problems downtown was that a lot of the homeless people were getting robbed by gang members or other homeless individuals, so a good homeless street person disguise was one of my costumes. We took an old wallet and stapled a couple of $5 bills inside with their corners showing. I wore an old Navy pea coat, rubbed in the gutter, dipped in a little Night Train wine. I had longish hair and a beard, both of which would look wild and unkempt if I let them. Then I'd find a park bench, or a doorway, or sit on the sidewalk beside a building, and wait for business.

Parked at the curb, usually no more than about thirty feet away, was our grimy undercover van, the "Trojan Pig," with at least two officers watching me. Up the street was another, and one or two would be stationed across the street. We all took turns playing the victim, rotating assignments.

It was very difficult work and sometimes emotionally exhausting. You've got to have the right mindset because you *know* you're going to be the victim of some sort of violent act! We were trying to catch the people doing the armed robberies, the felony "strong-arm" muggings, the worst street predators who used violence against the weakest citizens. These crooks were like sharks, cruising for victims, then attacking violently.

Very many of our arrests involved fights, foot pursuits, and officer injuries. Most of the time you had to deal with somebody armed with a weapon of some sort. I have been robbed with every imaginable weapon—guns, knives, bottles (broken and otherwise), tree branches, pipes, rocks, bricks, and sticks with nails protruding from the end. I've had people threaten, intimidate, punch, and throw me against a building, all to get control of me. And not just once a night but normally from *eight to twelve times* in a single shift!

A person who is willing to prey on others using violence and intimidation is a special kind of crook, a personality profile totally different from a burglar, for example. It is usually a macho kind of bully who takes perverse pleasure in seeing the fear in your eyes. A burglar doesn't want to have anything to do with you, but part of the payoff for street thugs is scaring and hurting victims. They were among the worst kind of criminal. When we did checks on these guys, their rap sheets often included convictions for rape, aggravated assault, robbery, assault with deadly weapons—and a lot were on parole from homicide convictions!

Typically, the way we'd get them was like this: I'd sit someplace, eyes down, apparently drunk, sleepy, or stoned. The wallet with the two $5 bills would be clutched in one hand, visible to the crook. The guy would walk past, about thirty feet or so, then turn and come back, like a shark circling prey. When that happens, and they start looking around at the ground, you know what's next. The guy is looking for some kind of weapon—anything handy.

Of course, the adrenaline is really pumping. Even though you've got your body armor on, and one hand on your pistol inside the jacket, you're in a very vulnerable position. If the crook really wants to slit your throat or shoot you, and some do, the backup officers can't prevent it—you're on your own for those first critical seconds! The crooks didn't know it, but I always had my pistol pointed right at them and ready to fire if they were serious about hurting me.

A good felony strong-arm arrest requires that the crook use force or fear to take the wallet, so we tried to hold on. The crook typically would start tugging on the wallet then punch you if you didn't let go. All this takes tremendous concentration and focus. Your heart is pounding; you're loaded with adrenaline; your mind is going a mile a minute, but you can't let the crook see any of that!

So the crook might be standing over you, with a broken bottle at your throat, cutting you a little just to show he means business. Then you have to let him take the money, and you *hope* he walks away.

As soon as the crook has the wallet, you use the hand signal to have him arrested, and the other officers come pouring out of the van and from across the street. This is when you're likely to have a foot pursuit and a fight. We always tried to keep the arrests very quick and to keep the decoy out of the action. Not only does the decoy have all the extra gear on, but you want it to look like the cops stumbled on something by accident and not blow the decoy's cover.

Even though we usually avoided it, I sometimes got so mad at the crook that I chased him down myself!

Hunting in the Duck Pond

The prostitutes were concentrated in what we called the "duck pond," an area about four blocks wide by two blocks long, just south of the downtown area. We decided to go after the prostitutes, the pimps, and their "johns," or customers. We figured that the fastest way to shut the activity down was to get the word out to the potential customers that buying sex and soliciting women on the street wasn't a safe thing to do in our jurisdiction.

We formed teams of five officers with a reasonably pretty female officer as the decoy. To avoid any charges of possible entrapment, our decoys didn't even dress up like hookers but wore normal, fairly conservative clothes typical of the college students at the university nearby, or something a woman might wear to go shopping— jeans, a normal blouse, maybe a sweater or pullover— but nothing tight or revealing.

Our unit would run a prostitution sting operation for about a month until the activity was pretty well suppressed, then work a robbery sting for a month or so, then maybe come back to the duck pond for another sting. Another team took over the prostitution-sting work as soon as we departed, so the pressure was always on.

When we were ready for one of these "john sting" operations, we'd book a room in one of the motels that normally catered to the activity. The ideal room was one at ground level, facing the street, right at the entrance to the motel parking lot. That room would be turned into a processing center with a uniformed officer and everything needed to completely book the freshly arrested and deeply disappointed john, each of whom would be handcuffed, searched, photographed, fingerprinted, and checked for outstanding arrest warrants, all in less than fifteen minutes. And speed was pretty important, because we had a *lot* of work for the booking officer to do!

Now, I believe the *primary* objective for somebody in law enforcement is to go home safe and sound after work. You're no good to anybody if you get hurt or killed. We want to make our arrests with the very lowest level of danger of injury to the decoy, the arresting officers, and the criminal. There is a tremendous amount of crime associated with prostitution, often directed at the prostitutes, either by pimps or customers. So our decoy officer was always armed, and she was always close to her back-up officers. She communicated with us with hand signals that indicated a solicitation, an arrest, and a threat-potential. She could let us know covertly if a weapon was visible—and sometimes it was—or if the john smelled of alcohol or marijuana.

The team involved the decoy, the uniformed officer in the motel, an undercover chase car parked nearby with two officers inside, and one or two officers on the sidewalk within close reach. We were all dressed pretty much like street people; in fact, we all looked like scum.

Part of my cover assignment was to act as a taxi driver. I learned how to drive a cab, and we bought a cab, and set it up for these stings, complete with meter and radio. The radio, though, was a police version. I could cruise around, or wait at the curb, and look perfectly normal.

If you knew what you were looking at, the area around the decoy was saturated with cops with plenty of backup support should anything go wrong. We were all wired for good communication, and we tended to blend into the woodwork.

Our basic tactic for the decoy was to have her walk slowly down the street or stand in one spot. And just having that one woman on the street produced an *amazing* amount of activity! It hadn't taken long for this neighborhood to get a reputation as the place to go to find a prostitute, so there was a lot of customer activity, and they were hitting on any woman in sight. Big mistake!

The real prostitutes quickly figured out what was going on, often within a few minutes, and cleared out of the area leaving all the business to us. The street people found the whole thing pretty entertaining and would hang around to watch. And it was pretty entertaining, too, if you knew what you were watching.

Doing the Circle Jerk

It was quite normal to make fifteen to twenty-five arrests in a two-hour period with just one decoy and one team, but on some Friday nights we'd run a "doubleheader" with two teams and two decoys. Then we'd have cars waiting in line, down the street and around the block, double-parked! Other cars would circle the block, cruising for action, doing what we called the "circle jerk."

When any of these guys saw a girl they wanted, they'd just wait their turn for her attention. Normally, a prostitute services a guy in about fifteen minutes, so they all knew she'd be back for another customer pretty quick, and that's just how it worked. The johns got a different kind of trick than they expected, though.

The normal procedure involved the john driving up to the girl standing on the curb and making a solicitation through the open passenger-side window. She would never actually get in the car with the guy but would come over and inspect the interior and the guy while negotiating. All the dialogue was recorded on tape, and once the solicitation had been made, our girl signaled that she was ready for the arrest. At the same time, she signaled if the guy seemed to have a threat potential and if he seemed to be under the influence of anything.

Two or three times a month, one of these guys would show a weapon and try to force the decoy into the car with him. When that happened, the whole team pounced on that guy immediately and forcefully, and he was placed in a "felony prone" position and handcuffed before he knew what hit him. It must have looked pretty strange to suddenly see all these scummy derelicts and winos pulling guns and badges and jumping all over the poor unfortunate john!

But normally, the decoy tells the john to meet her at the motel down the block, and she walks down the sidewalk while he finds a place to park. She guides him to the room, opens the door with her key, and lets him enter first—to be met by the uniformed cop who smiles and says, "You are under arrest."

Here Comes Da Judge

One of our municipal court judges was seeing a lot of these prostitutes in court and wanted to know more about what was really going on out on the street, so I invited him to come along with me on some undercover ops. I told him to dress like a "geek," so he combed his hair back, wore an old madras shirt, and put a Band-Aid on the frame of his glasses, then I took him downtown to meet the girls.

"Here's my cousin from Modesto," I told the women, and they fell for it perfectly. He talked to women that he'd sentenced in court, and they still didn't recognize him! He asked them about what the business was like, how much they made, and was hearing a completely different story than the one he got in court. One girl, I remember, told him she made over $90,000 in the previous year, and others had similar stories of making $400 to $700 per night on weekends. The girls were hitting on him. It was a real eye-opener.

Actually, he learned a lot more about the streets than just about prostitution. On one occasion, we watched a prostitute pick up a john, then lead him off to an alley for the deal. We noticed two guys follow the pair, and we went to investigate. We crawled up to the alley, and the trio was in the middle of what we call an "armed 211," or armed robbery. I pushed the judge out of the way, then "proned" all four out at gunpoint, called for a backup, and arrested them all. It was quite an education for the judge!

The Phantom Stutterer

When I first started working Vice, I really wanted to come up with a way to make good arrests, and the way to do that was to be sure the prostitute did all the talking. That's important in court because we often are accused of entrapping people in these sting operations, and I came up with a plan to make sure the girl talked herself into a solid conviction. Here's how I did it:

First, I got an old pickup truck from a drug-seizure case and plastered some San Jose State (the nearby university) decals on the back. Then I got some San Jose State Maintenance Department patches and had them sewn on some old blue coveralls. I loaded the truck up with some commercial mops, brooms, and cleaning supplies in the back. It was really grimy, and, suddenly, I was a janitor from the local college.

I completely sanitized the truck of anything that could

HANS HALBERSTADT

appear to be police-related, making what we call a
"cold" vehicle. Then, I wanted to create the impression
that I was anything except a cop, a two-stage plan. The
first step was to burn a small amount of marijuana in
the vehicle; the odor is unmistakable. Second, I used a
little bourbon as mouthwash. When I rolled up to a girl
on the street and she came over to check me and the
van out—bingo, she was ready to go!

But my technique went farther than that. Since I
wanted the girl to do *all* the talking, I invented a character I called "The Phantom Stutterer." I had long hair
and a beard at the time, and I didn't look, or smell, like
any cop the girl was likely to have met (on duty, anyway). With this getup, I was ready to hit the street.

You Are B-b-b-busted

At the height of the problem, we'd often have fifty or
sixty girls working the street on a Friday or Saturday
night, so it wasn't difficult finding one. I'd roll up to a
corner, and five or six girls would fight over me. Competition was intense!

That put the pressure on the girl to do a fast "safety
check." Before she'd get in the car, while negotiating
with the john, every hooker inspects the guy to see if
he's safe, not a cop and not a nut case. Any hint of
police equipment will warn her off; she looks for the
usual stuff, plus flashlight, radio gear, even dark socks.
But with the odor of dope and booze, and with me and
my scrubby beard and long hair, they were in the car
pretty quick!

"Hey, baby, what you looking for?" she would typically ask.

Well, I didn't want to get accused of leading her into
the bust, so I just stuttered nervously something like, "W-w-
w-well, I-I-I-I-I'm l-l-l-l-o-o-o-o-ok-k-king f-f-f-or . . . ," and

I could drag it out for a long time! She'd usually get tired of the delay and make the suggestion for me.

"Hey, baby, are you looking for a 'date,'?" and the term "date" is a euphemism for sex. "What kind of date you want?"

"W-w-w-w-h-h-hat I-I-I-I-I'd-d-d-d-d . . . ha, I-I-I-I w-w-w-w-a-a-a-a-nt is, is . . ." I would say, but the girl would always interrupt.

"You want some 'head,' baby?" Oral sex is always the quickest "car job" for these women, and the key to profits for them was speedy service.

"Yes!" I always said clearly because a clear response is important in court.

The girl then hugs you; the customer thinks this is affection, but the girl is actually "frisking" the john for weapons, body armor, radio, or a badge. I had a gun, but it was hidden, and the badge was under my seat. All I had actually on me was a police ID card, a set of handcuffs, and a microcassette tape recorder tucked in one sock.

Once the girl hugs you, she opens the glove box, checks the visors, looks at the registration, feels around under the seat, looking for anything that might reveal an undercover cop. She'll play games with you, asking, "Are you a cop? Are you *sure* you aren't a cop?" Your answer needs to be very convincing. I'd stutter through all these questions and tests and instructions.

Then you drive around for a few minutes while she checks to see if you're being tailed. Normally, too, the girl would demand that you touch her breasts or crotch area, something cops are prohibited from doing even in a sting operation. "Touch me," she'll usually say, "someplace a cop wouldn't touch me!" This is another test. If you do it, she will use it against you in court.

If you're reluctant, she'll take your hand and try to place it inside her top. The way I stopped that was to act very nervous and excited . . . and to drive *really* badly! I'd start weaving around, getting close to parked cars and other traffic. The girl would quickly get really nervous and freak out! I could act very nervous, and they were convinced I wasn't a cop. You could almost see the girl thinking, *This guy is a real freak; let's give him a quick head job and get rid of him!*

So we'd go to her favorite hideaway with two cover cars following on parallel streets. Just to seal the deal, I tried to get her to repeat the offer:

"N-n-now, wh-wh-what are we g-g-g-onna d-d-do?" I would ask.

"It's 'head' for forty bucks, honey," she'd typically respond.

"An-an-and d-d-d-do I p-p-p-pay fi-fi-first?"

"Oh, honey, you *always* pays first!" she said.

Then I'd take my police ID out of my pocket and hand it to her, saying, "D-d-d-d-do y-y-y-you t-t-take p-p-p-plastic?"

She'd look at the card, study it, see the San Jose Police Department logo, and start squealing, "What? You ain't the *po-lice!* You *can't* be a cop! What is *this???*"

And then I said, "H-h-h-h-honey, y-y-y-you are b-b-b-b-*busted!*"

The Trojan Pig

We had a lot of ruses to use with the girls, and one of the best was a beat up, old van we got from a drug-seizure case. Because of the way we used it, I called this van the "Trojan Pig."

Now, prostitutes *love* johns with vans. A van lets her "turn the trick" in the vehicle, rapidly and in private, with less risk from the cops. But a prostitute quickly learns to inspect every john, and every john's vehicle, for any hint of possible connection with a police undercover operation. She checks shoes to see if they look like cop shoes, the belt for a basket-weave pattern standard on our "leathers," the keys in the ignition for a telltale municipal tag. I sanitized the van and myself of anything that would connect me to law enforcement.

Well, the van had a curtain across the back, right behind the seats, for privacy. Naturally, the girl would always pull the curtain back to inspect the inside of the van to make sure no cops were hiding back there. And, in fact, there was a cop back there, right in plain sight, but they never noticed until it was too late! Here's how it worked:

The guy driving would be dressed like a typical john, but the guy in back, the arresting officer, would be in full ninja outfit—black from head to toe with just a little slit for the eyes. You could curl up in the back, right in the stepwell behind the passenger seat, and essentially become invisible! It was very weird to be sitting back there, have the girl pull back the curtain, and look right at you. But none ever noticed me.

All the Trojan Pig operations were memorable, but none more than the time we picked up a prostitute on her way home from the market. We were cruising the duck pond and noticed this woman walking back from the market with a bag of groceries. Well, she might have been coming back from the store, but she still had something to sell! She notices my partner, catches his eye, and he slows down. She solicits him, then hops in the van, complete with groceries, to seal the deal. As they all do, she pulls back the curtain, looks me right in the face without seeing me, then does a quick inspection of the van, concludes that it is safe, and turns back to talk to my partner.

Okay, we're cruising down the street at about ten or fifteen miles an hour. They make a deal. When the deal is agreed to, my partner gives the lady the bad news, "San Jose Vice—you're under arrest." At exactly the same time, I reached out and put my hand on her shoulder to restrain her.

She was so startled by both these developments that

she jumped up out of the seat banging her head on the roof of the van! Then she tries to bail out of the vehicle while we're still moving! My partner grabs onto her, across the big engine housing that was common in van design of that era, and tries to keep her in the vehicle and steer at the same time. She pulls him halfway across the engine housing until his feet can't reach the pedals. He's holding onto her with one hand, the steering wheel with the other, and rapidly losing control of both.

The girl is squealing and screaming bloody murder, as if she were being kidnapped, hanging out the door of this decrepit old van; eggs, milk, and groceries are flying everywhere; and the vehicle is wobbling down Reed Street, barely missing parked cars and oncoming traffic.

Naturally, I freak out. I'm trying to help haul her in, get my partner back in the driver's seat, all the while expecting the van to crash into some solid object and some good citizen to appear to rescue the poor damsel from us two apparent crooks! God only knows how, but we ended up on the sidewalk and in a hedge without hitting any cars or people. The poor hooker falls out of the van, my partner falls right on top of her, and eggs, milk, lettuce, and all sorts of other stuff fall all over both of them. That was a *bad* trip to the store!

Street Crime Follies

Sometimes, though, it worked the other way around. For example, we were conducting a "john sting" operation one night and the uniformed officer was a guy I'll call Fred for the purposes of this story. Now, Fred was an officer who invariably got hurt in every little skirmish and was always out on disability, or about to be. Fred was a black-belt martial artist who had studied how to fight, but it just didn't seem to work for him. And it didn't work on this particular night, either.

Now, the Street Crimes unit where we worked at the time was typically a very violent assignment. You were pretty well-guaranteed at least one good knock-down, drag-out fight every week and sometimes more. And it seemed that every time there was a fight, Fred was the guy that got hurt. He'd get glued back together, get some "comp time" to heal up a bit—and within twenty-four hours of returning to work, poor Fred would be beat up again!

Our decoy made a sale and led the john to the room. The whole team was in position, ready to take him into custody. The problem, though, was that this john really didn't want to be arrested.

The decoy unlocked the door with her key, stepped aside to let the man in, just as she was supposed to. The guy was huge, about six-feet six-inches tall, and about 370 pounds. He'd been a former college or semi-pro football player, and he pretty much filled up the doorway.

Fred took one look at this john and blurted out, "You're under arrest!" Well, the guy decided that, no, he wasn't interested in being arrested and turned around to leave.

Our standard procedure was for all the other officers to come in behind the john, in case of trouble, and the rest of us were hustling toward the room. So there were three of us coming in the door while this monster of a guy was trying to get out. If you added up the weight of all three of us, we just about equaled the john, who tried to get past us football style, first by straight-arming one of us (which hurt!) and then by just forcing past the rest of us.

My partner and I hit this moose, high and low, with everything we've got while Fred is pulling backwards from behind. A little brawl develops, but we don't have much area to work in because the entry is only about four feet wide. But we manage to unbalance the guy; he trips over the sofa, and down we all go in a heap. The sofa falls over backwards, the wall collapses, and a pile of bodies are squirming in the rubble. On top is our cute, little female-officer decoy, trying to grab one of the monster's wrists to restrain him. Below her were me and my partner trying to fight with this infuriated customer. And way down at the bottom of the pile is . . . you guessed it, Hard Luck Fred.

The monster is grabbing and thrashing around, and one of the things he manages to grab is Fred—by the testicles! Fred let out a scream unlike anything I have ever heard before or since. Maybe the scream startled the monster because he started to fade about then. We managed to get some cuffs on him, and we ultimately took him into custody, but it took about five of us and three or four sets of handcuffs to do the job. We had to pay for rebuilding the motel room, and Fred was out on disability one more time!

Knuckleheads
and Wolf Packs

New York has recently experienced a radical drop in crime of all kinds. Homicides dropped from 2,300 per year to about 900, with similar drops for other crimes. Much of the credit for this success story is the aggressive police work done by the NYPD Street Crimes units and their undercover officers. Sgt. John Politoski is one of those officers. He's been a New York cop for twelve years, four in the plainclothes Street Crimes unit.

The main focus of my unit was basically street crimes—strong-arm robberies, street grand larcenies, purse snatching, and similar crimes in public places. One memorable example took place a few years ago in the vicinity of Thirty-fourth Street in Manhattan. That's an upscale shopping district with a lot of large department stores. On Fridays and Saturdays this district is very busy with shoppers, people with money in their pockets. That makes it a pretty attractive area for "perps," as all New York cops call perpetrators of crimes. There are a lot of potential victims on the street, most carrying a lot of money.

My unit became very good at just walking around and spotting the perps and their likely victims. We worked in four- or six-man teams, and our shift typically began with all of us sitting down for breakfast together then moving out onto the street. One Saturday morning we had our usual breakfast. While we were paying for our ham and eggs, a group of five or six guys strolled past. We looked at them and knew immediately that these guys were in town to cause some trouble. Their timing was perfect for us!

Our standard procedure was to follow them to see what they were doing. Now, we didn't know for sure they were bad guys, or that they were going to do something illegal, but there are some behaviors that we learned are excellent cues that somebody is up to no good. This particular crew was showing us a lot of these—they would pass a likely victim, then stop, turn around, and size them up, check the location of the victim's pocketbook or wallet, and decide if they were a good risk.

We followed this crew for about twenty minutes, up to about Thirty-fifth and Seventh Avenue. I won't tell you the details of how we set up surveillance, but basically it involves splitting up into two-man teams, staying out of the way, and watching what's going on. If you do this long enough, you can start to see exactly what the perps are planning to do, and you can anticipate them. And one way to do that is to put some of our guys in position where the perps are likely to go when they try to escape.

Sure enough, one of these young punks decided to take on a young family—a mother, father, and baby in a carriage—all by himself. Only one of the crew was involved. He jumped the father from behind, got him in a headlock, went into his pockets, took his money, and then ran down the subway stairs. We had already figured that's what the plan was, and another officer and I were already down there waiting for him. When the robbery goes down, we get a call on our radios, and we know who we're looking for. The guy comes running downstairs, and we grab him with the money in his hand. We snatch him up in the subway, then send a female officer upstairs to secure the victims.

All his friends are still upstairs, and they have no idea where their friend is. We took the perp to the far end of the station, and called for a car to come collect the guy out of sight of the rest of the crew. We then continue surveillance on them for another hour or so while they move down to Thirty-fourth Street near the entrance to the subway down there.

I actually bumped into one of them on the stairway downstairs. He was trying to scope out his route of escape, looking for police, when he obviously notices me standing there waiting for him. Now, these guys are normally pretty good at identifying cops, but we were dressed pretty casually, and I thought maybe I could fool him. "Can you tell me where Penn Station is?" I asked him, acting like a guy from, maybe, Long Island.

He gives me directions. I say, "Hey, I really appreciate that. Thanks a lot!" and pat him on the back, shake his hand, and walk away. So I exit the place, run down a block, come back to my position.

This crew finally found a victim. They jumped a couple on the far side of the street from the station. The guy I had just spoken to pushed the man to the ground, took his money, and ran right toward me and three other officers standing on the stairway. They ran right into us! We snatched them all, recovered the money, and took them all back to the station house.

One by one, we marched these perps back to meet their friend from the morning. "We've got a surprise for you!" I told them. Then we hauled them back to see their buddy, who they thought got away with the money. "Yo! Yo! Yo!" they'd shout. They were shocked.

Now, we never told them how we caught them, and that was frustrating. When you make a good collar like that, you'd like to tell them exactly how stupid they were, but you also don't want to give them anything to make it easier the next time. The guy who told me how to get to Penn Station, just a few minutes before, didn't recognize me. I really wanted to tell him that we'd talked just five or ten minutes prior in the stairway, but I had to let it go.

Where Are the Cops When You Need Them?

Unlike most officers, I had an opportunity to actually witness a *lot* of strong-arm robberies. The normal procedure in police work is that the officer reacts to a robbery after it happens, secures the victim, then goes looking for the perpetrator. Very rarely will an officer actually observe the crime occur. But with undercover street crimes and transit operations, you actually have them happen right in front of you—if you're good at blending into your environment.

For example, one time I was standing on the subway platform at Fifty-ninth Street and Columbus Circle right in the middle of a bunch of young sixteen- and seventeen-year-old kids. Now, boys that age are notorious for committing robberies in the subways. They gang up on people and steal their money, watches, pocketbooks, and jewelry.

While I was standing in the middle of this group, two older kids walk up to a pair of younger kids just a couple of feet away from me. "Gimme all your stuff—all your jewelry, watches, all your money!" I stand there and watch while these little kids give up all their stuff, everything! I watch the victims hand over their property to the perps and I look over at my partner who was about ten feet away. He knew what was going on and, when they started to walk away, we threw them to the ground and cuffed them up right there. The perps didn't know what hit them!

I'll Take Manhattan

Two perps were doing gun robberies in Manhattan in the subways. They were working three or four stations in the southern end of Manhattan and, at the time, I was in a unit that went after "pattern" robberies like the ones these guys were doing. The lieutenant assigns me and three other guys to investigate the pattern and see if we can grab them. We start working during the hours they've been committing the robberies, and in the same areas where the stickups have been committed. We hope to find them by talking to the victims, reading the crime reports, and finding their pattern. We try to get a real good description of these guys, their MO, how they flee the station, and then we can use that to find them. After three or four of these robberies, we started to see the pattern, and the details started to come together.

My partner and I thought we knew how to catch these knuckleheads. We went down to Rector Street, on the N and R train, right down the block from Wall Street. Actually, we jump on the N and R train farther north, at Canal Street, and ride it through our target area just to see what's going on. As we are passing by Rector Street, we see two guys sitting on the platform who fit the description of the perps.

Now, there are only three basic kinds of people on the subway from a cop's point of view—you've got the perps, you've got the police, and you've got the riders. The *riders* get on and off the train at the platform every time the train comes in, and they leave and enter the station. The *perps* and the *police* don't do that. The perps stay in the station, and the police stay in the station. That's the pattern, and it is important if you want to catch the perps and not have the perps catch on to you.

So we notice these two knuckleheads. They don't get on the train when it stops at the station, and they don't leave. My partner and I decide to stay aboard and see if they get on. They don't move. I say to my partner, "John, these are the guys!" There are four of us on the assignment, and we all ride to the next station, Whitehall Street, run up the stairs like bats out of hell, and jog back over to Rector Street. You can be very effective with these operations if you're on foot rather than in a car.

It is difficult to watch these perps without being noticed by them, but we knew from our crime stats that they were exiting this particular station through the exit turnstiles at the remote end of the station. So, we figured our best bet was to wait for them upstairs, on the street, while we call for some reinforcements to set up a better surveillance. We also knew that we could check on them occasionally by going across to the other side of the platform, going down to the toll clerk, and getting a peek at them that way. They aren't going to notice if you do that, as long as you don't do it too often. And we often asked people—guys about our age, normally—if they'd noticed these people sitting downstairs on the bench. Frequently, they had noticed them and would say "Yeah, they're sitting right there on the bench!" This went on for about an hour, and we *knew* that these were our perps.

We watched them for about two hours. But here's the problem you run into with this kind of situation, you have nothing on these guys, yet. They fit the description and are hanging out in the subway. What do you do? We were sure they were going to do something, and we were sure they'd exit through the turnstile. Once they exited that way, there was no turning back. They would be trapped on the stairs.

Finally, they made their attempt. They tried to rob an elderly oriental male. But the victim didn't comply and ran off the other way toward the token booth, screaming and yelling. The perps say to themselves, "Okay, this is done, we're outta here," and exit the station, running up the steps in our direction. We can hear the commotion downstairs and are ready for them. We call for backup and head downstairs. The other two officers with us had been placed in the tunnel because perps often use that route for their escape, so John and I are on our own.

We get into a huge struggle with these two on the stairs. They are screaming that we're trying to rob them! They call people to help them fight off the robbers—us! At the same time, they are trying to get to their pockets—where we think their guns are. But we haven't actually seen their guns, and you can't exactly say, *Time out! Do you have a gun? Yes? Oh, okay, I'm going to take my gun out and shoot you, then.*

You can't do that, so I'm wrestling for my life with this guy, and my partner's doing the same thing with the other guy at the top of the stairs. It's a big, bloody battle. I'm pounding his head into the concrete, and he's screaming that he's being robbed. I get him in a full nelson, I have my gun in my hand, and finally our backup arrives. They cuff the guys. Both of these idiots do indeed have guns on them, with hollow-point bullets in them, and there was no doubt both were trying to "do" us. I received ten stitches in the forehead after we finished with the arrest. Both guys were picked out of four lineups, were convicted, and sent away for long terms. That was a satisfying arrest.

Wolf Packs

Crime is definitely down in New York, thanks very much to policies put in place by Jack Maples and Bill Bratton, former transit cops. Maples used to be in charge of the Decoy unit before he became Deputy Commissioner for Crime Control for NYPD. It all ties in! You've heard about the crime drop in New York. Well, as somebody who was there and watched how it happened, you can give the credit to these two guys.

There are new policies in place that made it happen. When we catch a perp these days, we heavily debrief him about guns, knives, homicides, and other robberies. And he's going to give them to you! Guns are off the street now as a result. The perps know now that the cops will pull up and arrest them on "quality of life" crimes like urinating in public, drinking a beer in public, smoking a joint—things that the cops used to let go will now get you arrested, and those little crimes will get you frisked, "thumbed," and if you're carrying a gun, you'll get charged with that!

My experience with these robberies has been that you find different kinds of perps in different areas. For example, right now I'm working in the Thirtieth Precinct, working all drug-related crimes. Robberies in Manhattan are committed mostly by males from Brooklyn, aged sixteen to twenty-five or thirty years old. We call them "wolf packs." Four, five, or six of these guys would come into Manhattan on the subway, looking for victims. They had a saying: "Manhattan makes it, Brooklyn takes it!" They'd come into town, do a crime spree of robberies, larcenies, then spend their money on boots and clothes, steal some boots and clothes, get something to eat, then go home. They'd start over again the next day.

We liked to wait for them at the subway. As soon as they came to visit us in Manhattan, we picked up on them and followed them. I enjoyed that—there is no pleasure like hunting down these perps. At the same time, it is stressful and frustrating sometimes.

Here is one way the NYPD started getting control of street crime in Manhattan. When a wolf pack of ten guys did a robbery, we could usually grab the guy who took the money, the guy who grabbed the victim, plus any of the perps that the victim or the officers could readily identify for prosecution of the case. But maybe seven of them would get away!

So we bring these three cretins back to the command, sit them down, give them their Miranda rights, then get them to give up the rest of the seven guys—make statements on them. The next day, we went out and knock on the doors of each of these guys and lock them all up for the robbery. Then we debrief the seven for guns, robberies, and violent crime activities. The information just snowballed, and it worked.

Tricks of the Trade

We always try to set things up so we are in total control of the situation, including the actual arrest. When a uniformed officer rolls past a crime in progress, the crooks will bolt and you'll have to chase them immediately, but if you are in plain clothes, you have this tremendous advantage, you can take your time.

A little trick we used was that, normally, I didn't jump on a crook right at the scene of the crime. Sometimes that wasn't avoidable, but often it worked better to do it like this: the actual robbery takes a second or two, then they are gone, running down the street. We tailed them; we let the guy run and after half a block he looks around and if nobody's running after him, he stops. Now he starts walking.

We get on the radio and set up the whole squad to converge on the guy, maybe two blocks away from the crime. When we take him down, he is totally surprised! For example, he's walking eastbound on Thirty-sixth Street between Seventh and Sixth Avenues. We get some undercover cops to come westbound on Thirty-sixth Street and run right into the guy. You walk down the street, la-de-da, like a couple of construction workers, and the perp is walking toward you, counting the money he just stole. Then, you do to him what he just did to the victim! You put your gloves on and "ring his bell," or the two officers just slam him to the ground and cuff him up! He is in total shock!

A good example of that happened when a Spanish army general and his wife were shopping on Canal Street in Manhattan. We picked up on two perps in the subway, figured out they were up to no good, and followed them. We could see them sizing people up. They wandered around for a while, then set up just outside the subway. They go up and down the steps, checking the place out. We know we've got these two clowns.

The couple walks by. One jerks the gold necklace off the neck of the lady, the other gets the man in a head-lock, goes into the man's pockets, grabs his wallet—and they both take off. My partner takes off after the guy with the wallet, down the subway.

I go after the guy who took the chain. He runs east on Canal, gets around the corner, then stops. As soon as he's around the corner, I run after him. When I get to the corner, I walk past the corner, right past the guy. I see him but cross to the other side of the street and start walking along with him, tailing him on the other side. He walks fast, but I keep up with him without being noticed.

Now, my partner and I took just one radio with us that day—*bad tactical move!* I was younger then, and why we did that I will never know, and we would never do that today! I got no radio, I got nothing! I decide to just follow this guy and make my move when I get the opportunity.

I follow this perp at least eight blocks! The guy sees me—he looks over three or four times, but he doesn't have a clue. I'm not looking over at him, I'm just walking down the block.

He's headed right for the First Precinct, he's walking right into a hundred cops, although he doesn't know that, the knucklehead! He gets to the Canal Street Station on the A-line subway and heads downstairs to the trains. I know that downstairs there is a transit-police precinct for District Two. As he goes down the stairs, I jog up behind, to get closer. We get downstairs, in a huge tunnel. He is only about fifteen feet in front of me, but I can't get to this creep there—if I make a move, he's gone and I am not going to catch him alone.

I'm right behind him: my heartrate going about 240! He walks to the trains, pulls a turnstile back, and sneaks in just as a train pulls in.

I have to make a tactical decision and, as it turned out, I make the right one. I have a choice—do I go get backup or do I stick with the guy? I stick with him. One thing I know—if you lose sight of your perp, he's gone!

There was a conductor in the car. I go up to him and say, "Transit police! No matter what, *do not move this train!* Make an announcement that you're down for mechanical difficulties."

"No problem, officer!" he says.

I spotted a transit employee, identified myself, and told her, "Go upstairs to the transit police and get them down here, right now!" Off she goes. I'm exhausted, but at least I know the cavalry is coming!

Now, I start working my way up the cars toward my perp. He has made his way to the first car, sitting down, and he is in the process of taking off his sweat pants. They use the pants to hide stuff and to change their appearance. I get to within five feet of this schmuck—I can reach out and touch him. He's got his pants down around his ankles—I decide that now's the time and I "kabong" him right there! "Police!" I say, "You're under arrest!"

He and I get into a fight, but I don't care because I know my help is on the way. Well, this guy and I are in the battle of our lives inside the subway car. He's got one hand on the threshold of the subway door, trying to pull himself out so he can run away—with me on his back! I'm prying his fingers trying to get him to let go.

Now, rarely do the wonderful citizens of New York, in my experience, assist a robbery victim. It may have happened on occasion, but it is unusual. But this time, some of the brave people on the platform move in to help the poor young man from Brooklyn who's being assaulted by the man with the badge and handcuffs claiming to be a police officer! They start trying to drag me off this schmuck! I was beating the heck out of this guy, trying to hold on to him, while these people on the platform try to save the perp.

But then I can hear the jingle of keys coming in the distance. Here comes the cavalry! They come down and cuff the perp. I'm exhausted! But even so, I let those people have it! "I have never seen one of you people ever help a victim being mauled by the crooks, but when you have me, a police officer—I told you I was a cop, you could see my equipment, I am screaming to you to get more cops—and you decide that I'm a bad guy and start dragging me off the guy! What were you thinking? Are you stupid?" Then I really lit into them.

Some of the ladies then chimed in and said, "You're right, officer, these guys should have helped you!"

Anyway, I didn't know where my partner was, but I had my perp. My partner shows up with the other knucklehead, and somebody else brings in the two victims. These victims were tourists from Spain and were supposed to leave that evening. Normally we'd keep the chain for evidence, but this time we were able to just photograph it and give it back to them. Then we drove them back to their hotel. It worked out really well, and the couple wrote a nice letter to the Police Department thanking us.

Undercover in Uniform

If you play things right, these thieves don't have a clue you're on to them. In fact, you can even do "undercover" operations while you're wearing your uniform!

For example, I'm in a uniformed assignment now. I was driving around last week, just me and a rookie driving around. A T-shirt vendor got robbed by two Dominicans and flagged us down. He gives us the description and hops in the car with us. We drive around looking for the perps, and then he starts yelling, "There they are! There they are!" We see two guys who fit the description of the perps perfectly.

"Okay," I tell him, "slide down so they can't see you." He slides down.

Now, my marked police car is in front of these two strong-arm robbery perps. I turn to the rookie and tell him, "Relax, relax. Get out of the car nice and easy. We're gonna walk over to that pool hall like nothing's happening. We're just going to check it out, like we got a call for something inside there."

The perps walk past carrying the jackets they just stole, but they've got their eyeballs locked on us. We get out of the car and start ambling over to the building. The question in the perp's peanut brain right now is, *Do I run? Does this cop know I just robbed somebody? Man, if this guy knew I did the robbery, he'd jump out of the car and come after me. But he's just walking over to that store behind me. He's doing something else.*

"Naw, I don't see anybody down here," I say loudly to my partner, so they can hear me. These two schmucks turn around, walk down the street, and the rookie and I grab them from behind, put them in headlocks, throw them to the ground, and cuff them up, bang! It was great! They had no idea!

A West Side Story

A subway line runs up by Central Park West, from Fifty-ninth Street to about 110th Street. That's a pretty exclusive area, and the subways aren't very crowded like they are in other parts of town. People who ride that line tend to have some money on them. It is a place where you get a lot of pattern robberies—four or five in a row, all similar descriptions for the suspect, all at stations between Eighty-sixth and Eighty-first Streets.

We were getting reports of such robberies, and my squad went up there to work on them. My partner and I set up at the top of the stairs to the station because the place is so empty normally that any perp would spot you immediately. When you stand up there and observe people fleeing the station at a high rate of speed, looking back over their shoulder, with a handful of gold chains and similar property, you stop them, question them, and hopefully the victim shows up to explain what's happened.

So that's what we were doing one night on the back stairway of the Eighty-sixth Street station. We observe an older lady coming up the stairs, looking back over her shoulder, then walking away. "John, this is a lady who's just been robbed," I said to my partner.

I approached her and asked if something had happened downstairs. "Yes!" she said, "Somebody just tried to steal my pocketbook!" She described a tall black male, indicated what kind of clothing, hairstyle, and other details. He was standing on the platform, by the turnstiles, way down at the end, she said.

I called the sergeant and the two other guys on the detail over. John and I run downstairs to the main exit. We believe he's still in the station because the train has left, and he has to either leave through one of two exits or go into the tunnel.

We make our way down to the platform and look around. "There he is! That's the guy! John, that's him!"

So, John and I start walking down that way, acting like a couple of drunk construction workers. We're the only people in the place. We're yelling at each other, clowning around, wrestling, acting like two idiots. The guy is looking right at us and has no idea who we are.

When we get up to him, bam, we take him down. What he tried to do to this old lady, we did to him! We cuff him up and bring him upstairs where we want the victim to identify her attacker.

We get to the top of the stairs. We have our shields out, we're carrying our police radios, and we have the guy in handcuffs. The lady suddenly decides she isn't sure if we're really cops! We later learned she was a senior executive in a bank, had lots of education from places like Columbia, but without a shred of common sense. She agrees that this is the guy, but she won't come down to the station to make a statement because she's decided she doesn't think we are really the police!

"Lady," I say, "you gotta be kidding me, right? This is the guy that tried to rob you, right? We got him in handcuffs, right? We have *radios, badges, guns,* just like *police,* don't we?"

"I'm not telling you who I am, where I live, or anything," she says.

"Listen, ma'am," I said, "you didn't give a thought to getting off the subway at this desolate subway station, walking right past this guy, and yet you're going to question that we're the police? We just brought the guy who tried to rob you up in cuffs. Who do you think we could be?"

She stuck her nose up in the air. "I want a uniformed cop here," she said.

As luck would have it, a police car came by. I hailed it and the guy pulled over. "You're not going to believe this," I told the guy, we just collared this guy after he tried to steal that lady's handbag."

"Good job!" he says.

"But she won't believe we're the police."

He turns to her and says, "They're the police!"

"Okay," she says, without further comment.

This is a classic example of what frustrates me about a lot of people: lots of education but no common sense!

Charlotte's Web

Ralph Kabernagel was a Maryland State Police officer for twenty-six years: twenty-three years in the Undercover Narcotics Division, and fifteen of those years on the street buying drugs. That's a lot longer in covert roles than most officers or agents are ever allowed to work.

To be successful in undercover work, you have to be a likeable person. That's the only way to win over the other people. That sometimes involves some acting, and it gets you into some things you'd otherwise avoid.

A good example is a case that came to us from another department in Maryland. They had been developing an undercover investigation against a wholesale drug distributor, but one of the two agents had to break off his role in the case because of concern that his cover may have been blown. The other officer, a friend of mine, called and asked, "Are you interested in getting into this organization?"

"Sure," I told him. We decided to work it together so we could provide mutual cover, and he had already established his credibility with the dealer organization.

I was introduced to an informant in the case, and that informant's identity is still secret. The three of us met and discussed the case. The informant was reluctant to get involved, but we talked him into it.

We were going after an organization here in Maryland that was importing tons of marijuana by truck up from Texas and Florida. We had been working on the group for years at this point, and we thought maybe now we'd get enough to prosecute the central figures in the organization.

One of those people was a man named Harvey; we didn't have a direct relationship with him at the time, but the informant knew his sister. I was introduced to the girl as a large-scale wholesale drug dealer with organized-crime connections from Delaware. She was a very nice looking blond lady named Charlotte, and we seemed to hit it off right away.

We put together the appearance of a large, profitable Delaware drug operation. That included a telephone number in Delaware that forwarded calls back to our office in Maryland. I gave Charlotte that number as the best way to contact me.

Once I became acquainted with Charlotte, we cut the informant out of the operation and began to deal with her directly. We began to go out to dinner several times. I met her at the airport under the guise of having just flown in from New York, although all I actually did was walk into the airport, and then back out with a couple of suitcases.

During all of this I was constantly attended by a "bodyguard" who was actually a six-foot six-inch state trooper. I threw a lot of money around, bought a lot of dinners, a lot of drinks, and ordered a lot of people around.

All of this finally convinced Charlotte that I was really the big shot I claimed to be. One time, as we discussed the possibility of a deal during dinner, she said, "My brother Harvey is the one you really want to be talking to." I acted surprised although I knew all along who he was.

Charlotte was obviously a nice person, besides being attractive, and we concluded that she wasn't deeply involved with the drug business. After the dinner and drinks and showboating on my part, she started to become attached to me. This became a problem for the investigation generally and for me professionally. I didn't want to have to make an excuse for not having sex with her, and that's where this relationship was headed.

She made her intentions clear, but I was always able to dance around them, saying I had an appointment, or had to leave, or that people were watching. The bodyguards were always present and that helped inhibit her—somewhat.

One night, after a date, I took her home. We'd all been drinking, and my bodyguard was crawling around somewhere in the backyard, getting sick. Charlotte and I were in the living room on the sofa. She pushed me down, climbed on top, and pulled her skirt up. Her blouse was still intact but in the process of coming off when the bodyguard crawled back into the living room. "What's happening?" he mumbled. Well, once he arrived, nothing.

We wanted Charlotte to tell her brother that I was a big-time dealer. To finalize the impression, we rented a motel room for a short, one-act play. She and I had been on a date and I said to her, "Come along with me. I need to stop by a motel to do a little business." She was willing to go anywhere. I had one of my undercover guys in a room and we dropped in on him. I started talking to him about a deal we'd allegedly done, talking about it in evasive terms but making clear that we were talking about a completed drug exchange. I acted like I was upset with him, then threw a bundle of cash at him. It was $10,000 and it fell all over the bed. Charlotte's eyes widened at the sight of all that money. Then we left.

"You ought to talk to my brother," she said. "I'll introduce you." That was the idea all along, but we wanted her out of the picture after the introduction. She didn't want to leave, apparently because of her attraction to me.

Finally, she introduced me to her brother Harvey. We met in a bar, and had some drinks, and talked for a long time. We agreed to do some business.

The deal was supposed to be a thousand pounds of marijuana for $276,000 in cash, and the exchange would be made at Charlotte's house. Getting the cash was a big problem, though, and we had to beg, plead, and promise to be careful with it. The money came from the First National Bank of Maryland, and this kind of use hadn't been done before. Cash loans for drug buys had previously only been for much smaller amounts. Our stress level over this cash was so great that when we went to collect the cash from the vault in the main branch in Baltimore, I had people guarding me! My supervisor, who had never done anything like this before, put additional surveillance on me in case I decided to take off with the money.

Well, I knew he was nervous about it, so I called him and said, "I've got the money and am headed for the airport! See ya!"

"Don't kid around with this!" he said, highly upset. I found out later he hadn't slept for the two previous nights, he was so worried about the cash, and wouldn't sleep again for a third until the money was safely returned to the bank.

So I have this $276,000 in a briefcase and head for the meeting. About forty undercover police surround me, strategically located around the house where we are going, and we even had a helicopter providing surveillance overhead.

Our intelligence information indicated two potential threats from weapons in the house. One was supposed to be a pistol kept by Charlotte in the kitchen; the other was a concealed pistol carried by Harvey. This created a dilemma, and the other undercover officer and I discussed this during the night before the meeting.

I said, "I can't shoot Charlotte." Something can always go wrong in these deals, and the whole thing could go to hell. If it did, and Charlotte came up with a gun, I knew I would not be able to kill her.

"Well," he said, "if it comes to that, *I'll* shoot Charlotte and *you* shoot Harvey." And that was good enough for me.

I was so sure someone was going to get hurt I hand-wrote a will and told my best friend where to find it. I also wore my best underwear that day!

We showed up at the house with the briefcase. On the way in, I noticed the surveillance helicopter was far too low. You could hear it, and its presence was obvious. "Get the helicopter up! Get the helicopter up!" I said into my body wire, hoping the guys monitoring the transmitter could hear me and do something about it. They didn't.

Harvey was already there. Charlotte answered the door, looking worried. "Get in here! Something's wrong!" She was in a panic, and Harvey was moving quickly and nervously around the house. I couldn't tell what they were worried about.

"Man, the cops are all over this area!" he said. "I don't know who you told or what's going on, but you better take that money and get the hell out of here!"

So the deal fell through and we left.

Charlotte was highly upset. She thought somebody in her brother's group was informing the police. She was also upset because she understood me to be an organized-crime guy and was afraid I would kill her brother. She cried and pleaded that I not hurt him or her because the deal went sour.

All this was actually encouraging. Our credibility was still good with them, and they didn't suspect us, at least directly, although we discovered that they thought the cops might be watching me.

I called her. "Listen, I'm really upset about this deal. I don't want to hurt your brother, but I think he brought the cops in." That forced them to take the defensive and, hopefully, make concessions.

Charlotte and I met for dinner and drinks again, and then I talked to Harvey. He was still convinced we could make a deal. I managed to cut Charlotte out of the action this time and made an appointment to meet in another motel with the money.

I had a gun in my boot and was wearing a body wire. The room was wired for sound, with a surveillance team in the room next door. Undercover officers were again stationed discreetly all around the place, some watching for a U-Haul truck loaded with marijuana. I had along a fifth of Jim Beam whiskey to ease any tensions that might develop. We were ready for business.

I got to the room first. The money went under the bed. Harvey arrived and sat down. "My people want me to count the money," he said.

"Fine, but let's have a drink first," I tell him.

"I don't drink," Harvey replied.

Now, normally, the dealer will make a quick inspection of the cash and make an estimate of the amount without bothering to count every bank note—but not Harvey! So he sat there and counted every single bill I brought along, the largest of which was a $100 note. It took him two hours and twenty minutes!

In the meantime, since I was pretty nervous myself, I had the bottle of Jim Beam to myself. I drank about half the bottle all by myself, but I was so edgy that I never felt the effect of the alcohol.

Finally, he finished the count. "Okay, it's all here. Let me go call my people." He got up and walked out to a pay phone down the street. We had an undercover officer in the booth next to him who overheard Harvey say, "Look, the guy is legitimate, I've known him for a while. The money is all here. Can we do the deal?"

The undercover officer couldn't hear the response, but it was apparently favorable. Harvey hung up and walked back to the room. He said, "Look, my people want me to bring them the money so they can count it. Then we'll bring you the drugs."

I started ranting and raving. "Here we go again!" I said. "Do you think I am some kind of idiot? You want to walk out of here with $276,000 of my money and have me sit here waiting for you? It could be a long wait!"

"I'll leave my car with you," he offered.

"So what's your car worth, a few thousand dollars? What's your life worth?" We went around and around on this for a while, then he goes back to the phone booth again.

When he got back to the room he said, "They won't budge. They want to see the money first. This is our first deal. You've got to trust me and you've got to trust them. After this one, we'll have smooth sailing; we won't have to do it this way again."

"Well, I am *not* doing the deal that way."

Harvey was off to the phone booth again. When he came back, it was with another message. "The people I work with are so big that they really don't need your business," he said. "They say that if we can't do the deal this way, the whole thing is off." So the deal fell through. We packed up our cash, our half-empty bottle of bourbon, and our hopes for the case, and went home.

Even though no drugs were exchanged, Harvey and Charlotte had violated federal conspiracy laws by offering drugs for sale. The U.S. Attorney took the case over. Both were indicted in federal court. Both were arrested about five months later.

The case was very sticky for me at several levels. For one thing, the informant who helped at the beginning was (and still is) a very valuable source and personal friend. If his identity became known, he would be in serious danger. On the day I was scheduled to testify, I told my supervisor that there was a good chance I might be sent to jail that day for refusing to identify a confidential source.

Happily, it didn't come to that. But both were tried, convicted, and Harvey was sent to federal prison. Charlotte got probation. I moved on to other cases.

A few years later I was visiting Ocean City, Maryland. I walked into a bar, alone, and heard somebody call my undercover name, Frank, from somewhere behind me. I didn't turn around but walked to the bar.

"Frank!" the voice called again. I turned around, and it was Charlotte. She was sitting by herself at a table. I walked over and sat down. She wasn't as chummy as she'd been. "Well, I didn't know what to call you," she said. "I saw in the indictment papers that your real name is Ralph, but I just knew you as Frank."

"How are you doing?" I asked.

"Well, I'm on probation, thanks to you! And my brother is in jail!" She wanted to vent and was doing a good job. I was waiting for somebody to join her so I could escape, but her friends had already left. So we started to talk, and I tried to explain to her what had happened.

"I tried to keep you out of it," I told her, "if you will try to remember the conversations where I told you I wanted to talk to Harvey alone! You would never allow that. Remember?"

A couple of drinks went down, and by the end of the evening we were both laughing about it all. I went over the case and listened to her talk about how she felt about it. I told her my side of the story.

We got up and parted friends. It has been a few years, and we are still friends. We talk on the phone a couple of times a year, and I have been introduced to her current boyfriend.

All this makes it an unusual case. I was responsible for her conviction and putting her brother in jail, but she clearly still thinks highly of me, and I think highly of her, too. She really is basically a good person.

The Block

The Block is a unique place, known around the United States for its strip joints and bars. I started working undercover there many years ago, playing the role of a derelict and buying drugs from the bouncers at the clubs. After a while I became fairly well known in the area, and one of the club owners approached me with an offer of a job. I accepted but with some reservations.

I went to my boss in the police department and said, "I'm going to work as a bouncer and doorman at this club. I'd like to know what my parameters are from the department. If I throw somebody out of the club and they get hurt, I don't want them to come back at me or the department."

"Well, you'll just have to use discretion," he said. That was a lot less support than I was hoping for, but I went ahead with the job anyway.

I worked as a bouncer and "bar back" and from then on I was in with the criminal element on the Block. I bought drugs from a lot of the bouncers and some of the strippers. They were paying me cash under the table, and I turned the money in to the department.

After a while, it was time to make arrests. We arrested some of the strippers during their acts, while they were performing onstage pretty much in the nude. The arrest team went out on stage and put the cuffs on the girls right in the middle of the performance!

Survival Skills

Undercover work can be extremely hazardous for many reasons. The best protection is an ability to think well on your feet and to be able to talk your way out of trouble. For instance, I was working undercover out in western Maryland, a rural area very difficult to infiltrate. Another officer and I were in a bar and had both gone to the bathroom when a guy walked in clearly under the influence of PCP. He produced a pistol and started aiming at us, waving it back and forth from one to the other. We played him off, somehow, by saying, very calmly, "Don't shoot us, go outside and find somebody else to shoot." He went outside and shot somebody else, in the face. He was arrested and sent to prison.

Wire Taps

Getting authorization for a wiretap is a long, involved process. It is essentially a last resort, and you can't get one until you've been through a process called "exhaustion." You have to exhaust most other means to develop the information first, then go before the judge with a lengthy *ex parte* order before the court will grant the authority for the tap. Taps are authorized for short periods—thirty days, sixty days, or a similar period.

While you're listening to a tap, you try to figure out the codes these people generally use. One time we heard a guy make frequent reference to "boogers." We interpreted that to mean different kinds of drugs. Unfortunately, when we ultimately did a search warrant on this guy's house, we found several jars of the real item stored in his house.

Another time we had a guy on the wire who said to an associate, "Don't talk about drugs to me on the phone, I think there's a tap on the line."

There was a hesitation from the guy on the other end of the line. He was thinking hard. He wanted to talk about a drug deal, but whenever he did, his friend said, *"Don't talk about drugs on the phone! It's bugged!"*

There was another pause while he tried to reframe the question. Finally, he said, "Okay, do you have any R-E-D-S?" I guess he thought cops couldn't spell.

My very first wiretap was quite interesting. Normally,

you have a "monitor" officer who sits there and listens to every conversation. At the same time, you have other officers who are busy transcribing previous conversations. You have surveillance teams ready to jump out of the bushes when the opportunity for a bust develops.

We had an authorization for a round-the-clock wiretap, and I was the monitor officer. At about three in the morning I heard the receiver pick up. All the other guys are lying on the floor, asleep. I put the earphones on and also had the loudspeaker on, at the request of the other agents. Since I was new at this, I didn't know what they had already found out: every time the subject of the wiretap, a young woman, went out on a date, as soon as she got home she called a girlfriend with a blow-by-blow account of all the steamy action she had on the date. Well, the guys were ripping the earphones off my head, hoping to hear the conversation more clearly.

Sadly, there is a provision of the regulations called "minimization," spelled out in the court order for the wiretap. If a conversation isn't pertinent to the investigation, you have to turn the recorder off, then turn it back on every thirty seconds or so to check if the nature of the discussion has changed. We all got an earful, even so! This girl's dates clearly had a good time and, according to her accounts, so did she!

Pagan Rituals

I worked a group called The Pagans, an outlaw motorcycle group. We had several chapters here in Maryland, although their numbers have since diminished. I didn't know anything about motorcycles and didn't pretend to when around the members of the gang. That's one of the cardinal rules about working undercover, you should never pretend to know something you don't. My dealings with them were strictly related to buying drugs, but after a while they started asking me to "prospect" for them. These outlaw biker gangs require a prospect to do something clearly illegal, though, and as a police officer I couldn't do the kinds of things they wanted me to do. So I hung around the edges of the club, buying drugs.

When you first start working undercover, you think everybody can tell who you really are. The first time I went to a party as an undercover officer, everybody turned and looked at me as soon as the informant and I entered the room. I turned to him and whispered, "I'm burned—everybody recognizes me!" But they didn't, it was just the natural curiosity everybody has about anybody new walking in the door. We stayed and had no problems with anybody.

About this time the Pagans started assigning the drug sales to their women, so I started making the buys from them. Some were real characters. One of these women was arrested and brought into a police station. During the booking interview we routinely ask if the arrestee has any tattoos, scars, marks, or other identifying features. Well, this woman had them *all over!*

She decided to show off her favorite, a skull and crossbones on her chest. She popped off her top, displaying this artwork. On top of the tattoo, hanging in her cleavage, was a little baby rat, alive and squirming. It was suspended by a piece of rawhide inserted through the rat's jaw and had been there for some time. We noticed the smell before we identified its source. The woman's nickname was "Grand Canyon," for reasons obvious to all present.

Marital Survival Skills

I've never been married, but I have been through a lot of girlfriends. Undercover work is hard on a relationship. You might have to spend most of the night in a strip club and come home at three or four in the morning, reeking of perfume and covered with lipstick—if you come home at all! I've seen a lot of married guys become separated and divorced as a result of their undercover work. One guy I worked with would be out all night partying—off duty—then go home. On the way, he'd stop at an all-night pharmacy and pick up a small package of aspirin or other unmarked white tablet! He'd wrap these in a little piece of tinfoil, and come in the house at six or seven in the morning. His wife would be sitting there waiting for him. He'd throw them on the table and say, "All night we worked, and *this* is all we got for it!"

Information, Please

One of the biggest problems we have is with informants. They can be very dangerous if they turn on you, as they sometimes do. An informant can easily set you up to be ambushed, if he or she wants to.

That happened to me once when an informant and I went to a popular bar. He was talking to a couple of guys on the other side of the room and since I can read lips a bit, I caught him telling these two that I was a state trooper. It cost me some money to "burn" him back, but I walked over and, in front of the two, tucked a twenty-dollar bill in his shirt pocket. I stage-whispered into his ear, just loud enough for these two guys to hear, "Thanks! That information you gave me really paid off. Call me again the next time you've got something to share!" I walked off and never saw the informant again, although I hear he's still alive. Getting burned by your informants is one of the things that upsets undercover cops the most.

We normally get our informants when they are arrested and they then "turn" or "flip" and offer to help us work against their former friends and associates in hopes of getting a better deal when the case goes to court. These deals are negotiated through the State's Attorney's office, not directly with us. Often, the informant will escort us to meetings with her dealer or contacts and introduce us as another member of the underworld. We try to cut the informant out of the relationship with these dealers as soon as possible so we can work the case alone.

There is a lot of drinking involved in working most of these cases, and that can be a problem. Often you'll be working with a female informant. Maybe she has a crack cocaine problem, she may be unhealthy, and her kids will often have been taken away from her. Her pimp is beating her up, and she's living on the street. She has nothing in her life—then you show up, driving a half-decent car, a reputable person with some money, and some typical cop charm. Well, that girl will naturally want to latch onto you. We have lost many undercover officers to this kind of situation when the officer begins to develop a personal relationship with the girl.

A lot of times the informant will become more of a problem than the dealers. For example, it often happens that while they're working covertly with us, they will get arrested for drug possession by our department or another agency. When that happens, she or he will often say, "Oh, I'm working with Sergeant Ralph Kabernagel, and I just bought these drugs for him!" When that happens, the arresting officers aren't sure what to do; we've had people released after such stories.

Sometimes, too, these informants will get a "police complex" and start to identify with us. They will buy a phony badge someplace and, after drinking in a bar for a while, might start to tell people that they're an undercover officer. People who do that tend to get beat up, and we have to go clean up after them. So now we have the informant sign a contract with us before we do anything with them. Everything they can and can't do is enumerated in the contract. Working with informants is like raising children—it is a lot of work, and you have to clean up a lot of messes.

Undercover Split Personalities

One of the biggest problems for many undercover cops is the need to have a strong sense of who you really are. You need to play the role of three or four different personalities in this business, and some cops have difficulties with this. You have an undercover personality that you have to practice, to be comfortable and natural with; you have to behave naturally and spontaneously in this role, even when you are doing things like buying drugs. Then you have your overt police personality, a role that is supposed to keep you honest and prevent you from crossing the line to genuine criminal conduct. Finally, you have your off-duty personality and your relationship with your wife and children, if any.

This becomes a problem because some cops don't know when to turn one role off and another role on. When I used to come home to my girlfriend's house, she knew to avoid talking to me for a while. It usually took an hour to transition from my undercover role to my off-duty role, and then I could have a normal conversation with her. We spend a lot of time developing stories and scenarios to support our undercover roles, lies about who and what we are. I noticed that I was starting to do the same thing in my off-duty role, playing another kind of undercover role with my girlfriend. I found myself telling an elaborate lie, and I had no idea why I was doing it!

All this is one reason why many departments limit the time an officer is allowed to do covert work. If you stay in it long enough, you'll be tempted to take a little money here, then pocket some drugs for resale there;

then you might try some of the drugs yourself instead of turning it all in. That's why the Baltimore Police Department doesn't let its officers work undercover for more than three years, although the Maryland State Police doesn't have a similar restriction.

RICO, "Rough Rider," and Radio-Free FBI

FBI Special Agent Tim McKinley brings a different per-spective to the story of undercover work. Tim is a special-ist in dealing with outlaw motorcycle gangs, particularly the Hells Angels. The highlight of his career has been working with the legendary Anthony Tait, a civilian who volunteered to penetrate first the Brothers outlaw motor-cycle gang, then moved on to become the Security Officer of the Hells Angels. McKinley spent three years supervis-ing and surveilling Tait, spending hours in the back of an old Toyota camper, changing tapes, and making pho-tographs documenting criminal activity.

Operation "Cacus" was the third major campaign mounted by the federal government against the Hells Angels. The first effort ended in the Racketeer-Influenced and Corrupt Organization (RICO) trials of the late 1970s and early '80s. This was largely a Drug Enforcement Agency (DEA) and Bureau of Alcohol, Tobacco, and Fire-arms (ATF)-led effort, and it happened about the time the Hells Angels were just getting into methamphetamine manufacture. Prior to this time, the gang had been making phencyclidine, the "shake and bake" of dope. The Angels were brokering labs, and some were cooking dope themselves. A few of these Angels were getting quite good at making the drug, thanks to the help of professional chemists. At the same time, the Hells Angels were also involved in racketeering in the food-catering industry.

The prosecution in the RICO trials was based largely on the highly paid testimony of "fellow travelers," former members and associates of the gang with a low reputation for truth and veracity. The trials quickly deteriorated into a liar's contest.

Many Hells Angels can be charming and compelling personalities when they want to be. They performed well on the stand. As a result, the trials were not particularly successful. The primary defendants were either acquitted or had hung juries. Very few Hells Angels went to jail after the RICO trials.

The major result of the RICO trials was that the federal government learned a lot about the Hells Angels, particularly what didn't work when trying to stop their unlawful behavior.

Then, in the early 1980s, the Hells Angels were harassing and threatening a couple of federal judges. About the same time, the Banditos outlaw motorcycle gang made an assassination attempt on an assistant U.S. Attorney named Knerr in Texas. The Banditos pulled ahead of the U.S. Attorney's car in a van. Knerr recalled under hypnosis that the van didn't have any rear windows—just curtains across the back. He saw the curtain part and an M2 thirty-caliber carbine, the fully automatic version of the weapon, poked out and started firing at him at very close range. The only thing that saved Knerr's life was that he fainted; he slid under the steering wheel and the bullets impacted on the engine block and firewall.

Shortly thereafter a San Antonio, Texas, judge named John Wood was assassinated by rifle fire. The judge was known locally as "Maximum" John Wood for his inclination to hand out hefty sentences. At the time of his killing there were several cases pending before him, one involving the Banditos and another involving the Jimmy Chagra narcotics cartel. It turned out that Jimmy Chagra was good for it. The shooter was Chuck Harrelson, the father of the actor Woody Harrelson.

But it took a while to develop that information. Massive investigations were launched and interest in outlaw biker gangs went way up. Several of us in the FBI who had been involved in biker investigations previously were pulled back to Washington; we sat around a big table, playing "what if?" Ironically, one of the things discussed was how wonderful it would be if we could get somebody inside the gangs to actively cooperate.

Some of the agents present had been involved in mob investigations. They said, "If you twist a guy that hard, frequently he's going to be disloyal; he's going to be a hard-core crook, and not very reliable." So that was the way it was about 1981.

Shortly thereafter a guy named Vernon Hartung contacted the FBI in Baltimore, Maryland. He had escaped from a federal prison and wanted to turn himself in. At the same time, he wanted to establish himself with federal agents. He knew a member of the Hells Angels, Gary Edward Kautzman—also known as "Frisco Gary" or "Little Gary." At the time, Kautzman was president of the San Francisco chapter of the Hells Angels.

Operation "Rough Rider"

A deal was struck with Hartung. He was put in contact with Kautzman, and he brought with him an undercover FBI agent. The undercover agent never really worked out; he just didn't have what it took for this kind of investigation. He certainly had all the guts in the world but just didn't have the right personality for the work.

If there was a slow spot in a conversation, he'd start talking, the hallmark of a poor undercover agent. You've got to just sit there and listen! The jury doesn't want to hear you yapping; they want to hear the *crook* yapping.

This agent also failed to understand that there are certain elements you must have for a successful prosecution. The whole thing doesn't count unless you get those elements, and this FBI agent wasn't comfortable bringing them up in conversation.

The agent was successful at developing probable cause to ask a judge for a couple of wiretaps. Unfortunately, though, wiretaps on sophisticated criminal groups like the Hells Angels are notoriously ineffective. You'll hear a conversation that sounds like this:

"I love you, bro! You want to party?" the first Hells Angels asks.

"Yeah, sure, come on over and let's party!" another Hells Angels responds.

The first is really asking, *Do you have any meth to sell me?* And the answer means, *Yes, I do. Come on over— usual price.* They just won't use language that will sell in front of a judge or jury.

About this time, another FBI agent, Kevin Bonner, was brought in to work with Hartung. Bonner's undercover role was a crooked sports attorney who needed to travel hither, thither, yon, and about, supplying drugs to his various sports clients. Hartung and the Hells Angels were to be the conduit for the drugs, and it worked fairly well. Bonner turned out to be a very good undercover agent who understood the elements of a crime very well. Things started going much more smoothly, and the FBI started collecting useful information. The operation became known as "Rough Rider."

The emphasis of the investigation shifted from San Francisco to upstate New York around Troy and the eastern seaboard. The operation continued in this mode for about two years. It went so long, in fact, that the

FBI lost our "probable cause" to conduct search warrants because the original foundation went stale.

Then, as "Rough Rider" was winding down, the San Francisco office of the FBI put in a bid to shift the focus of biker gang investigation back out to the West Coast. That request was honored.

Hartung started buying dope from a New York City Hells Angel, Howard Stephen Wisebrod ("Howie" to his friends), who transferred to Oakland, California.

Radio-Free FBI

We wanted to put a bug on Howie's phone, but we in the FBI had already learned that phone taps alone weren't terribly productive. That was largely due to the telephone companies being infiltrated and corrupted by Hells Angels' plants. A technique that was extremely productive, though, was to combine a microphone and transmitter with the phone tap; often, a Hells Angel would have a coded conversation with an associate on the phone, then hang up and explain in plain language to somebody else in the room what had been discussed.

Hells Angels' houses, though, are notoriously difficult to get into when you want to plant a bug. For one thing, they are guarded against such possibilities. There is almost always somebody home.

In order to get around that, the FBI commissioned two stained glass windows with the Hells Angels trademark logo, a death's head profile, featured in the design. One of the windows was for Howard Wisebrod and one was for Sandy Alexander, president of the New York City chapter, and both contained sophisticated radio transmitters in the frame, each operating on an unusual frequency. Hartung gave these windows to Alexander and Wisebrod. Both hung these windows up inside their carefully guarded homes and became operators of "Radio-Free FBI."

Super Bowl Sunday

The information we got from these bugs gave us even more information to justify additional bug plants and surveillance, one of which was to go in the home of Albert Perryman. The ruse we used to get him out of the house was that Bonner, our crooked sports attorney, offered Perryman four tickets to the Super Bowl. We called up the Super Bowl security people, explained the situation briefly, and they came up with four tickets on the fifty-yard line, four rows up! Several of us wanted to use them!

The tickets got used but not by Perryman, much to our chagrin! But Albert was going on a motorcycle run with his wife and would be gone from the residence. We learned that a girl would be left to keep an eye on the place during his absence, however.

Since I had done this sort of thing quite a bit before, I knew that there was a pattern to the typical behavior of people guarding Hells Angels houses. Normally, the guy motorcycles off into the sunset, then calls back about sunset to make sure the guard is on duty. The guard would have to be in the place all weekend, or even for a week, until the Hells Angel returned. Well, that puts a certain amount of "cabin fever" pressure on somebody, and we noticed that very often, just as soon as the guy left on the trip, the guard also left to go shopping, or to pick up videos, or whatever was going to be required for the duration of the time they were locked into this house. That meant the place would be unguarded for a short time and during this time we might be able to plant our bug.

So, sure enough, Perryman isn't more than five miles down the road when our surveillance team watches the girl disappear out the gate, into her car, and down the road. We had a court order authorizing us to make the plant and were ready to go.

King, the Wonder Dog

Since we knew Albert Perryman owned a Bull Mastiff guard dog named King, we brought along the only FBI veterinarian-assistant specialist to deal with the dog, if necessary. This would be done with hot dogs laced with tranquilizer, or a syringe on a stick, or a dart fired from an airgun, or a tazer, or a silenced twenty-two-caliber pistol, if necessary, as a last resort.

We had all the "black bag" experts out from Washington, the alarm specialists and the lock specialists. All of us were lurking in the woodwork as Perryman leaves. As soon as the girl leaves, we all swarm over the fence into the compound.

King, The Wonder Dog, takes one look at this motley crew, many of whom are bombarding him with hot dogs, and concludes something is *very* wrong. King runs at high speed around the outside of the house twice, runs up to the front door of the house, and smacks the door very hard with the top of his head. The door flies open, and the poor dog runs and hides under his master's bed while a platoon of FBI agents are running around calling, "Here, King, here, King!" and trying to get him to eat a hot dog.

The alarm guys look at each other, the lock guys look at each other, shrug their shoulders, do their magic, and we all walk in and go to work. We put the bug in place with no interference from King or the girl guard, and we picked up our tools and departed. The bug worked perfectly and provided a lot of useful information.

Breakthrough

About this time (1985) we were seeing some intelligence information in the San Francisco FBI office that indicated that somebody, somewhere had a person inside the Hells Angels, but we had no idea who it was. Then

I got a call from Washington asking if I would be willing to meet a potential source and evaluate him for a long-term investigation of the Hells Angels. It turned out to be Tony, Anthony Tait, who had been working for the Anchorage Police Department and then for the FBI Alaska State office for several years by that point.

The problem for the FBI just then was that the Anchorage field office had very limited experience with outlaw biker gangs. They also had only fourteen agents covering the entire state. Their monthly field-support account to fund such investigations was a total of just $2,400, not enough to buy you much of anything!

I met with Tait and his "handling agent" Ken Marischen in Las Vegas. Tait showed up in a three-piece blue suit; his hair was short, and he looked like he was headed for MBA classes at Cal or a job in a bank. He looked like anything *except* a Hells Angel. He was obviously very bright. I thought he might be a double of some sort. He was too good to be true.

Tait was the Intelligence Officer for the Alaska chapter of the Hells Angels at that time. He wanted to just turn over all their records, leave the Hells Angels, return to the continental United States, and find a job as a cop someplace. "Oh, *no!*" I told him, "please don't do that!"

Now, with twenty-twenty hindsight, I regret that a lot. This has not been a kinder, gentler world for Tony Tait as a consequence. He has accomplished a tremendous good but, in a way, at the sacrifice of his personal life.

Anyway, Tait agreed to keep swinging with the Hells Angels. What I proposed to the FBI was that we turn him into a walking surveillance platform. The court-ordered break-ins we'd been doing were very hard work; the typical affidavit for such a break-in might be ninety or a hundred pages long. That request might take two or three weeks to get through the FBI system; then you have the sheer joy of trying to break into one of these Hells Angels places to plant the bug. Once you got it in, you could bet they'd change the meeting location within a week.

But how to make Tait a productive source with a life expectancy of more than a month? The Hells Angels have been very diligent in their countersurveillance techniques and were good at catching and cleaning infiltrators. We set him up with a transmitter installed in a conventional pager.

This transmitter had a very limited range, so somebody had to get in close to wherever Tait was working in order to pick up the signal. That meant that I and a couple of other guys had to hide out in an old Toyota camper, the kind with the pop-up shell on the back. We left the top down to keep it looking inconspicuous. You crawl in there and lay inside, feeling like an idiot. In the winter you freeze and in the summer you roast.

Also, we sometimes set up fixed-site surveillance points on a rooftop, in a basement, or in the trunk of a car—whatever it took to get close enough to listen to the transmitter and change tapes in the recorder.

Since transmitters and electronic equipment of all kinds have an eerie way of not working, we normally used redundant recording devices. Not only would we record the signal from the transmitter, Tait would also often carry a microcassette recorder. Every half hour or forty-five minutes he would get up and excuse himself to go to the john where he'd turn the tape over or put in a fresh one. So in any critical conversation we might have as many as three recordings of a single transaction. We got pretty good at it.

Undoubtedly, though, the primary reason for the success of Operation "Cacus" was Anthony Tait. He was a unique personality, easily the finest undercover operator I have ever worked with! You'll have guys that are dumb; Tait was real bright. You'll have guys that are chickenshit; Tait was pretty damn brave. You'll have guys that are *too* brave; Tait had the uncanny sense of where that line is in any situation, and he stays about two or three feet on the right side of the line. And he would follow instructions, religiously! While other agents had to be tracked down and throttled to produce receipts we needed for reimbursement, Tait handled the paperwork just as he was supposed to.

Another reason for our success was that we teamed up with a small number of agents from other agencies. Ted Baltas from ATF added humor and his considerable weapons expertise. Tim Bobbit of the California Bureau of Narcotics Enforcement (BNE) added guts, monumental surveillance skills, and raid planning. Bob Barnes of the FBI added wisdom. Jay Colvin, also of the FBI, added a willingness to do detail work. We all worked long, long hours. Ken Marischen in Anchorage was the heart and soul of the Alaskan facets of the operation.

Money flow was a constant problem with this investigation and with many FBI undercover operations. Tait was frequently reaching into his own pocket to keep the case going. He would ultimately get reimbursed, but in the short run it was creating big problems for him. It created problems for us, too. In fact, during Operation "Rough Rider," the other agents and I got $27,000 into our own pockets to keep the case going. It was around Christmas, we were buying dope like crazy, and the Bureau was paying extremely slowly. As an example of how these things sometimes work, the other agents and I came within two days of missing a mortgage payment because all our savings and checking accounts were fully drained to support the operation. Tait had similar problems.

Anchorage got authorization for Tait to carry a firearm. That was considered extraordinary criminal conduct when it was done by an undercover operator who was not (and Tait wasn't) a sworn law enforcement officer. That authorization only applied to Anchorage, though. So, when Tait traveled to California or elsewhere, our deal with him was that he could keep a gun in his hotel room but that he wouldn't carry it when he went to make buys. That didn't make him happy, but he was responsible enough to follow the instructions.

Well, Tait and I and some other agents were back in Kentucky for the funeral of John Cleve Webb, an Anchorage Hells Angel killed by members of the Outlaws motorcycle gang. We had been going nonstop for about forty-eight hours and were utterly beat. Tait had the uncanny ability to sense when you were at the end of your rope and would invariably try to bring some levity to the situation. The stress level was high for the Hells Angels, too, because a gang war was imminent. Officers of the club were detailed to stand guard, and Tait's turn came up. He relieved another Angel on the security detail, and we listen as the other guy hands Tait a pistol which, of course, he is prohibited by our agreement from carrying.

Tait walks off into the shadows, looks over to where I was parked, and says into the wire, "Tim, are you out there?" I was about five hundred yards away and flashed the parking lights to answer.

"Well, you're not going to like this, but a guy just handed me a gun." He reads off the serial number and tells me the make and model and caliber. "And I *know* you don't want me to keep it! *Okay,* well, I'll take it back!" Then he took it back to the guy and returned it, telling him he didn't need it and having it was just asking for trouble. That was typical of him, turning a situation around so that it played well with the FBI's organizational requirements. The fact that he returned the weapon saying he didn't need it increased his stature within the Hells Angels organization, too.

How important was Tait? Well, I think he set the Hells Angels back about ten years. After the operation was over, when I was writing up a recommendation for an award for him, I pointed out that Tait took something like $165 million worth of crack off the street. One hundred sixty-five million dollars! How many robberies does that represent? How many muggings? How many burglaries? A thousand burglaries? Ten thousand? Probably something over 100,000 burglaries! And in the course of the commission of these crimes, how many people would have been murdered? And as a result of people using all that crank, how many rapes and assaults would have been committed? There isn't any easy way to accurately evaluate the importance of what Anthony Tait accomplished, but it was tremendous. It changed the face of the Hells Angels, particularly in the San Francisco Bay Area, because they lost their major cash cow, Kenny Owen. It is ironic that one criminal could have contributed so much to the Hells Angels organization.

As a result of all this, unfortunately, the federal government has backed off on the pressure we applied to the Hells Angels and outlaw biker gangs. That's too bad. We haven't done that with the Mafia. It was almost as if somebody said, "Okay, we got what we were after. We declare victory and now we're going home."

There are a lot of guys in law enforcement who talk trash about Tait—claim to have met him, claim to have done things with him, claim that he's a lying scumdog. None of them will say that to his face. They are afraid of him, and rightly so; he'd eat their lunch. They are lying. One federal officer from another agency, incredibly, nearly exposed Tait during a Missouri visit. It was an amazing example of unprofessional conduct by a federal agent. It came close to getting him killed and the whole operation compromised. This same federal officer continues to tell anyone willing to listen that Tait was a crook, working off a beef or some other lie. Why? I can only think that he's one of those rare, self-serving assholes one sometimes encounters in law enforcement.

Tait has been testifying every year for the past ten years. He recently contributed to the conviction of Gerald Michael Lester for four counts of murder, including the execution of a seventeen-year-old and a five-year-old child.

Tait always makes himself available to help law enforcement personnel with their investigations. Several highly successful operations against outlaw motorcycle groups have Tait's fingerprints all over them. Tait talks the operation over with the officers involved and knocks the rough edges off whatever they have in mind until it aligns with both the *real* world of the Hells Angels and with the *unreal* world of the gang's manners, morals, and traditions.

After the case went overt, I wrote up a reward recommendation for Anthony Tait's contribution to the operation. It was approved. As a result, he was awarded the largest cash reward authorized by Congress for such a role: $250,000.

Inside
the Hells Angels

Anthony Tait wasn't a sworn officer of any jurisdiction or agency at that time, but he has probably done more for law enforcement than any other single individual recently. Tait volunteered to penetrate the Hells Angels motorcycle gang, and he succeeded. He quickly rose to become an important national officer of the group while working for the FBI. During the course of a three-year federal operation, Tait took large quantities of drugs, automatic weapons, explosives, and criminals off the street.

Tait worked closely with a small handful of FBI, ATF, and California Bureau of Narcotics Enforcement (BNE) agents, including Tim McKinley, Ken Marischen, and Timothy Bobbit.

Tait was never an "informer," term that normally applies to someone (usually a criminal) within a group who provides information for revenge or to get better treatment from law enforcement agencies. Instead, Tait was a hugely successful spy who penetrated the gang and collected information specifically designed to reduce criminal activity. It was an amazing acting job, and hard, dangerous work.

Tait was a "hang-around" for several months before being invited to join the Brothers motorcycle gang. This first story is from his "prospect" stage, a year-long period

*where prospective members are tested and evaluated be-
fore being accepted as full members. The rules for a prospect in any motorcycle gang are usually the same: you
attend all events, are assigned menial jobs, and do anything a sponsor asks. A prospect must fight anybody who
attacks a member or the club's name.*

The Price of Admission

"Prospecting" for any motorcycle gang can be hard
work. You've got to defend your sponsors in fights, do
anything they tell you to do, and generally act like a
slave. Ed Hubert, my sponsor, and Charlie Potter decided to visit a stripper bar, the Wild Cherry, and another prospect and I went along to do their bidding.

The Wild Cherry was the kind of place soldiers and
airmen like to visit, especially on payday, to get drunk
and to engage in their favorite sport, barroom brawling.
The bar was full of young soldiers from Fort Richardson,
all being loud and rowdy, but we got inside and up to
the bar without major incident. Our hairy little group
(looking out of place with all the close-cropped soldiers)
assembled at the bar, ordered our beers, and proceeded
to absorb one after another.

I was chatting with the manager of the club (soon to
be indicted for murder) when I noticed that Charley Potter has one of America's Finest jacked up. He's got the
kid by the collar, his feet a few inches off the floor, and
they are having an intimate discussion, nose to nose. I
put my drink down, ambled over, and used my best bar-
room-bouncer voice to reassure the gathering crowd of
the guy's soldier-friends. "Sit down, shut up, and there
won't be any trouble," I told them. They sat, they shut
up, and there wasn't any trouble for the moment.

Charley, whose interpersonal communication skills
were the envy of most of the club, pushed the kid down

back into his seat. "Mind your fucking manners and nothing will happen to you," he said. And the lads did just that, for a while.

But I could see they weren't entirely charmed by Charley's efforts at diplomacy. They were muttering among themselves, apparently planning something. We went back to the bar and our beers, and I resumed my conversation with the manager. Or tried to. The sounds of two drunks scuffling made me turn around. A couple of soldiers decided to make a move on Charley and Ed at the bar while my back was turned.

So there was Charley; he punched one of the guys. Another was standing near me, and I took him down with one punch—drilled him right on the nose, and he hit the deck.

Then I ran over to the rest of the group, four guys sitting at a table but in the process of getting up and joining in. I threw the table over and started punching and kicking as fast and hard as I could. A couple more were out of commission for a while, but then I noticed one guy had Potter in a headlock and was doing a good job of helping Charley make his mark on the bar, banging his face into the wood. I hopped over and chopped the trooper on the back of the neck a couple of times; he let go of Potter and wobbled there for a moment while I whacked him a few more times.

Then a couple of them caught me from behind, and we all played "pinball" for a little while, bouncing off the walls until we crashed against one of the fire exits, and we all fell outside into the snow and slush in a squirming pile.

There is just about nothing as refreshing after a good bar fight than falling into a large quantity of snow and slush. It will really perk you up. I would have felt more refreshed if I hadn't been pinned by the semideadweight of two of my recent competitors laying across me. One was holding me down, yelling to the other, "Break his fucking legs! Stomp on him!" Well, I wasn't feeling too

perky. I had taken some punches, my knuckles hurt, I
was sore all over, and I was lying in six inches of slush.
One guy was kicking me in the knee, trying to break
something, but when that didn't produce the desired result, he shifted his aim to my side. He managed to boot
me once or twice but accidentally scored on his partner
at least as often.

About this time, I was able to look around a bit and
noticed, through the open door, that Charley Potter was
still standing at the bar, a shot of tequila in one hand,
grinning and enjoying the floor show he'd started. He
was enjoying it a lot more than I was.

Frankly, I was just about used up. But before calling
King's X, I worked my hand down to the pocket where
my secondary weapon, a blackjack, was stashed. It
wasn't easy with these guys working on me, but I helped
things along by grabbing a handful of gonads owned by
the guy holding me down. A hard squeeze and he
yelped, then rolled off, more concerned about personal
matters than beating on me. That left one soldier to
deal with.

I got up. The guy saw me pull the blackjack out and
started to backpedal as I closed in on him. I started
chasing him—not easy on all that ice and snow after the
beating I had just received—and we started running laps
around cars in the parking lot. It must have looked like
an episode from the Keystone Kops. We were falling
down, getting up, swinging, falling down, yelling and
cursing with me bringing up the tail end of the parade
swinging my little weapon. I got some good licks in on
him once in a while and an occasional kick. Finally, he
surrendered and ran off, his buddy following. Trust me
on this, I was not about to chase them!

But wait, there's more! While trying to recover a little
bit, my sponsor and liege lord, Ed Hubert, saunters outside with his beer. He had been a bemused spectator to
most of this, but the actual fighting is the responsibility
of the prospect, so he stayed aloof during the brawl.

"Somebody punched me," Hubert complained, as if I was his mommy.

"Oh, hell," I replied. That meant I had to go defend his dubious honor, and I was just about out of gas. While we were standing there, a big Samoan bouncer from the club came out and, without even saying hello, sucker punched Hubert in the side of the head knocking him down. I gathered my pitiful, remaining resources and charged the Samoan. I must have looked pretty bad because he did a great imitation of a rabbit and took off at high speed. I tried chasing him for about half a block, but that's all. I was *thrashed!* But that kind of thing was pretty typical. The full members would start something, and then the prospects would have to get in and fight it out.

Famous But Incompetent

This picks up the story about two years into the program, after Tait had been working informally for the Anchorage Police Department (APD) strictly as a volunteer and using his own money for expenses.

As long as I was working with my friends at the APD, we weren't buying any dope or bombs or weapons. For one thing, we didn't have any money for it. For another, it would have been quite illegal under those conditions. We had no mission statement from the agency, and the whole operation was quite informal.

I hadn't had any real trouble penetrating the Hells Angels, had collected on the bet I made with Robbie and Ron, and had gathered about all the intelligence information I could under the circumstances. I'd been using my own money for expenses, and my dad had been great about subsidizing the operation, but it cost us something like $50,000 of our own money, and I was running out of resources. Besides, I was getting worn out and used up and starting to feel exposed and alone.

I was just gathering intelligence information and passing it along to the two cops. They, in turn, put it out within the police department as something they'd picked up from somebody on the street. That was the general cover story. But it was just a matter of time until somebody put two and two together and realized that these two cops were coming up with an awful lot of hard information about biker gang activity—more than they could pick up on the street. Then, somebody would start looking for me, maybe successfully.

I told them that I had just about had my fill of the operation. "Look," I said to Robbie, "I've done everything I promised—I got the gang's security file, developed a profile on each and every member, you know exactly what each of them is doing—it's time for me to quit the club, sell my bike, load up my truck, and go down south and find a law enforcement job."

Their response was that we'd been far more successful than any previous attempt to collect information on the gang, and that the operation should not be abandoned. "Let's go visit the 'I' instead," they told me, meaning the FBI.

Now, even though most cops will tell you the initials FBI stand for *Famous But Incompetent*, I held them in higher regard than the DEA, another federal agency that might want to work with us. DEA's security was notoriously lax, and when they wanted to execute an operation all the street scum seemed to know about it two days in advance. In fact, DEA agents managed to lose three handpacks, radios that could be used to monitor their tactical frequencies. Those handpacks turned up in a Hells Angels' clubhouse. I did not want to be associated with DEA. You couldn't trust them with routine security issues, and they had a reputation for burning people.

So my friends made the initial contact with Billy Andrews and Ken Marischen in September of 1984. Noth-

ing much happened until early December. I continued
to work as a bouncer at the Arctic Fox, a Hells Angels'
bar, three nights a week while working a construction
job weekdays. Finally, in December, Rob told me that
somebody at the FBI wanted to talk to me and that we'd
hook up sometime in January.

One night at "church" I was told that the club was
having some problems with people in Japan, and since
I spoke a little Japanese I was elected to go fix it. I went
to work getting my visa and called Robbie to give him
the bad news.

Finally, a meeting was set up at the FBI office in the
Federal Building in Anchorage. I wasn't real happy
about being seen around the place, but we met in the
evening after everybody else had left so the risk wasn't
too bad. I showed up about six in the evening, but I
wasn't quite what the FBI guys were expecting. They
were looking for a biker-type scumbag, with long hair
and wild beard, instead of normal-looking construction
worker with sawdust in his pockets. But they got over
their disappointment and we sat down to chat.

Biker 101

We talked for about four hours. It didn't take long to
discover that these guys, who were the FBI biker task
force for the area, knew nothing about what was happening in the gangs. So I just started briefing them on biker-
gang criminal activity in the Anchorage area—a four-
hour version of Biker 101. They took lots of notes, listened carefully, and then it was time to go home. "We'll
be in touch," they said, and that was it.

I went to work the next day and the next. We were
building a big warehouse, in the middle of January, and
it was bitterly cold. A week went by, then another, and
I didn't hear anything from the Bureau guys. Finally, I

got a call; Ken wanted me to drop everything, take time off work and come in—the beginning of a pattern that caused me a lot of problems and ultimately got me fired from my job.

We met at a bowling alley and sat in the car in the parking lot, talking for three or four hours. He took lots of notes and asked questions trying to verify that I knew what I was talking about. One of the things Ken wanted to know about was the death of Michael Moore, and it was a homicide I knew quite a bit about.

It had happened in December of 1982. Moore was a low-level drug dealer who'd been lured to the home of a Nomads prospect. Moore arrived expecting to sell a quarter-pound of cocaine to the prospect, but instead of the money he was expecting, he got a bullet in the back of the head. I was also a prospect for the gang at the time, and I found out about it when my co-prospect called and asked me, "How do you get rid of blood stains?"

"You can't," I told him, "Bloodstains are forever. Why?"

He didn't tell me right away but invited me over to help him move, and I could see why he was moving. He showed me where he killed Moore and told me how it happened. There was a hole in the wall around which was spattered blood, tissue, and bits of hair. There was a big splotch of dried blood on the carpet, too, and the colors clashed badly.

Here's what happened. He lured Moore over to the house with an offer to buy a large quantity of cocaine. Then, when Moore showed up with the big bag of coke, he pulled a gun on him, marched him downstairs to his roommate's photographic darkroom, and made him kneel facing the wall. Then he shot him in the back of the head. There was brain tissue splattered all over the photo gear, too, which pissed off his roommate who owned the stuff. Another Hells Angel, was asked to help get rid of the body. They took it up to the garage, loaded it into a pickup truck, and dumped it in an Anchorage city park. Somebody found it a couple of days later. The prospect kept the dope with the intention of selling it. The idea had been to make some money from the dope, but another Angel ended up snorting all the stuff before it could be sold.

About this time, the chapter chartered an airplane to take us all down to California for a big party to celebrate the chapter's acceptance into the Hells Angels.

Monterey Pop

The trip to California in January of 1983 was a very big event for the chapter, a celebration of our new status as a chapter of the Hells Angels. Although I was still just a prospect, I got to go along. In fact, I had work to do if I wanted to earn my colors. My duty was to fight for the honor of my sponsors whether they had any honor or not.

The chapter bought airline tickets for everybody, and when we got to San Francisco, we chartered three Lincoln Town Cars—two were baby blue, and one was pink—to get around the Bay Area. We drove around in a caravan looking for adventure.

We found some adventure in Monterey, and it got me arrested for the first time. Some local Hells Angels hosted us, and we drove around the area in our big Lincolns looking for fun. "Where can we find a little 'action?'" somebody asked the locals, meaning a strip joint where prostitutes would be available. "Not around here," the locals told us, but they suggested a different kind of action as an alternative.

The alternative was a bar called The Brick House, with Mexican Mafia ties. There was a gym nearby, and the guys who worked out at the gym came to the bar for their drinking. "We *always* get in trouble when we visit this place," the local chapter guys told us, and he said it with a twisted grin that made it sound like an endorsement.

"Hey, not a problem," the guys from my chapter replied with a laugh, "we've got the prospect, Tony, with us!" When I heard that, I thought, *Aw, shit, here we go again!*

Our little convoy of Lincolns pulled into the parking lot, and we crowded into the bar. We had been at this place no more than ten minutes, and I was just standing at the bar with a fresh drink in my hand, thinking that it seemed like a pretty nice place, when I heard a noise toward the front door. I turned just in time to see a body fly through space, slam against the front of the vestibule, and slide slowly down to the ground, just the way it happens in movies but without the music.

Hmm, I thought, *this is interesting.* So I took my drink and ambled over to the door expecting to watch somebody else's fight out in the parking lot. Just as I walked out the door, still holding my drink, somebody "sucker punched" me. My head snapped around and my glasses went flying. The loss of the glasses really pissed me off!

I recovered in time to discover a big bruiser, apparently from the gym, standing there, mouth agape, waiting to take me on. Without bothering with small talk, I snap kicked him in the sternum. Now, you can deliver a *lot* more force with a kick than with a punch and even after the sucker-punch, I planted a pretty good one on this guy. It rocked him back and took all the starch right out of him. I threw him against the wall and was punching him, whipping his ass. Another prospect came out somewhere along the line and was getting in a few licks on this guy, too. It's not nice to sucker punch a Hells Angel, even a prospect, and the two of us did our best to correct this big lunk's manners.

While I was busy with this, though, I heard the sound of approaching vehicles in the parking lot—screeching tires, car doors slamming, and the pitter-patter of many running feet, getting louder. I looked around to see a half-dozen police cars and a small horde of cops running in my direction. *Well, isn't THIS wonderful!* I thought to myself. I had been holding the guy up against the wall with one hand while punching him with the other, but it seemed time to drop him, and he slid to the ground, inert.

I turned to face the charge of all these cops. One guy was in the lead, baton raised over his head, ready to take my head off. Well, that's not the correct way to use the baton, as he was about to discover! As he closed on me, bringing the baton down, I blocked his swing with my left forearm, deflecting the force of the weapon away from my head. As his arm continued the swing, I just rolled my hand up, around his arm, under his wrist and elbow, and then he was trapped, and I had him locked to me, unable to move the baton.

Over the cops' shoulder, I could see his buddies closing in, waving their batons. It wasn't a reassuring sight. So I just grabbed the cop by the front of his body armor with my right hand, kept his other arm trapped with my left, and pulled him in close to use him as a shield. I backed up against the brick wall, with a bush on one side, and told him, "I'm not resisting, but I am not going to let you guys beat me up, either, so *you're* going to be a human shield!"

It was, looking back on the incident, hysterical. His buddies, in their zeal to beat my brains out, were whacking this poor cop with their nightsticks. They were nailing him on the arms, on the torso, trying to get to me but pounding their poor pal. I started laughing at them, which didn't help. The poor cop was wincing from pain every time his pals laid a blow on him, and he started screaming, "I've got him, I've got him! Stop, stop!" And they stopped.

I was arrested and spent the night in jail, a first for me. I was arraigned the next morning and went to court for trial. The judge fined me $50 and gave me six months unsupervised probation. I told him I was going back to Anchorage, and he told me to be a good boy. I said, "Yes, sir, I promise," and that was it.

North To Alaska

During the trip to California, the Moore murder kept coming up in discussion with the other Anchorage guys; and people were talking about it, around the edges of the facts. There was a lot of bitching about the way it was done, particularly how the dope had gone up an Angel's nose, and pretty soon the details of the killing were common knowledge within the club.

When I got back from California, I gave Robbie a call and made a report on the murder. I was thinking that the prospect who did it would get picked up for the murder, but it didn't work out that way. A few days after he moved out, the owner of the property decided to bulldoze the place and sell the land for a parking lot. All the evidence was gone before the APD could search the place, so there was nothing to support the case, and it was dropped.

As much as I regretted the arrest, it was another "ticket punch" with the gang. They really enjoyed the way I fought the guy who attacked me, and they especially loved the way I used the cop as a shield against the other cops. It was the sort of performance that really raised my stature with them, but it created a problem, too.

Sometime later, after I moved down to Oakland, California, to be closer to the Hells Angels headquarters, Chico "The Man" Mangenello called me with an ominous demand, "You've *got* to come over to my house. I want to talk to you RIGHT AWAY." He didn't sound like he wanted to tell me what a great guy I was, and it left me feeling very apprehensive. I met with McKinley downtown at the Hyatt Regency, and I told him, "Tim, there's some serious shit going down here. I have never gotten a call from him like that." I got the idea that it was the same kind of visit Mike Moore had made to the other place, but I didn't want to get the same reception. Tim set up some troops to provide security if it turned out I needed help, and we planned the visit as a kind of hasty and ad hoc operation.

I had recently sent my three-fifty-seven magnum to a law enforcement armorer to be tuned and tweaked, and it had just come back better than new. This seemed like an appropriate time to put it to work, so I stuffed it full of hollow points, tucked it into my waistband, and—with a small mob of invisible FBI and BNE (California Bureau of Narcotics Enforcement) cops watching from a discreet distance—drove over to Chico's place. I carried a microrecorder, just in case. I knocked on the door not knowing what was coming next, a bier or a beer.

Mangenello had been partying for three or four days straight, and was deeply under the influence of meth, but was on the downside of his binge. He was very tired, and he looked old. Apparently, he felt old, too, because he started to explain why he asked me over. "Look," he said, "I know I've only got a few years left in me, but I'd still like to impress the young guys coming into the club."

"What do you mean?" I asked him.

"I want you to teach me how to do the kinds of moves you used down there in Monterey, and some of the other fights you've been in. If you don't mind telling me, I would really like to know how to do that stunt with the cop's baton."

Well, that was a relief! I half expected to be asked to take a bullet in the brain, but instead he was asking me for a little show-and-tell time. We talked for about an hour, and I promised to come back when he was feeling better for more instruction.

I did come back, and that visit almost caused big problems, too. I noticed a plastic model of the president's helicopter in his living room. Chico didn't seem to be a big fan of the president, or of airplanes, so I asked him why he had it. "Oh, that's so I know how to take that fucker (meaning President Reagan) out, if I ever need to," he laughed.

It wasn't a laughing matter when I reported the conversation to McKinley, even though I thought he was kidding. McKinley, naturally, had to quickly write up a report and get it to the SS, the Secret Service, for a threat assessment. The SS immediately wanted to go have a chat with Chico. McKinley explained to them that if they did, they would blow the case, and my relationship with the Hells Angels, too, and the whole program would be over. So the SS told me that I had to make the call. Was there a genuine threat, or was the guy just BS-ing? I thought he was just being sarcastic, not serious, and the incident passed. But an autographed photo of President Reagan showed up not long after.

The Frozen Few

Every April Fools' Day the Anchorage chapter of the Hells Angels sponsors and event called The Frozen Few. It is a motorcycle run from Anchorage, in the sunny tropics of southern Alaska, up to frigid Fairbanks, and it is a very cold, miserable ride. Alaska in early April is never very balmy, and when you experience it on a Harley at seventy or eighty mph, it is downright nippy.

The Frozen Few run for 1987 was scheduled to terminate at Cheena Hot Springs, a nice little resort about forty miles outside Fairbanks. The local chapter had reserved cabins, arranged for catered meals, and laid in a large supply of booze and drugs but didn't bother with the canapés or the caviar on toast.

After a day on the road (some riders miserable on their bikes and yours truly in his cozy car), we finally arrived, checked in, and I hauled my bedroll to my room. Shortly thereafter I was propped up against the bar with a drink in my hand and a nice warm glow amidships. We arrived around three in the afternoon, and by seven or eight in the evening a lot of drugs and booze were being consumed.

I noticed a couple visiting with some of the members during the afternoon and evening. It was obvious that they were all acquainted, but it was not obvious just how or why. I was watching them when one of the other prospects ambled over, and I asked who they were.

"Oh, she's a 'hype,'" he told me, meaning somebody who does intravenous drugs. "Charley and another guy went over to their motor home to do some coke, and the couple wanted to shoot up; so Charley and the other guy bailed out." Even Hells Angels have their social limits, it seems, and IV drug users are not considered acceptable company.

I drank with the guys until 2 A.M. or so, by which time we were all pretty ragged, and I staggered off to bed.

The next morning dawned bright and clear, a beautiful cloud-free day with a deep-blue sky. The snow was deep and fresh and still clean, except for the parking lot and walkways where it had been plowed. I checked the thermometer—twenty degrees below zero, so cold that even the inside of your nose hurts! But I was dressed for it and was comfortable: lots of layers of clothes; good boots and gloves; and my favorite fashion accessory, my shrouded-hammer snub-nose five-shot thirty-eight-caliber revolver, tucked discreetly in a jacket pocket. I trooped down the icy trail, over toward the restaurant for breakfast about 8 A.M., but on the way I noticed the odd couple from the night before having a heart-to-heart session with one of the members.

As I approached, I could hear them "motherfucking" each other—never a good sign—and tensions seemed to be getting high. As I got closer, the guy made a quick gesture, and the three members of our group jumped back out of the way. I couldn't see what he was holding at first, but as I got nearer and asked what was going on, he turned toward me and took a quick swipe with a nasty little blade.

I was wearing heavy leather gloves that offered pretty good protection. I blocked his swing easily, and my first punch caught him on the nose. The result was a literal explosion of blood! I had broken his nose, and the blood sprayed all over everything. It would have been bad enough under normal conditions, but on the snow it really looked spectacular. Then we danced a little and he went down on the ground. I put my boots to him then. Its not nice to try to carve up people to whom you haven't been introduced.

I continued to kick him three or four times, in the ribs mostly, to remind him that he'd been bad. By now the knife was long gone, but while I was busy punting him along the trail, he was clawing for something else in his waistband. I noticed an object pop out of his clothes but didn't pay a lot of attention to it as it flew into a snowbank.

This little discourse was interrupted by the unforgettable sounds of somebody chambering a round in a rifle followed by a feminine voice screaming, "Get away from him, you motherfucker, or I'll kill you!" I turned to see his girlfriend about thirty feet away, holding an M1A rifle, the civilian version of the M14. Both chamber the three-oh-eight round, effective against targets at half a mile, and I was a lot closer than that.

I stood up, popped my glove off my right hand, and stuck it inside my jacket and around the thirty-eight special. That pistol is designed to shoot right through your pocket, if you need to, and I had it centered on her chest. I was thinking, *I can pop this bitch right now if I need to end this.*

The other three guys had evaporated as soon as that

rifle showed up, and I was standing there by myself, surrounded by three sets of tracks headed away. I talked to her and tried to get close enough to grab the rifle, but her man started yelling to her to keep back. She backed away, pointing the rifle at me the whole time.

By now some reinforcements have arrived, and they start yelling at her to throw down the gun. They are backing this up with guns of their own, and the woman takes cover behind a fifty-five gallon oil drum. This seemed like a good time to hide, so I did, behind a woodpile. While she's negotiating with the cavalry, her beloved is busy looking for something in the snow—and it isn't his watch.

Other members show up with shotguns, rifles, pistols, and they're all yelling at this girl. Now, she and the guy were both lightly dressed for the occasion and were obviously cold. I finally yelled to her, "Let's go inside and talk about this! I give you my word nothing more will happen to you!" The couple thought about it, then agreed. We walked toward the lodge together with me escorting them. She still had the rifle, and the members still had their guns pointed at them. As we walked past the club manager I whispered, "Call the police. Get me some help out here, now!"

We found a table in the lodge and ordered coffee. She sat across from me with the M1A pointed at my chest; I had my hand in my pocket, wrapped around my snub-nose thirty-eight, pointed at her. We sat there with her bloody boyfriend, chatting like old buddies.

"Look," the guy said, "all I want is my forty-five back." I didn't know what he was talking about.

"When you knocked me down and kicked me, it came out of my belt and Charley stole my gun. I want my forty-five back and my knife, too!"

"I'll do what I can, but no promises," I told him in my best bouncer style. "And you can see that things have gone to shit around here, and you're going to have to leave. You can't stick around or there's going to be more trouble." After twenty minutes and two cups of coffee, they realize the party's over and it is time to go home—and without the forty-five or knife.

"I'll walk you out to your truck to make sure there's no more trouble," I told them, "and I'll look for the forty-five but if it's in the snow, it is probably lost till spring."

"No, Charley stole it—and I want my knife back, too," he said, but he wasn't going to get either.

We walked out to his truck, and the two of them pile in. Five Hells Angels are providing security, spread out around us, waiting for an opportunity for more excitement.

He turns the key and nothing happens. The truck is frozen solid. The guy is having a very bad day. "Don't worry about it," I told him, "we'll fix that." I sent two prospects off for a couple of Ready Heaters.

While we were waiting for the heaters, the lodge manager ran up. "I did what you told me," he said breathlessly, "I called the cops and they will be here in about half an hour!"

"You did *WHAT?*" I screamed at him. "We don't need any cops around here!" It is a very rare event indeed when a Hells Angel calls the cops for help and admits to it.

The two prospects show up with the heaters, a common item of equipment in Alaska. They are essentially big blowtorches used for space heating. We fired both up and pointed them at the radiator and oil pan of the pickup. In a few minutes the engine was warm enough to cook on; the guy turns the key and it fires up. After a few minutes for the truck to warm up, he put it in gear and the happy couple disappeared down the road.

Now, if you are thinking that our troubles were over, you'd be wrong. The real trouble is down the road, headed our way, "code three," in the form of an unknown number of Alaska State Troopers. The relationship between these fine lads and the friendly local chapter of the Hells Angels was not good on the best of occasions, but when guns, knives, bloodshed, and mayhem were all part of the equation, you can appreciate how they might be a little tense. And I still hadn't had any breakfast.

"Okay, everybody, put your guns in the trunk of my car," I yelled at the guys, "then get undressed and into the pool! The cops are going to be here in a few minutes, and it'll be safest for everybody if we're obviously unarmed and not a threat to them." There was some argument at first. "Look," I told them, "if you're in the pool, the cops aren't going to consider you a threat. They are coming out here with a bad attitude, and they've probably heard about some gunplay and violence. They aren't going to shoot you while you're soaking in the hot tub."

Most of the guys buy into this plan, except for a few still in bed, and we all get into our suits and hop in the water. Within a couple of minutes, we're all soaking in the hot springs, enjoying the company of our peers, and flirting with each other's old ladies. After simmering in one of the hot tubs for a bit, I got up to go to the swimming pool and, while walking the short distance between the two, noticed somebody standing at the door to the enclosure. He was a nervous trooper holding a twelve-gauge shotgun and was pointing it at me.

"I'm not armed," I told him and turned around, ". . . except for what's between my legs. Wanna see it?" I started to pull down the front of my trunks.

"No, no, no, I am not interested in it," he said. He calls for cover. The troopers held us in the pool while other troopers searched the locker room. They came up with small amounts of marijuana—legal in Alaska at the time—but only found a small amount of cocaine, a few bindles of dope (legal at the time), no guns, and just a few knives. Potter had some coke behind his patch, so they confiscated that but nothing substantial enough for an arrest.

Then we could get dressed, and they marched us into

the lodge where they could keep an eye on us. Finally, I got to order something to eat and had my breakfast and coffee while the troopers were poking around in everybody's rooms.

The troopers tried their best but just couldn't come up with anything to charge us with, and ultimately said good-bye, climbed into their cars, and left. The club manager had had enough of us, and we were invited to leave, too, and the party was over. The 1987 Frigid Few run was now just another page in the Hells Angels Anchorage Chapter scrapbook. Memories, memories!

Later, I found out that the couple who started all this were snagged in a roadblock the troopers set up on the highway. The gal got picked up for some outstanding warrants; the guy went to the hospital for a broken nose and broken rib. All in all, a weekend they probably wanted to forget.

Explosive Developments

On August 16, 1986, John Cleve Webb of the Anchorage Hells Angels, was shot and killed by two members of the Outlaws motorcycle gang at Shepardsville, Kentucky, just outside Louisville. As you can imagine, the membership was not pleased. So we all got together at the clubhouse to plot and scheme revenge.

As security/intelligence officer and sergeant at arms for the club, I was in perfect position to know what was happening and to defuse some of it. We had a meeting to discuss the incident and how we ought to respond. There was talk right away of using explosives to blow up the Outlaws clubhouse, preferably during some important social function when it would be full of Outlaws. Of course, the FBI cannot permit something like that to happen; so, it was up to us to defuse the situation.

Hells Angels members love to collect weapons of all

kinds—guns, knives, and explosives. Everybody seemed to have a little stash of exotic fireworks hidden in a garage, or trailer, or in their "old lady's" underwear drawer. "Okay," I told them, "if any of you guys have stashes of explosives, bring them in and turn them over to me. You'll be compensated for them."

After the meeting, one member came up to me and said, "Listen, I have some stuff out back. Want to take a look at it?" We went out to his car and in a briefcase he had some TNT, white phosphorus grenades (very nasty things), some mining explosives, some dynamite, and a two-and-one-half-pound block of C4—a veritable mixed bag of high-grade fireworks.

All this would have made a nice haul but a poor foundation for prosecution. That's because there were no blasting caps in with the explosives and, without them, most of these items were almost inert. You can set fire to C4, TNT, and dynamite without much fear of detonation—that takes the sharp jolt of a cap. So an ATF guideline for such buys specifies that blasting caps should be part of the deal.

"Yeah, I'd like to buy it," I told him, "but I need caps with it."

"Okay, no problem. Six hundred bucks for the lot," he said, and we made an appointment to do the deal a couple of days later.

I huddled with the FBI and ATF guys to plan the buy. I was supposed to visit the guy's house, collect the explosives, pay him the $600, then bring the stuff back to a safe-house apartment we maintained.

On the day of the deal they wired me up like stereo store with a microcassette and a transmitter to provide play-by-play coverage. I ambled over to the guy's place and he popped open the briefcase. The dynamite was in a paper sack, and the bag had a little oily residue on it—bad news!

Now, normally dynamite is safe and stable to handle. It is a mixture of nitroglycerine—a very, *very* sensitive explosive—and a binder like clay or sawdust that makes it far less sensitive to shock. But dynamite needs special handling during storage to keep the nitroglycerine from leaking out of the binder. Typically, the cases are turned over every few months to keep the stuff from leaking out. Well, my friendly explosives vendor hadn't bothered with that, and the nitro was leaking out. All it would take to detonate the whole mess would be for something to strike a sharp blow on that residue on the paper.

So we made our trade, I collected the briefcase and its contents, and I very carefully placed it flat on the front seat of my pickup truck. I strapped it down with the seat belt and drove off, slowly, making wide detours around potholes and bumps in the road.

Once I got to the safe house, I unstrapped the briefcase and carried it gingerly inside, flat, and watched my steps very carefully. Inside, I set it down on the kitchen counter and opened the latches. "Here you go, guys," I told them.

Ron Tarrington, the ATF agent, acted like a kid at Christmas. It was his first-ever big explosives case. He started pulling things out of the briefcase, then got to the dynamite and said, "Oh, shit! I really get nervous about this!"

"What do you mean?" Ken asked. "What's to be nervous about?"

"This dynamite is leaking nitroglycerine all over this paper bag," Ron said.

"You mean we've got nitro in here?" Ken exclaimed.

"Well, fellas, I guess my part of the operation is all done now. I think it's time for me to be leaving. See ya!" I said, laughing at them.

"Wait—don't leave now," Kenny said.

Ron said, "We need a plastic washtub and about ten quarts of motor oil to neutralize this material, *RIGHT NOW!*" The oil suspends the nitro and makes it safer. He called the office and got two other agents to bring the stuff over. They showed up after a while and left the tub and oil outside, refusing to come inside. And about this time I decided my role in this explosive little drama was over, and it was time to make my exit, stage right. "Bye, guys, have fun!" I said, and left.

Kenny called later to report that both he and Ron survived the incident, no thanks to me. "We took it out to Fort Richardson, put it in the burn pit, and set fire to the stuff. We have enough other stuff to prosecute with, and the risk from the dynamite was just too great to keep it around."

I guess all of us were lucky with that one. The guy who was selling it did everything wrong with it, including leaving it outside where it could freeze and thaw, another good way to make it unstable. But the operation was just one part of a risky business.

Fighting Words

I went to "church" for our regular weekly meeting the night of September 5, 1986, and sat down, waiting for the festivities to begin. A bunch of us were sitting there, drinking beer and laughing, when Ed Hubert, the club president, walks in. He looks right at me and says in an accusing tone, "FBI, huh?"

My blood ran cold. I didn't flush or get nervous, but I thought I had been discovered and wasn't sure what was going to happen next. If he was serious, they would not want me to get out of that room alive. And he didn't seem to be joking.

There were about a dozen of them in the room, and it would be me against them all. We were all sitting around the pool table, and I had my back to the wall. Four of us were on an old sofa, one guy was on my left, two on my right.

This was at a time when the whole club was gearing up for war against the Outlaws, and a lot of us showed up for meetings loaded for bear, including me. My Browning Hi Power nine-millimeter automatic was in a shoulder holster under my vest. The Hi Power's nine-milimeter round isn't particularly powerful and its knockdown ability is limited, but it holds fourteen (thirteen in the mag, one in the chamber) rounds and I might need them all. There were two full-spare magazines on the right side of the shoulder-holster harness, if there was ever a chance to reload. For backup, I carried a little shrouded-hammer snub-nose thirty-eight-caliber revolver in an "appendix carry" Holster inside the front of my pants. And for dessert, I had a nice, little Cold Steel tanto-fighting knife in a cross-draw position.

There were eleven guys waiting for church, some armed and some not, but most were experienced fighters. I knew I could shoot the guy on my left—he was the closest, and he'd be first—then the two on my right. I would have had to kill all eleven guys in the room to get out alive. I could have gotten out of there, but it would have destroyed our case and all the work we'd been doing.

While those words were hanging in the air, I casually put my hand in my lap, then ran it up inside the vest to the Browning. I unsnapped the holster, got a good firing grip, and waited to see what happened next.

"Yeah," he said, "the FBI stopped me outside my house and questioned me. They wanted to know who killed J.C." That's why I was late." And that was it—a little joke, at my expense, and not very funny.

I kept my hand there for a bit, put the safety back on, and tried to laugh politely at the remark. Then, after a decent delay, I got up and went to the bathroom and tried to throw up. It didn't work. I washed my face and hands with cold water, trying to recover. That worked. I snapped the pistol back into the shoulder holster, got myself back together, and went back out to the meeting as sergeant at arms. The meeting was called to order and we began, just like always.

That was one of the most frightening moments of the whole three years' work for the FBI.

Kenny Owen, the Mad Scientist

Kenny Owen was well known by the FBI, DEA, and many local agencies as one of the major methamphetamine producers in California, a brilliant chemist, a sociopath, and a very important—and untouchable—criminal. These agencies had taken many runs at Kenny but were never able to get what they needed to convict him.

They called Kenny "the Mad Scientist" because he could cook up just about anything he wanted, and what he wanted to cook were drugs that could be sold for lots of money. All of this, naturally, made Owen a prime target and, just as naturally, Owen knew he was being hunted. He was extremely cautious about everyone he dealt with, and everything he did.

Owen was a meticulous chemist. While almost anybody can cook meth, given the chemicals and some fairly common lab apparatus, Kenny routinely did what was supposed to be impossible—he produced virtually one-hundred percent pure methamphetimne while the best others could make was only eighty-seven percent pure. Even the FBI lab was impressed.

One of the BNE (Bureau of Narcotics Enforcement) agents mentioned to me one day that Owen was his priority one target, but that nobody had ever been able to get the goods on him. "Well, why don't we try?" I told him.

Making a drug buy from Kenny Owen didn't seem like much more than a regular dope buy to me, but it certainly was to them. Owen was somebody they'd been trying to get for years, but he was too careful for them. We decided to try to set up a buy sometime in the future, and to do so I was going to drop in on Kenny and see if he was willing to make a deal.

Anyway, they wired me up with a recorder and transmitter, and I drove over to Kenny's woodshop. As usual,
I had a couple of agents monitoring the transmitter, providing documentation, and covering me. Another couple
of agents set up surveillance on the location, both to
protect me and to document what I was doing when the
case ultimately went to trial.

The shop was right across the street from the Oakland
Hells Angels' clubhouse, behind a chain-link fence and
normally locked gate. The gate was open and I went in,
knocked on the door. "Hi, Kenny here?" I asked the
guy that came to the door. It was one of Kenny's employees, and he recognized me from the incident with
the Oakland police raid when I defended Kenny.

"No, he's at his house," was the reply. "You can go
up there, but he's probably upstairs, and you'll have to
let yourself in the gate."

"Okay—what's the combination?"

"It's 2001."

I thanked him, got in my car, and drove up to his
place in the Oakland hills, off Golf Links Road—losing
my cover in the process, and taking the transmitter out
of range, too. But I found the place, parked, ambled
over to the fence, and tried to visit with the four barking,
snarling Doberman Pincer dogs patrolling the yard, then
pushed the intercom button to announce myself. "Hey,
Kenny, are you in there? It's Tony."

"Hi, Tony, come on in," Kenny answered.

The dogs refrained from chewing on me, and I went
in. Kenny was upstairs, in his bathrobe and, with his
long hair and beard, looking just like a friendly old so-
ciopathic Benedictine monk.

We sat down and visited for a while; then Kenny
handed me a small bag of crank, the way most folks
would offer a guest a cup of coffee. I simulated taking
a snort, then passed it back to him. "Hey, that's pretty
good stuff!" I told him.

We visited a while longer, then I said, "Kenny, have

you got one of these?" and patted my elbow. He looked puzzled. "You know, *'LB',*" I said, using a code-word gesture for a pound of meth, one Kenny wasn't apparently familiar with. "I'd like to get one."

"Oh, yeah, sure," he said, "wait a couple of minutes," and disappeared into another room. I could hear creaking and banging as he fished around in secret compartments for his stash. Then he reappeared with a package wrapped in brown paper. "Here you go," he said.

"Oh, shit, right now? I don't have the cash on me. It's back at my hotel," I said.

"Just take it," Kenny said. "Pay me later. I'll give you the Oakland member price—$10,000 a pound."

Well, this was an operation that suddenly got way out in front of its planning. We never anticipated that he'd hand over the dope so quickly and easily. I didn't have any cash, I had lost my cover and my surveillance, and I was suddenly in possession of a pound of pure, illegal crank with a street value of maybe $100,000.

I walked out of Owen's compound elated but worried at the same time. The meth went into the trunk of my rented car and I drove off. "Okay," I said to the transmitter, "whoever is out there chasing me, you'd better get up here on my ass, right now! I have a pound of crank with me. He fronted it to me, and there's no way I could get out of it without creating suspicion! Come and get this stuff!"

As soon as I could, I started talking into the transmitter and recorder. Successful prosecution of drug cases requires that the custody of the drug be documented every moment, from the time it leaves the hands of the dealer until a government agent takes possession and documents the deal. This means that there couldn't be any gaps on the tape in my recorder or on the recorder attached to the receiver for my transmitter.

Well, nobody showed up. I got all the way back to the hotel—still no cover. I removed the bag of crank from the trunk, took it upstairs to my room, still mumbling to the recorder and transmitter. Finally, I grabbed a magazine and started reading into the recorder to maintain continuity; the article was "The Charge of the Light Brigade," in *Military History* magazine. I was really concerned that, for a lack of a documented chain of evidence, we couldn't use this evidence to prosecute—it happens all the time—and our good luck would be wasted. Keeping up this running dialogue was the only thing that could prove that we didn't somehow plant the evidence, a charge often made by defense attorneys in court. Another problem in such cases is that informants will sometimes open a package of dope bought for evidence, then steal some of it for their own use—for sale or personal use. The tape recording and transmitter provided some evidence of what I was doing every second the dope was in my custody.

Finally, there was a knock at the door. It was the BNE agent, and the deal was done. He was laughing his ass off. "I never thought you could pull that off," he said, "but you did it perfectly! This is a very prosecutable case!"

I returned to Kenny's place that night, meeting him at the wood shop, and handed over the $10,000. "That's good stuff," I told him. "We need to do it again."

"Whenever you want it," he said, stuffing the cash in his safe.

We went back for more, just before the November arrests, just to make sure we had Kenny's case airtight. I bought another pound for $10,000 and he "fronted" me another pound for the same figure, but he was arrested before he got paid.

Bobbit said it was a prosecutable case, and so it was. Kenny was arrested in the big sweep that followed, on November 10, 1987, and was finally sent to prison. He'll be eligible for parole in 2012 but with special, "searchable" parole for the rest of his life.

I guess I still owe him that ten grand!

Working Undercover

First Sergeant Pete Edge joined the Maryland State Police thirty-two years ago, back in the days when undercover operations were somewhat more improvised—and sometimes safer—than they are today. Pete worked all kinds of undercover jobs all over the state for many years, and he is still called on occasionally to participate in operations. Rather than describe in detail specific cases, Pete tells about a life undercover.

Unlike some of the other officers and agents who've provided stories for this book, I am not comfortable providing names and details that could reveal the identity of the people I worked with and my relationship with them. If I didn't have to surface and make an arrest—which was often the case for me, since I was gathering background information for later use—these people never knew what I was doing, and they still don't. And I would like to keep it that way.

I started in narcotics a long time ago. The policy at the time seemed to be that the command assigned the bizarre guys to that kind of work. There wasn't much screening or interviewing. I had been a drama major in college, and that's about as close to acting as I am ever going to get. I loved doing covert work, and that's why I am still a police officer. During the day, I'd work my uniform assignment and at night I went down to D.C. and to Georgetown to make buys for the District of Columbia police. That agency had run out of undercover people so they used me to buy peyote buttons for them; they'd put the event on film, and we'd go to federal court. That's how I started working undercover.

It was a less brutal time, back then. You could expect an ass-whipping once in awhile, but it wasn't like today when a seven-year-old will shoot you just for drill. That part has changed very radically. But I enjoyed it. We had a small unit and had to do all our own surveillance, our own wiretaps, our own investigations, so each of us got to rotate through the assignments.

We did all kinds of cases—small buys of marijuana down at Ocean City, in the beginning. I used to walk the boards down there, in casual summer attire, and find somebody dealing. "Raise your right hand and swear you aren't a narc," they would sometimes demand. I did it, then bought the dope and made the arrest. My very first undercover arrest was at the Purple Moose on the boardwalk; the dealer had stuck a joint inside the mouth of a stuffed moose inside this place.

I did just about every kind of case you can imagine. One time I drove a fuel truck for a guy with a federal contract to deliver fuel oil to impoverished people. He was selling the oil instead of delivering it to the poor folks who needed it. It was a horrible assignment. I worked for this guy during a long, freezing cold winter, with leaky hoses and decrepit trucks that were always breaking down. And when the truck broke down, the driver got charged for it! I worked over ninety hours one week and made just $25.

But the funny part of the job was that while this guy was cheating the people he'd been paid to serve, his drivers were cheating him! The drivers were mostly on work-release from jail, and they were giving lots of the fuel to their friends and family for free. So the guy who was trying to cheat the poor folks was getting cheated himself, and the fuel was going to the community where it was supposed to go in the first place! I got a big kick out of that. The hard part of the operation was having to stand by while this guy beat up his secretaries. He would smack these gals in the face, and there was nothing I could do to intervene.

The whole operation, with the exception of me, was black. They should have had a clue, since I was the only white guy, but didn't. Anyway, one night one of the other drivers and I were walking along the sidewalk when a little boy, under ten years old, confronted us. He had a little twenty-five-caliber pistol and said, "Gimme all your money!"

The guy with me said, "Go fuck yourself!"

The kid shot him. The bullet hit him right in the forehead! But the mechanic didn't fall down. The bullet didn't even penetrate the skin. I took off after the little son of a bitch who ran off at 8,000 miles an hour. I almost caught him, though, but he stooped over and I went right over the top of him. He got up and disappeared through a hole in a fence. We called the police, but that was the end of it. If that bullet had hit me, I'd have died of shock!

The owner of the fuel-oil company doesn't know, to this day, that I was "working" him. Ultimately, the guy was arrested and tried on federal charges. He was convicted but served a minimal sentence. He bullshitted his way through it. And that was all too typical of many of the cases we worked—you'd get the goods on somebody, work hard and long to do it, and then little or nothing would happen. No charges would be filed, or they'd "cop a plea," or be acquitted. That is the frustrating part of covert police work.

A lot of the cases were very small-time vice jobs, but one of my most interesting covert cases was a long-term operation against an old Italian organized-crime figure.

I spent a lot of my life with this guy and was just starting to make major inroads when he very rudely died on me—of cancer. He was quite a character. Even though he was very evil, he was extremely interesting! He had done *everything* criminal you can imagine.

This man was a great spaghetti eater, and he always fixed me spaghetti with milk and fresh bread, which I enjoyed at first. But I wondered why nobody else in the organization would eat at the man's place. Then one night I got to his place early and was waiting for him to fix dinner. There was some spaghetti left over from lunch, still in the big iron pans he used to cook it. He came in, said "Sorry dinner's not ready yet," and put the pans on the floor. He called in his big Doberman pinschers, and they quickly ate up the pasta, licked the pans clean. And he just threw them back on the stove and started cooking dinner! I cut down on the spaghetti after that.

A lot of situations that seemed initially to be quite dangerous turned out, after awhile, to be not so bad. I became friends with these people, and I think that happens pretty often. If you're working deep cover, or long-term covert ops, you find that some of these people have redeeming qualities. I started working with this old, Italian guy after his teeth were pulled. He had a much younger girlfriend—about a quarter his age—and that was typical of this kind of guy. She was a stripper, and he was in love with her. She was nuts, and he was nuts, and they'd throw knives at each other in front of me. Knives would be sticking in the walls.

Even so, he was *fascinating,* like a Damon Runyon character. He was a major fence, and people brought in all kinds of stuff. He hid stuff all over—money in the walls, in a truck buried underground. And he trusted me. Then he got very, very sick.

His dark side was very dark; he had friends who did contract murders; he sent whores from one state to another. There was no illegitimate activity in which this man did not participate. He was nasty and yet very well respected. He was charming in his own crude way.

And he was very crude. He didn't have a bathroom in his place, in the heart of Baltimore City. When he needed to go, he just went out in the backyard and went on the concrete—he didn't care. If he didn't like you, he'd tell his dogs to bite you, and they would!

A lot of undercover work I did was like that—a bit confusing. One of my first cases was a heroin buy in a nice bar in Baltimore City. It was a gay bar, and this was at a time when the gay world was even more covert than I was. My contact for the deal was the maitre d'— the guy was a real "flamer"—and while I was waiting to make the buy, a gorgeous creature, apparently female, walked in. I was young and handsome at the time, and she invited me upstairs. The maitre d' said to go ahead, and I went along. I expected to buy dope, but this "girl" had other things in mind. I really didn't know *what* this creature was, and I wasn't going to get sexually involved in any event. We talked, though, and she got undressed—and looked to me to be a fully authentic woman. Anyway, it was clearly time to depart.

I made my excuses and started down the long staircase, hurried along by shoes and other solid objects the scorned "woman" hurled at me. Then something landed on the top of my head. I thought it was acid. Instead, it was a cat she had dropped on me from above. Its claws were imbedded in my scalp; I could *not* get that damn cat off my head! It was still there when I went out the door. That was the kind of thing that happened working undercover back then.

One guy whose name I will mention is Robert Michael Wilson. Wilson is the guy who allegedly killed Albert DiSalvo, the "Boston Strangler." That happened in Walpole State Prison during a fight over a pound of bacon.

Robert Michael Wilson was responsible for eight or ten murders that police agencies knew about. He had

-cut people's heads off and burned them. He was a very nasty guy.

We knew Wilson was planning to visit a horse farm owned by a wealthy gentleman in Maryland, and we planned and executed an operation to take him. I was placed in one section of the building, and Wilson came into my sector, where we had a little encounter. I tried to shoot him, but some of my guys were behind him, in the line of fire. I had a shotgun and tried to get him by firing low at his legs, but he jumped out of the way just as I fired.

Wilson shot at me; the shot just grazed me and went into a box stable. Wilson ran and got away for the moment, but we caught up with him later that night and one of the other guys shot him. He lived. He's a tough little son of a bitch.

We finally got him into court, years later, for the shooting and a whole raft of other crimes he committed. A young prosecutor was able to get him charged with trying to kill me.

Wilson came to court wearing the bullet he'd been shot with on a chain around his neck. "Here, motherfucker," he said, holding up the mangled slug, "look at this—I'm still alive!"

After the trial, at which he was found guilty, I was given the bullet he'd fired at me. It wasn't damaged at all. I had it put on a chain and when he came in for sentencing, I held it up to him and said something like, "Here, motherfucker, mine's prettier than yours!" That was fun, but you don't often get to do that.

We were convinced we were making a difference. We worked for a guy named Frank Mazone who told us we were putting a dent in crime in our state, and we believed him. There was no overtime pay when I started, but we worked twenty and sometimes twenty-four hour days with no extra compensation except a little meal money. It cost me two families. We worked everything from murder-for-hire to liquor violations out in western

Maryland, around Cumberland. Out there we hung out in red-neck bars, got in fistfights, and went after liquor violations.

One of the more enjoyable assignments I had was working the Mitiki coal mine, out in western Maryland. The Mitiki is a nonunion mine, and when the unionized coal miners in nearby West Virginia went out on strike, they'd go after the nonunion mines by blowing them up. We lived in West Virginia for six months investigating the attempts to dynamite the Mitiki. We hung out with the coal miners, went to meetings, found out when they were going to attack the mine—and then, somehow, the Maryland State Police Tac Squad would be waiting when the miners went to blow the place up. They *never* figured that out. And while hanging out in the miner's bars, we discovered that the bartenders were fences; one thing leads to another.

The West Virginia assignments were fun for me— chewing tobacco, doing all kinds of things we wouldn't ordinarily get to do on covert assignments. And I got to experience things that would never happen to me during a conventional assignment. For example, I was sent out to a small town to investigate a guy operating a federal program intended to help poor kids. I just arrived in this little town when I got pulled over by the local cop.

"You were doing twenty-five in a thirty-five zone," he said, writing me a ticket.

"But I was doing ten under," I told him.

"You heard me, didn't ya?" he said. "If ya don' believe me, look at my granpappy!" His grandpappy was sitting in the car holding the radar gun—in his pajamas! The display on the gun indicated twenty-five.

"Look," I said, "it says twenty-five, and the limit's thirty-five!"

"Don't you know better than to argue with the police?" he asked, finishing the citation.

I signed the ticket, which turned out to be great cover for the assignment. I got pulled over in front of the town bar, and all the locals saw what happened. They welcome us, saying "That son of a bitch get you, too?" Some of them turned his car upside down, as payback. It ruined the light bar, and all the oil dripped out. The next morning the cop and his grandpappy got some friends together, and they turned the patrol car back onto its wheels. That was fun!

I really enjoyed some of cases we worked. Besides the dope deals that went bad, the long surveillances that didn't pay off, the hours of wiretap recording we did, it was very rewarding and satisfying work. The hardest part was when I had to bust a police officer, something I had to do several times. Serpico I wasn't! And I hate to work other cops—the worst assignment in law enforcement. But I would still like to be doing those jobs, now mostly reserved for the younger guys and gals. A lot of old, hard-ass crooks don't want to deal with kids; they are more comfortable with their contemporaries.

My assignments were probably pretty small in the grand scheme of things, but they entertained me, they were fun, and I believed then and now that we made a difference.

Just Like *Mission Impossible*

Graham "Des" Desvernine, Special Agent, FBI (retired), spent a career working organized crime, undercover, white-collar crime, and surveillance. He formed and supervised a regional special operations squad. He now heads a private investigative service and works cases around the world.

I had a lot of cases going on at the same time, but I never got into the long-term, deep-cover kinds of operations that some of the guys who worked with me did. Some of them were in the Weathermen movement and were in there for years; the only time they came out was for occasional FBI meetings. Other than that, they lived the life for years on end.

But I was able to maintain pretty much a normal life. I maintained contact with people through post-office boxes and special phone numbers where I could be contacted without being identified. I worked that way for many years.

One of my roles was Harry Silverman, a New York fence. I used that role anyplace and said that I just came into town. I had a telephone number in New York City, a business address, stationery, my name on the door—

everything. And if they tried to contact me there, they could. I dealt in stolen property, securities, and jewelry.

Another role I played was Vic Rossi, a Mafia boss, also from New York. I used that one for money-laundering schemes and anything relating to organized crime.

I had complete sets of identification for each personality—American Express card, driver's license, business cards, and the works. The nature of the roles I played, and the way I set them up, let me live a pretty normal life most of the time.

I owned a bar in Alaska for two and a half years, in Valdez during the pipeline days. We opened that bar in November of 1974, just as the pipeline was getting rolling. The bar was part of a scheme by a guy in the San Francisco Bay Area who set up a prostitution and gambling ring to service the pipeline workers. The workers were paid cash, by union agreement, and they were paid well. They didn't have much to do after work, and it was a natural environment for prostitution and gambling.

Nobody ever "made" me during the whole time I was doing undercover ops, even though I lived a pretty normal life and was out on the street a lot. My wife was in the restaurant business; I met a lot of people through her, and it would have been pretty easy to bump into somebody who knew somebody.

One of the ways I protected myself from such situations was to always walk out in front of a group. If we were entering or leaving a restaurant, I went through the door first. The first thing I do is to scan the room to see if there's anybody present I know. If I do recognize somebody (and that does happen), I avoid conversation with them. If they know I work for the FBI, there's a tendency for somebody to mention that in conversation, "So, how are things down at the Bureau?" kinds of comments. You can get burned that way in a hurry! So if I did spot somebody I recognized, I excused myself saying, "Excuse me a minute, there's somebody over there I need to talk to." Then I approached the guy and asked him to be cool and not say anything more to me. And that worked.

In every one of the cases I worked I made it a point to be in control the whole time, to never let the crook call the shots. If you let yourself be subject to the whims or instructions of other people in undercover operations, you're dead. Some agents will tell you that you should go along with what the crooks want, that you should get them to like you. They don't need to *like* you; they only deal with you because of greed. So if you understand what motivates them—money—you can conduct yourself accordingly and stay out of trouble. Once these guys start giving you instructions, it is time to walk away from them. It was an interesting career.

The Victor Nash Gem Heist

Some years ago a jewelry salesman named Victor Nash lived in San Francisco and traveled from city to city throughout the western United States, carrying a large number of unmounted jewels with him. Nash would visit large jewelers in each city and show his wares—rubies, emeralds, jade, and other colored stones outside the normal gemstone distribution channels—to potential customers of the jewelers. These customers would buy the gems from Nash and have the local jeweler mount them. Nash made the deal even more attractive for the local shop by giving back a percentage of each sale as a commission.

Nash had a big show for a large jeweler in Beaverton, Oregon. Because of the value and exposure of the gems, Nash felt he needed extra security for the event and hired a local police officer to help out during his off-duty hours. Well, the police officer saw a great opportunity to augment his income even further by taking down Victor Nash and stealing all the jewels. The officer contacted his brother—about to get out of prison—to help with the project.

The cop and his brother intended to rob Nash of his briefcase full of gems after the Beaverton show, but they missed him and Nash went on to his next stop, Seattle. They caught up with him there, though, and accosted Nash in his car at gunpoint. They pistol-whipped him, beat him up, and made off with the stuff.

A few weeks later a woman approached the FBI with information about the case. She said her cousin, just out of Oregon State Prison, had approached her in an effort to line up a "fence" to dispose of a large number of unmounted gemstones. The cousin had given her a few pieces as a gesture of friendship.

The cousin, though, didn't realize that he had earned this woman's eternal anger and resentment by turning his niece—her daughter—onto drugs earlier. She hated him for this but had never said anything to him about it. Turning him in was her revenge.

The agents from the field office brought her in to talk to me at the FBI San Francisco district office for an interview. After we talked for a while, I asked her to introduce me to the guy as Harry Silverman, a "fence." She agreed, and we set up the operation.

I had a special phone line just for "Harry." This telephone was set up in another part of the Federal Building, away from the usual office conversations but where I could still get to it quickly.

The lady called her cousin from my phone and made the introductions. I talked to him for a bit and quickly concluded that the jewels were from the Victor Nash robbery, a significant case. And it became clear that they wanted to trade the jewels for narcotics.

"I don't deal in *junk*," I told him. "I deal in cash ONLY! If you've got cash, you can get anything in the world." We went around and around on this for three or four phone calls but all within just a few hours on the same day. It was a little complicated because the cousin was acting strictly as an intermediary; he wasn't involved in the actual robbery. We didn't know then who had committed the robbery, but it was obvious he was in touch with them.

Then, finally, we made arrangements to get together and let me take a look at the gems. "We'll show you the stuff," he said, "but only in a moving vehicle. Can you meet me in half an hour?"

"Sure," I told him, "but I'm not playing games. I won't have any money with me. We'll take a look at what you've got and see if we can do business." There is always a fear with these things that you're being set up, that you'll be killed for the cash, and that they never had any intention of giving you anything.

"Okay," he said. We agreed to meet at Fort Mason.

I was driving a big, black Lincoln, a drug-seizure vehicle. Before leaving, I tried to put my squad together, the guys who would do surveillance and cover. I didn't have time to put an airplane up—the best surveillance technique under these circumstances, but one that takes a while to make happen.

I drove down to Fort Mason and met the guy. He was driving a little, beat up Volkswagen sedan. I parked my car and climbed in with him. He immediately takes off, doing eighty miles an hour around the Marina, then going the wrong way up one-way streets—"dry cleaning" himself of any tailing vehicles. I look over my shoulder occasionally and discover that he's succeeded, and that I no longer have a surveillance vehicle covering me. I'm on my own.

That was unfortunate. I had worked out a set of signals with my cover squad, if they could have kept up, that would have allowed us to bust these guys. In this case, if I took out my handkerchief to blow my nose, that was their signal to come in and take them down.

We drove around, all over the city. He stopped several places, got out of the car to use a pay phone, then got back in the car. Off we went again. This continued for about an hour and a half. Finally, we ended up at the parking lot at Coit Tower on the top of Telegraph Hill sometime before midnight.

The driver parked near a black van. We got out of the VW and climbed into the other vehicle. This van was one of those fully customized things with a fancy interior. It also had four other guys in it.

As soon as I climbed in, one of the guys pulled out a pistol and put it to my head while the other guys searched me. Not only did they pat me down, looking for a transmitter, but they had an RF meter used to detect radio transmissions and they frisked me with that, too.

Earlier in the day, the guys in the office wanted me to carry a wire. "No way in hell," I told them. I've worn them many times in other situations, but this time I wanted to go in clean. That decision saved my ass. They were a ratty bunch of criminals and nervous, too, but they relaxed and we sat down to talk.

"Why are you going through all this business?" I asked them.

"You gotta be careful," one of them replied.

Then they started bringing out a large load of gemstones. I had previously been trained by the Bureau to identify and evaluate gems. I wasn't a gemologist, but I knew enough to be convincing as a potential fence. I took my loupe out of a pocket and started inspecting some of the gems. I found an empty paper bag in the van, ripped it open, and started inventorying the collection.

"What are you doing that for?" one of the guys asked.

"If we do a deal, I want to make sure that what comes back is the same stuff I'm looking at right now." They thought that was really smart.

After evaluating the stuff and inventorying it all, we started to negotiate. We finally settled on $65,000 for gems worth well over $1,000,000, but they understood that you don't get much for stuff on the street. If you offer them too much, they start to smell something.

They wanted to do the deal right away, that night. "Go get your money," they told me.

"Wait a minute," I said, playing for time. "I don't keep that kind of money at home. That's in a safe deposit box at the bank, and I can't get it until morning." They agreed.

"Where do you want to meet?" one of them asked.

"Right here is great. Nothing happens here in the morning." So they agreed we would all meet back in the parking lot at Coit Tower.

We got back in the VW, and the first guy drove me back to my car at Fort Mason. I got in my car and took off.

I spent the rest of the night getting the bust team together and planning the operation. We got agents from the office to start showing up at Coit Tower, men and women wandering around like tourists.

I had told the crooks that I would show up at 10 A.M. Instead, I arrived a little late just to make them sweat. I parked seven or eight spaces away and went over to meet them.

They had me climb in, and we went through the whole routine from the night before. They frisked me, looking for a wire or recorder. Then they brought out the jewels. I checked them all out—some pieces were missing.

"Where's that nice apple-green jade bracelet we talked about last night?" I asked them. "That thing is worth at least $30,000."

"Oh, yeah," one said, "it's here someplace." And they dug it out.

I went through the same routine, inspecting the stuff and checking it all against the inventory. The same four guys were watching me, but the driver from the night before was missing. Finally, I told them the deal was okay.

"I'll go with you to get your money," one of them said.

"Oh, no you don't!" I told him. "Nobody goes near

my money but me! You wait right here." And that's part of the way I always run an undercover operation. You control the situation all the time; never let the bad guys take control of what you are going to do. You have the one thing the crooks want and need, and that is cash. The whole thing is motivated by greed, and since you have the money, you call the shots. If you get into a situation where the bad guys won't let you call the shots, drop the deal and let it go. Somebody will get them another time.

The signal to the bust team to move in and arrest these guys was when I went to my car and raised the trunk lid. When I did that, they were supposed to hit them.

I put the key in the truck lock, raised the trunk lid, and nothing happened at first. I lowered the lid, then raised it again—and it seemed like World War III had just broken out! Agents started running in from all over, carrying shotguns. Two of the crooks were standing outside the van, watching me, the other two were still inside.

All the jewelry taken from Nash was recovered. The four guys all went to prison, and I was able to testify against the police officer up in Beaverton at the state trial, but he wasn't convicted.

I was completely confident during that whole operation, despite being out on my own. If I wasn't, I couldn't have done it. I never, in this case or any other, felt really in danger. I felt I had control of the situation just as in all the others. And in all my undercover operations, I was never "made" or discovered by the bad guys.

Undercover on the Cuff

The FBI didn't think much of undercover operations when I first started. The administration, including Hoover, really discouraged it. The feeling was that you'd lose control of people, that agents would become corrupted. And there was and still is a danger of that happening. So there was no support for these kinds of operations— no budget, no props, no encouragement.

I'm from New York and I sound like it. And I was part of the first squad to work Mafia cases, right after their Appalachian meeting in 1957. In the fall of that year, the New York State Police raided a house up there, the beginning of operations against the Mafia.

Hoover had died before I started working undercover operations, but the old ideas were still in place. I didn't have the suits, the Rolex watch, the cash to throw around, or the car to look like a Mafia boss, but I could sound like one, and that was one of my characters. We were scrambling all the time. So I came up with a more relaxed Mafia figure who was a "nickel-nurse," a cheapskate. Instead of wearing a fancy suit to meet the crooks, I wore nice golf clothes. I like to golf and already own the stuff, so that was no problem. I had a pair of phony alligator shoes and a black silk shirt. And I borrowed some stuff—a big gold chain, diamond horseshoe ring, and beautiful gold bracelet watch that I got from one of my informants who was a real Mafia guy—since deceased.

From the same guy I got another diamond ring— twelve carats, a real one! I carried that one around in my pocket, and when you pull out a sparkler like that and ask somebody, "Would you be interested in this?", it really gets their attention and they know you are a *serious* fence! I couldn't sell it, of course, so I always told them, "This thing came from a heist of Zsa Zsa Gabor's place. There's a guy in Vegas who's got first right of refusal, but if he doesn't take it, the ring will be available." That let me impress them and still gave me an out—and you always need to have an out! So that ring was very useful for connecting with people we suspected of dealing in stolen property. Once I offered them something that looked like it was stolen, then they started offering stolen property to me. People can be very, very gullible because of greed.

One of the things I often did was to fly around the country looking at stolen property, and a lot of times I would turn down their offer. That drove them nuts. A lot of times I would be offered stolen stock certificates. You can't sell them, but you can take them into a bank and use them as collateral on large loans. The banks didn't check the ownership of these things, only the current market price for the stock.

Some crooks would offer this stuff to you at close to normal prices. "Forget it," I told them, and walk out on them. They followed me out every time! They'll never let you go. I got as far as the elevator once at a hotel down in Florida. The guy came out and apologized, and we did business.

Another thing they tried to do sometimes was impress you by saying, "We're gonna check you out," or words to that effect. That was pretty common, particularly if I was in my Mafia role.

"You're going to check ME out?" I told them. "Who the fuck are *you* to check *me* out? If you don't want to do business with me, forget it." You embarrass them this way. "You came to me, remember? I didn't come knocking on your door! How the hell do I know who YOU are?" That always worked.

Vic Rossi, Mafia Boss

I used the Mafia-don character on a lot of cases, a personality I named Vic Rossi. One of the best cases was up in Alaska; they kissed my ass black and blue up there. After that, I understood why somebody would want to be a Mafia figure—you can't do anything wrong, everybody thinks you're wonderful. The people around you cater to your every whim. And that's because you represent money and power—violent power!

One important thing about working undercover is that you need to make the personality of your character as close to your own natural character as possible. That way you don't have to act very differently from your normal personality. I was from New York, I talk like a New Yorker, and that's the way a lot of Mafia guys sound. It's a tougher way of speaking than you find in other parts of the country, and it fit the image.

A good example of that happened one night up at Anchorage. I spent most of my time in Anchorage even though our bar was down at Valdez. The primary subject of the case at that time was a local lawyer who carried a lot of weight.

The lawyer had a dinner party in my honor one night. He was the lawyer for a union up there, so some of the union leadership was invited along with a few other people of mixed reputation in the Anchorage community. During dinner much of the conversation turned to hunting, a very big subject up there. I used to hunt but gave it up as a one-sided kind of contest.

The informant who introduced me into this operation was at the dinner. He was a "gofer" for the Mafia. Later, he became the very first person relocated under the Witness Protection Program, and a movie was made about him called *Hide In Plain Sight*. He did burglaries and stickups.

The lawyer and the others thought I was the informant's uncle. We told them that I moved out to San Francisco because of "problems" in New York involving my brother, a heavyweight guy. Rather than get a war going between New York factions, I moved out to handle business on the West Coast. And these Anchorage people all bought into the story.

We were having dinner. During all the talk about hunting, the informant mentioned that he wanted to go down to Kodiak island to kill one of the big Kodiak bears. I turned to him and said, "Listen to me, you shoot *no bears*. You know, I'd rather shoot five men than one bear." I said it as kind of a joke, but the table went deathly silent. Suddenly everybody was examining their fingernails or plates, and nobody said a word.

Well, I didn't intend to scare anybody, but that was the effect. To break the mood, I excused myself and went to the bathroom. When I returned all was back to normal, and everybody was chatting away in friendly fashion.

The informant told me later what happened at the table as soon as I was gone. One of the guests said, "Whew! Did you see the look in Vic's eyes when he said that! Can you imagine that? *He'd rather kill five men than one lousy bear?*"

Another said, "Yeah, the chills ran right up my spine!"

The Acres Bar

I became partners with "Jake," a guy who first owned a bar and ran a construction business in Fremont, California. He also ran a bookmaking operation from inside the bar. He was the kind of guy I call an "angle-shooter," someone who's always looking for some easy angle to make money.

He moved his construction business up to Alaska to make money off the pipeline project, and he decided to open a bar. Then he figured he could make real money by getting into gambling, which he was doing anyway. He was the kind of guy who associated with hookers and gamblers, and this seemed to him the perfect place for both kinds of operations. Realizing that it was too big for him to set up and run on his own, he reached out to his friend Paddy, who had substantial organized-crime connections. He asked the informant to line up some people with the muscle and resources to "get in bed" with him on this deal. That's when I got brought in on the deal.

The Acres Bar operation went on for about a year and a half. We gathered what we needed for evidence, and we had lots of taped conversations. Our focus had been primarily the local Alaskan politicians—like a guy up in Fairbanks, a Democratic National Committeeman who owned part of an airline up there, a bar, and was a real man about town. He and the Anchorage lawyer were primary subjects, along with some others—people who were willing to sell out their entire state. The other guys, like Jake, were just opportunists, chiselers, and bit players.

One of the problems I had with Jake was that I knew he was stealing from the bar, and I had to find a way to keep from knowing about it. If I *had* known about it, I would have had to kill him, beat him to death, or have his legs broken—and I certainly couldn't do that. But it was a difficult act to keep up sometimes.

We leased the Acres Bar, just outside of Valdez, as the location for our sting operation. My partner in the deal didn't know who I was. We used the informant on the deal at first, then moved him out and brought another FBI agent in to actually run the bar. I couldn't do that. It was completely out of character for Vic Rossi, mob guy, to be running a bar. But nobody else knew who we were. The local FBI office gave us no real support, although they knew what was going on. We had no resources to help, no cover. The two Alaska state troopers assigned to Valdez didn't know anything about the op, either—except that we were Mafia, and that they had problems. Just a couple of people high up in the Alaska state police knew what was going on, but everybody else thought we were Mafia, and we were strictly on our own.

The agent who actually ran the bar was Cosby Morgan, one of my closest friends today. Cosby is from

North Carolina and retired as the head of the FBI office at Asheville. But he needed a better Mafia name, so I renamed him Cosmo Morgante.

I had been dealing with the organized crime section at FBI headquarters in Washington and was trying to find somebody to go up to Alaska to run this bar for me. Not only did I need somebody on the scene, but I needed another witness when it went to trial. I knew a couple of guys in New York who'd done undercover operations with me before but neither was available.

Normally assignments like this are handled very carefully. The different offices are very jealous of their responsibilities and roles and don't allow much freelancing by district offices. But this operation was way outside everybody's normal turf, and the undercover guys at headquarters told me to see if I could find anybody in my own office for the role.

So I started looking around my office for somebody suitable. I put the phone down and started walking around the office. There were a few guys I had used on a few jobs, but they didn't fit this one. Then I spotted Cosby. I didn't really know him well at the time, but he was a *dangerous* looking guy with a big handlebar mustache. He looked like he could be Italian or just about anything. And he was a *real* tough guy! He'd started in the Bureau working in the gym at headquarters, teaching defensive tactics, so he was very capable.

But I didn't know Cos well at the time; besides, he was on the accounting squad then. Usually the guys who end up with that assignment don't make good undercover agents. They're too precise, the "eye-shade and pencil box guys," and not typically very adventurous. So Cosby was a little suspect in my mind just then, as far as this assignment was concerned, even though he looked right for the part.

I asked one of the other guys in the accounting squad, "You know anything about Morgan?"

"Why do you want to know? What's up?"

"I'm thinking of using him in an undercover operation," I told him.

"Oh, you better stay away from Morgan then. He'll get you in trouble!" the guy told me—and I knew I had my man. So I walked up to Cos and asked him if he'd like to get involved in an undercover job. "I've been wanting to do that for years!" he laughed and said. "What do I have to do?"

"You've got to manage and tend bar up in Alaska. Have you ever tended bar before?"

"Sure!" Cosby said.

"Okay, you're on. Tomorrow I'll send you up to Sacramento to get your phony ID and credit cards."

Two days later we got on a plane and flew up to Anchorage. Cos had a bartender's guide along—he had not really tended much bar before—and he read it on the plane, getting ready for his new role, but he shouldn't have worried. In the bar we ran, a shot of whisky with a beer chaser was considered a fancy drink.

Despite all the money spent on the pipeline construction project, there was never any attempt by organized crime to get into the project directly. One of the main reasons was that the Mafia was already up there keeping track of things, and the word got out in a hurry. So newcomers had a very limited area of opportunity. However, they could get involved in businesses around the major camps outside Fairbanks and near Valdez.

Cos was setting up the bar one morning when a local contact guy walked in. This guy was a wanna-be criminal; his family owned some local businesses there at Valdez. But this guy was attracted to the criminal element, and he helped out around the bar doing little favors for us. Andy walked in with two other men, both dressed too well for Valdez.

After introductions, these two guys spread out blueprints on the bar. They explained that they had purchased a large ferryboat and wanted to put it out in Valdez bay, set up for gambling and prostitution. "We're gonna have the "21" games *here,*" one guy said, "and the dice games over here. The hookers will hang out over in this area, and they will service tricks in their staterooms." They laid it all out for us.

"Well, what are you showing all this to me for?" Cos wanted to know.

"We thought we ought to get your permission before going ahead with the deal," they told him.

"That's a good idea. Come see me tomorrow. I need to call my people back in New York."

Cos called me at home that night. "Jeez, Des, these guys have all these plans, and they've bought this God-dammed ferry; they're gonna put it out here in the harbor!"

I told him, "Cos, when they come back in the morning, tell them that your people say 'no.' It would bring too much heat down on all of us. Tell them we don't need the competition at this point. If we change our minds, we'll let them know. But for now, tell them no."

The next morning the guys came back to the bar, hats in hand. Cos says, "I talked to my people. They say no. It would bring too much heat on us." And they walked away.

Naturally we reported this to the Bureau. These guys had paid a lot of money for the boat, hundreds of thousands of dollars, and then they had to sell it at a distressed prices. But we kept them out of there. And, in fact, no one in organized crime came into Valdez or anywhere along the pipeline while we were there.

FBI Greatest Hits

One of the biggest problems I had while working up there was a murder contract somebody wanted us to do. There isn't a whole lot to do up in Alaska—drinking, gambling, and killing animals was about the extent of it for a lot of people. And there was a *lot* of gambling.

128

A guy came in the bar one day and wanted to talk to me. He had a problem with a competitor, a guy who'd owed him a lot of money and welshed on the deal. He wanted the competitor wasted and came to me to do a contract killing. This created big problems for me. For one thing, if I refused the contract they would just give it to somebody else, and they would kill him. We are supposed to prevent that kind of thing. For another, it would look pretty suspicious to decline the job. "I'll talk to my people," I told him. "Come back tomorrow."

You *always* have your "people" to talk to; you never want to get put in a position where you have to make a final decision right away. That technique is really important—you've always got to talk to your partner, the bankroll guy, or somebody else.

He came back. "I talked to my people about this," I told him. "They say, 'no, we don't do this. Not only that, *you* don't do this. We got too much at stake up here, too much money we're bringing in here. You do a hit on this guy, it's gonna produce too many problems. So they tell me to tell you—nothing personal—if *anything* happens to that guy, *you* go on top of the list. Understand?"

"All right, all right!" he said.

"You can talk to him, try to get your money, but if you lay a hand on him, you go next. That's just the way it is."

"Fine, sure, Vic, no problem!" he said. The intended victim was never harmed.

Surprise Time

After two years, it was time to wrap the thing up. Cos and Jake and I went to lunch at the Rusty Pelican, a restaurant on the Alameda estuary across the bay from San Francisco. We finished lunch and walked outside.

"Jake," I said, "I've got a little surprise for you. Cos and I aren't who you think we are. We're FBI agents."

He thought it was a joke. "You might as well be," he said, "I've had a lousy day."

"Really," I told him, and we showed him our credentials. "Listen, I know you've been stealing from me, cheating me and Cos. We let you go because I didn't want to take you out and kill you."

We didn't arrest him, though, but we "counseled" him—explained to him that his best option was to testify for us against the principals.

We indicted the subjects in San Francisco but on appeal the defendants got a change of venue to Anchorage. The chances of getting convictions for charges as "unimportant" as gambling and prostitution in frontier Alaska, especially in a case where Alaska citizens are being pursued and persecuted by nasty, old federal agents, turned out to be negligible. We knew we had little chance of getting convictions, but we tried anyway. The trial lasted two and a half months, starting in January. I testified at length; the jury acquitted them.

The Cancelled Contract

On one case, a couple of guys put out a contract on my life. The story began in Los Angeles. I did a couple of undercover jobs for the LA office, this one involving three guys. These men had all been in trouble before, and two had previous murder charges filed against them. The third was just an opportunist. One of the trio had a business repairing bank machines, the "check-protector" kind that imprints information on checks. These machines are typically used in banks, and these guys would get called into a bank to fix one. Well, while they were there, they were stealing blank cashier's checks. Now they've got the imprinting machines and the blank checks, and they had a ton of this stuff! They wanted to unload it all to the criminal element, and that's when I was introduced to them.

I flew down there and spent a day visiting with them, finding out what they wanted to do. Then we negotiated a contract for all the stuff—$60,000 for around a million dollars worth of checks.

When a lot of money is being exchanged, it is not unusual for the bad guys to bring along a gun and take the cash without handing over the goods. Sometimes the guy with the cash gets shot, sometimes not, but there's not much he can do about it either way. So I had a way to prevent that from happening.

I always arranged to meet guys for a payoff at an airport, inside the security checkpoint. The x-ray machines don't care about money. It goes right through. But you can't get a gun past security! These guys have to show up clean, and you can make the exchange without getting into a shoot-out.

So we arrange to meet at the American Airlines gate at LAX. They hand over the checks; I hand over the $60,000. When these guys walk away, bang, the Bureau "bust team" arrests them on the spot.

Now, maybe you think that's the end of the case, but that's not the way it works. The three guys are out on bail in a few hours, and they know who I am, a Special Agent for the FBI, and they know what my real name is.

The next thing I know the two guys with the bad backgrounds start calling me up, offering to deal. "Listen," they said, "we can help you out with a lot of cases. How about going to bat for us?"

"Sure," I told them, "but first you gotta give me something to use. You do that and I'll go talk to the United States Attorney and see what we can do for you." We talked like that a few times.

In the meantime, the third guy, the opportunist without the violent record, tells his attorney that these first two have hired a hit man to knock me off—and paid him fifty percent of the fee up front.

Now, that actually made a lot of sense from their point of view. Without me around, there's no case against them. They'd walk. I had done all the negotiations with them, and I would do all the testimony in court. Nobody else had much contact with them.

Anyway, we got a report by teletype on this. The lawyer reported the information to the U.S. Attorney, and they notified my office immediately. I was worried at first but not for the usual reasons. I thought the Bureau would transfer me out of San Francisco for my own protection. I had just bought a new home and was about to get married, and the idea of moving seemed like a disaster.

While we were all trying to figure out how to deal with this, the two guys continued to call me, playing *Let's Make A Deal*. They said they were coming up to San Francisco and wanted to meet with me. Some people in the office objected, but I agreed to meet them, alone.

We made an appointment for dinner at Phil Lehr's Steak House in the Hilton Hotel. Of course they were very friendly and solicitous of me, still trying to get me to put in a few good words with the prosecution. I had a drink with them, and we had a nice dinner.

Then I said, "I got to have a little talk with you guys. We get along all right, but I got to let you know that I am *ashamed* of you two!"

"What do you mean?" they asked in all innocence.

"Look, you guys have been around. If you don't have the balls to take a guy out yourself, *never* hire somebody else to do it for you."

"What are you talking about?"

"Listen, I know who's supposed to take a run at me. I might do the same thing, if I were in your situation. I know it's nothing personal. I know it is just a matter of practicality. But just the same, you don't do anything like this. What's going to happen if he succeeds? This guy is going to own you. What are you going to do then? Hire somebody to take him out, too? So, it all comes down to if you don't have the balls to do it yourself, don't get involved."

They were shocked. "No hard feelings," I said, "but it's not going to work. If you think you've got the balls to try it yourself, I'll give you each a chance—one on one. I don't want this thing hanging over my head. What's it going to be?"

They fell all over themselves apologizing and reassuring me that nothing would happen. We stood up, shook hands; they paid for dinner, and we left on good terms.

A few days later we got another message from the LA office. According to the third defendant's lawyer, the two guys cancelled the hit, got their money back, and everything was back to normal.

The case went to trial a few weeks later. While waiting for the jury to be impaneled, one of the defendants came over to say hi. He asked me how I was going to testify. "I'm going to tell the truth," I said.

"*I TOLD you he was going to tell the truth!*" one said to the other. Then he said to me, "Well, how should we plead?"

"That's a question for your lawyers," I told him. They went over and huddled with their lawyer. As soon as we went into court, the two pled guilty.

Tony Romano, My Pal in the Mafia

I had a Mafia informant, Tony Romano, who helped me on a lot of cases. Tony has since passed away, so I can talk about him. We became close over the years, and he was involved in all kinds of shady deals.

I arrested Tony twice, the first time in 1969 back in Buffalo, New York. He was living in Florida but was part of the Buffalo faction of the Mafia. He had $10,000 in his pocket when we grabbed him; we picked him up at the airport, found the money, and seized it. We gave him a receipt for the money.

Tony and I got along fine right from the beginning. People who aren't involved in law enforcement don't realize that you're still dealing with human beings in these cases, and you can still get along with these people and be polite to them. In all my career at the FBI and all the undercover cases, there was only one time I had any animosity toward anybody, and that was a Houston attorney we nailed on a big money-laundering case. But other than that, I never had anything but friendly, decent relationships with the people I nailed. That's because I never broke the rules, never framed anybody, always told the truth.

So we were interviewing Tony later on the day we busted him, and Tony said, "Look, I owe that money to Babe." Babe was a notorious and very dangerous loan shark. "If I don't give him that money tonight, my ass is grass."

The mob got him out on bond almost immediately. We could have held onto the dough, and notified the IRS, and maybe he'd get some of it back someday, and maybe not. But I told him, "We'll meet you over at the Hilton." My partner at the time, Joe Griffin, and I talked to Tony some more, and we decided to give him back the $10,000.

I called my boss, Neil Welsh, a great guy who would later become head of the FBI in New York City, at home around midnight. I said, "Neil, I need that ten thousand right away."

"Where are you?" Neil wanted to know, and I told him. "I'll be there in twenty-five minutes."

Neil showed up with the cash, and we handed it back to Tony. He was very relieved, and from that time on we became great friends and associates. I did a lot of cases with Tony, one of which involved an attempt to steal torpedoes from the U.S. Navy.

Just Like *Mission Impossible*

The government of Taiwan managed to get two submarines from the United States, World War II–vintage attack submarines. At first, the United States didn't want to make the sale because of the friction between the People's Republic of China and Taiwan. But finally the Taiwanese government conned the United States by saying that they didn't want the subs for military purposes but rather for undersea research only. On that basis, the U.S. government agreed to the sale with the stipulation that the subs be deactivated of all offensive military capability.

Two American businessmen were involved in the deal as agents for Taiwan. One of these guys was a retired U.S. Navy captain who'd worked on subs. He oversaw the deactivation process. What he did was to have the torpedo control cables removed where they were visible, but he left all the rest of the fire control systems in place. They cut some of the cables and covered up some of the displays with sheet metal. It looked like the stuff was gone, but the guts of the fire control system were still in place. Okay, so the subs are handed over to the Taiwanese who hooked everything back up again. Now they have functional attack submarines ready to go!

Well, ready to go except that they don't have any torpedoes at all to fire from these submarines. The Taiwanese started shopping around for torpedoes. They started with NATO nations, but none would sell the weapons because of American policies toward Taiwan and China. Then they went to the Whitehead Company, in Italy, where the torpedo had been originally developed. Whitehead could build Mark 37 torpedoes at the time and was willing to sell some—at about $200,000 each—with no guarantee that they'd work in the old subs Taiwan owned.

Finally, as a very last resort, the Taiwanese representatives decided to approach the Mafia. They'd seen the movies, and they figured the Mafia could get anything, including torpedoes. They knew about Tony Romano from some other deals, knew about his Mafia connections, so they went to Tony. He says, "I'll call my people."

I was sitting in my office when he called. "I got some guys trying to buy some Mark 37 torpedoes, Des." I didn't know anything about them, but a guy in the office who'd been in subs filled me in.

Tony introduced me to the two businessmen who were trying to do the deal. We started having meetings with these two guys, both of whom were from the Los Angeles area. They wanted us to come up with thirty Mark 37 torpedoes, and they would pay $100,000 apiece for them.

I contacted the LA office, just to let them know what was going on and that their district was involved. We also asked for some help from them in checking up on the two businessmen. A stiff-necked, old supervisor told me, "We don't have time to waste on this case! This is a con game, and you should know it."

"Pal," I told him, "I've been working con games all my life. It isn't a con game *when somebody is planning to give YOU money for something that's not available on the street!*" So they gave the case to somebody else in the office, and we started working on it.

We wanted to get higher up in the chain of command of these guys. We were just dealing with a couple of American businessmen, small-time operators. But we wanted to find out who was behind them, and that took some effort. I also started doing my homework on these torpedoes, finding out where Mark 37's were stored and anything else I could.

During the course of this case—and it went on for months—these people never knew my full name. They only knew me as "George." I wouldn't tell them a last name. We met often, generally in LA. I told them, "Listen, we can get these things for you, no problem. We can grab these things for you, there are lots of them at New London, at the sub base in Connecticut. We got the 'grab' up there, we got lots of people on the base, servicing the PX, and working on the base. But my people up there say, if you grab the stuff and don't sell it, you got problems. You can't sell it someplace else, like a load of liquor or cigarettes. We need some kind of guarantee, and we need to get to know the people you're working for. Nothing personal, but I don't know you. What am I gonna tell my people, 'A couple of guys out here need a little favor'? We're talking about millions of dollars here. It doesn't work that way. I gotta talk to somebody so I can tell my people who will guarantee we're gonna get paid for this stuff."

"Oh, no!" the two guys said. "They don't want to get involved directly. You have to deal only with us."

"Fine, then," I told them, "forget it. Try stealing the damn things yourself."

Well, the next thing I know we're down at the consulate in LA, meeting with a guy who's official title is Assistant Commercial Attaché. I know from the Bureau that this guy is actually a high-ranking Taiwanese Intelligence official for the western United States. We go to the consulate, and the Bureau guys are outside all the time, taking pictures of me going in and coming out. Tony and one of the businessmen wait outside while I go into this guy's office with the other businessman.

He gives me a little spiel: "I have been authorized to inform you that Mr. 'X' here is good friend and trusted friend of Taiwanese government!" He sat back and smiled at me as if that was going to take care of the problem.

"What's your job here?" I asked him.

"I am Assistant . . ."

"Look," I said, "DO YOU WANT THESE TORPE-DOES WE'RE GONNA GRAB OR NOT?"

He recoiled in horror. He didn't want to hear anything like *that!* He wanted complete deniability.

"Look, pal . . . we grab these things, we can't put them back, we can't sell 'em someplace else, and they're too big to hide easily. Listen, do your people really want these torpedoes or not? These guys (I indicate the U.S. businessmen) tell me your premier wants 'em."

The intel officer recovered a little. "Ah, yes, we are interested in these . . . things." He still didn't want to say the word "torpedo."

"So how am I going to get the money? Who's going to pay for the torpedoes?"

"We will pay money," he told me.

"And tell me again," I said, "what did you say your position here is?"

"Assistant Commercial Attaché," he said.

"Forget it, mister! Am I gonna go tell my people that the Assistant Commercial Attaché gives me his personal guarantees? You're not a boss here—you're *nothing*, right? You're doin' a nice job, probably, but you're not the boss, and you can't make the decision to pay us for these torpedoes." And I got up and we left.

A short time later they called me back. They'd smuggled in a real nice young Taiwanese naval officer, Tony Han, their expert on torpedoes and submarines. They brought him in under the cover that he was going to a trade show for Ford tractors. We flew down to LA to meet him at the airport, then we all went up to the attorney's home in Northridge where we held a meeting with Tony Han.

While we were chatting, I learned that one of the businessmen had stolen the classified blueprints for the submarine fire-control system from a Navy library at Seal Beach, and he delivered them to Tony Han.

Now, this guy Tony Han was a really nice young man. During the evening he took me aside and said, "I sure hope this works out. You have no idea what things are like in Taiwan right now. It's just like Nazi Germany. If this thing gets screwed up, they will take me out and shoot me!"

Later that evening I did my same act for them: "Listen, I can't go back to my people and tell them that a *lieutenant* is making this deal with me! They aren't gonna go for this at all." So they agreed to make other arrangements—they set me up to meet with an admiral, the Naval Attaché for the government of Taiwan in the United States.

One of the businessmen and I flew back to Washington and met Admiral Chiu and his aide. They were dressed in civilian clothes, and we met in a car at the parking lot of the big shopping center at Tyson's Corners in the Virginia suburbs. The admiral explained the meeting in the car by telling me, "The CIA and FBI are everywhere in Washington! When you go to a restaurant, the waiter is CIA or FBI. You and I sit down in restaurant, right away the waiter comes over and places a listening device under the table and records all our conversation! But we know this and have come up with solution that drives your CIA and FBI crazy! We order food, and as soon as it comes, we ask to move to other table! You can tell they get mad because of the microphone under table!"

While we were going through the deal, my companion starts getting anxious about getting this deal going. His slice of it was going to be hundreds of thousands of dollars, and he already had it spent. Trying to put pressure on them, he tells the admiral that we've already grabbed the torpedoes! "We got 'em," he said. "They're waiting for you!" I went along with that.

"How you get torpedoes?" asked the admiral.

"These torpedoes are stored in wooden crates," I told him, "with one torpedo to a crate. They are stored in Quonset huts. We went in there at night and unbolted the back of one of the Quonset huts, and took the thirty torpedoes out of their crates, and replaced them with dummy practice torpedoes. We put them in the back of a truck, then bolted the back of the Quonset hut back on, and drove off the base. They'll never notice those things are gone until another war breaks out!"

"AHH!" exclaimed the admiral, "just like *Mission Impossible!*" He loved it! "Can you get nuclear weapons, too?" he wanted to know.

"Give me a shopping list, and what you're willing to pay, and I'll get you anything you want," I said.

I wanted these guys prosecuted and put in jail, but that's not the way it worked out. The case provoked an international incident, though, and it went all the way to President Ford to make the final decision. The FBI wanted the case to go forward, and an emergency session of the National Security Council was called on the matter. The problem was that if the case was allowed to go forward, some embassy personnel would be arrested and others declared persona non grata for violations of the Neutrality Act and Foreign Agents Registration Act. And if that happened, the United States might have to terminate diplomatic relations with Taiwan. I was told that President Ford cast the deciding vote against going forward. Nevertheless, the administration decided to issue a demarche, an extremely serious diplomatic message from the head of one nation to the other. The U.S. ambassador to Taiwan, the highest-ranking member of the United States in that country, delivered the demarche to Cho Ching Quo, the son of Chaing Kai Chek and then premier of the country.

I saw the message and remember that it began "The United States has incontrovertible evidence that the following situation exists . . . ," going on to describe Taiwan's attempt to contact organized-crime elements and buy the forbidden torpedoes in violation of laws and treaties. Admiral Chiu was declared persona non grata, and the assistant commercial attaché was reassigned to Pago-Pago.

Operation "Deadfall"

Special Agent Dave Leiting joined the FBI in 1979 and initially worked white-collar crime cases out of the Milwaukee office. He worked on the "Bellweather" organized-crime investigation, undercover operations "Safe Bet" and "Incubator," several abduction-murder cases, and the Tylenol murders before being assigned as the sole undercover agent for Operation "Deadfall," a campaign against corruption within the Chicago, Illinois, Police Department. The story of "Deadfall" reveals one of the dark sides of law enforcement—the sometimes sad, unrewarding assignments of "working cops," namely, going after corrupted police officers.

I was newly assigned to the Public Corruption squad in the Chicago office of the FBI and anticipating some significant, "fun" work; there are few cities which have more corruption to work than Chicago. I had just come off working on two long undercover operations lasting over five years, and was looking forward to working some "regular" investigations not associated with undercover-type operations. Within a few weeks, however, my boss handed me a complaint-call write-up that another agent had taken and asked me to check it out. I didn't know it then, but this would lead to my working on one of the strangest and most bizarre undercover cases I'd ever heard of. The case would ultimately record more police officers taking bribes than any investigation in U.S. history.

The complaint came from Service Corporation International (SCI), a Texas-based Fortune 500 company which I later heard referred to as the "McDonalds of Death." SCI is the largest company in the U.S. funeral industry with hundreds of mortuaries, cemeteries, flower shops, and similar businesses in operation around the country.

SCI was venturing into the Chicago funeral industry for the first time. The way they planned these types of market entries was to buy up the best funeral homes in a market but make the transition of ownership invisible to the general public. For example, if they bought "Brown's Funeral Home," a third or fourth generation business, they would keep the name and perhaps even employ Mr. Brown as the funeral-home manager for a few years. SCI wanted to buy that nice, friendly reputation the funeral home had developed over the years along with the building, contents, and clientele.

During our initial meeting, the SCI people told me that Chicago was potentially a great market for them; the area's strong ethnic character and traditions favored more elaborate and expensive funerals. SCI was considering buying a lot of homes and even some small funeral chains within this market.

In order to evaluate these businesses, SCI reviewed their books and discovered a pattern of accounting entries that really surprised them. The most common name for these strange entries were payments to something called the "Chicago Club." These payments were typically $40, sometimes as low as $20, and a few as high as $100 or $150. As it turned out, these payments were payoffs to Chicago policemen for bodies. And these bribes weren't coming from a single business but from most of the funeral homes SCI was interested in buying. It was clearly a business tradition within the Chicago market.

The payoffs were part of a long-time practice by the Chicago police. When somebody dies of natural causes, usually in their home, the police respond just as they do to any death. If there are no suspicious circumstances and the person had been under a doctor's care, a release is obtained via telephone from the coroner's office. The police then tell the family that they are free to make arrangements for the body. As a service to the public, the Chicago Police Department routinely transports the bodies in their paddy wagons, called "Squadrols" in Chicago, saving the family the cost of an ambulance, typically $150 or more. The body should then be taken to the funeral home of the family's choice.

In actual practice, the body would be transported only to a funeral home that was making payoffs. If your Uncle Lennie died at home of a heart attack, and you asked the police to take him to Brown's Funeral Home—and Brown wasn't making the payoffs—they'd tell you to make your own arrangements for transport.

What usually happened, was a little more subtle, a practice called "steering." The family sometimes didn't have a funeral home in mind and would ask the responding police officers (two officers were always assigned to a squadrol) for suggestions. Depending upon whether the family was black, Polish, Jewish, or whatever, the cops would suggest a "suitable" funeral home, but always one that was known by squadrol officers to be making payoffs. If the family mentioned a home that was known to not make the payoffs, the officers might say, "Well, okay, if that's what you want, but I've heard some bad things about the way Brown's handles the bodies. . . ."

If the family didn't ultimately change their minds and direct the body to a "paying" funeral home, the officers would back off and not transport the remains at all. Or, in some more egregious cases which were discovered later, the cops would actually take the body to a "paying" funeral home other than that specified by the family and collect their money. Later, the "intended" funeral home would have to pick up the body from the funeral home the cops took it to and pay various "fees," which included the payoff. Obviously, these charges were passed on to the family.

This "discovery" of payoffs to cops presented a dilemma for SCI. One option was for them to continue paying the bribes just as the other homes in the area were obviously doing, something the company refused to consider for both legal and ethical reasons. Another was to simply refrain from paying the bribes, but that would certainly result in such a significant a loss of business (estimated at 20–40% of revenues!), that few funeral homes would be able to stay in business, let alone be attractive for acquisition. Then again, SCI considered staying out of the Chicago market, but they didn't want to do that because it was potentially so profitable. Finally, SCI had the option of doing something to bring a halt to this practice in the local industry, and that's why they came to see the FBI.

SCI had researched the practice and discovered that this police transport service had been offered since at least the 1920s, and charges of widespread payoffs had been made in the 1950s and 1970s. After these scandals had occurred, the payoffs stopped for a few months while the heat was on, then they began again. Rather than go to the media and risk another "short term" solution, SCI came to us with a request to investigate the payoffs and put an end to them.

We took a hard look at the problem and considered a variety of investigative tactics. It was obviously an industrywide situation throughout the Chicago market. An investigation of a single funeral home wouldn't do anything to stop it citywide. We discussed the matter with a very trusted, high-ranking Internal Affairs Division

"You've been a bad, bad boy," Sergeant Jim Lilley *(left)* tells a bank robber he has just nabbed. *(Photo by Jeff Taylor)*

Trick or Treat! Sergeant Jim Lilley's crew, ready for a night on the town on Halloween. *(Photo courtesy of James H. Lilley)*

Sergeant Ralph Kabernagel with 1,500 pounds of marijuana seized by his unit. *(Photo courtesy of Sgt. Ralph Kabernagel)*

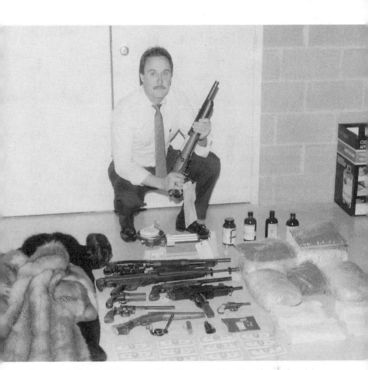

Sergeant Ralph Kabernagel with a small collection of evidence: illegal weapons, stolen fur coats, PCP ingredients, and a lot of cash. *(Photo courtesy of Sgt. Ralph Kabernagel)*

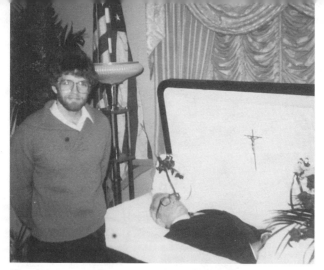

Special Agent Dave Leiting with an example of his undercover-assignment handiwork: the freshly embalmed body of a major Chicago mob figure.

Blank Santa Clara County, California, sheriff's ID cards discovered during a raid on a Hells Angels residence; the cards were stolen by a "plant" in the sheriff's office. *(Photo courtesy of Ron Martinelli)*

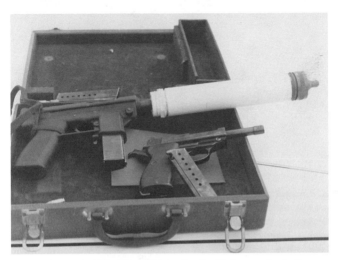

Fully automatic KG–99 machine pistol with improvised silencer seized by Ron Martinelli and the "Slime Crime" team. *(Photo courtesy of Ron Martinelli)*

Radio scanner and log of police transmissions found in a Hells Angels residence during a raid. *(Photo courtesy of Ron Martinelli)*

Fake arrest/booking photo of Officer Ron Martinelli, used as part of his undercover-identity kit. *(Photo courtesy of Ron Martinelli)*

Marijuana seized during an undercover bust by U.S. Customs.

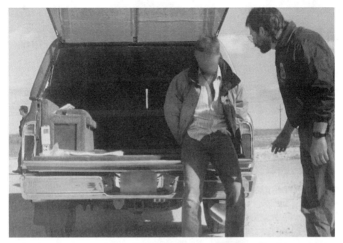

U.S. Customs agent Don Daufenbach interviews a freshly caught and very unhappy drug smuggler after a long undercover pursuit.

Agent Don Daufenbach *(kneeling at right)* has a little chat with a suspected drug smuggler moments after the "bust team" pounced on the Cessna and its load of dope.

After delivering the "bust team" to a remote airstrip, a UH–60 Black Hawk hovers nearby while a drug smuggler is "pruned out" on the dirt and the arrest team compares notes.

(IAD) officer of the Chicago Police Department. When we considered referring the matter to the Superintendent of Police for administrative handling of the matter, he told us he shared our lack of confidence that the practice would stop for long. He also told us that virtually all Chicago police officers work on the squadrols for at least a few months, usually at the beginning of their careers, thus many of the police brass may have accepted these payoffs years before.

We later found out, too, that at least in a few cases, these payoffs were explained to new recruits at the police academy during training. The payoffs were reportedly not described within the department as bribes but as "tips" for providing a legitimate service outside of their normal police duties. So, possibly, the investigators to whom we'd make the complaint may have been just as involved in the past as the cops taking bribes at the time of the complaint, and they would have had a hard time cracking down on the practice. Anybody who had ever been assigned to the paddy wagon—and that was almost all of the 12,000 cops in the Chicago Police Department—had likely been exposed to the problem and had possibly taken these bribes.

The United States Attorney's (U.S.A.) Office expressed a lot of interest in our initial meetings with them and encouraged us to consider an undercover operation (UCO). The U.S.A. and the Bureau viewed this practice not as a bunch of $40 or $50 bribes, but rather the diversion of thousands of $3,000 to $10,000 funerals to companies willing to pay these bribes. A preliminary study led us to believe that though only $200,000 to $400,000 per year was probably being paid to the police, potentially $20 million to $40 million of funeral-home revenue (interstate commerce) was being diverted. It was agreed that the problem was substantial, pervasive, and had to be stopped.

The U.S.A. believed the only way to stop the practice was to make a major splash out of the case with lots of media attention (and likely embarrassment to the police department). But the U.S.A. would not commit to exactly how he would charge the police officers whom we would acquire compelling evidence on. The intimation was that serious felony ITAR (Interstate Transportation in Aid of Racketeering) charges would be leveled at them as well as against a representative number of the funeral-home operators. We kicked around the scale of the arrests we'd need to make to show how pervasive the practice was and came up with the indictment and conviction of a minimum of ten officers.

FBI undercover operations work like this: first, you've got Field Office oversight. The Undercover Operation (UCO) must be reviewed and approved by the Principal Legal Advisor, the Field Office UCO Review Committee, and the Special Agent in Charge (SAC). Then, a UCO Review Committee at Bureau headquarters in Washington, D.C. must approve every operation, and they approve that operation for up to six months at a time. The "substantive desk" (which could be the Organized Crime, Public Corruption, White-Collar Crime, or other headquarters unit associated with the primary criminal activity the UCO is targeted at) is a key part of that review process. During these reviews, tactics are analyzed; entrapment and other legal issues are studied; dangers to agents, the public, or subjects recognized and minimized; chances for success assessed; and an attempt is made to predict and plan for every possible event that could occur which could might prove an embarrassment to the Bureau. One screwed up UCO, or even a good one that is portrayed by the media as foul, can wipe out the terrific results and hard work of hundreds of agents and support personnel on ten other UCOs.

There are two FBI "classes" of undercover operations, Class I and Class II. In general, these classes don't have anything to do with how many people are involved or the perceived quality of the cases but rather how much money you need to run them. At that time, a Class I operation was one that spent more than $50,000 per six-month period; a Class II anything under that figure. It was easier to get approval for a Class II operation; so, we determined to go forward with our proposal for a low budget operation.

The finances of these operations can be an important consideration. For example, as we started to structure our case, we thought that we could put an agent into a deep-cover role in the industry. He or she would also be getting paid a salary from a funeral home, and so we could use that salary to offset the additional costs for an apartment, car, and other living expenses. That way we could keep the operation under the "magic" $50,000 cutoff.

Another problem was: How would we actually get the undercover agent into the industry? We considered buying a funeral home, but that wasn't economically feasible or probably necessary. One option was to put somebody in at an entry-level job, but the problem was in that kind of job they wouldn't be around the payoffs because those interactions are typically handled by managers. There was another problem with all of this, too. You need to be a graduate of a mortuary science academic and training program to work as an undertaker, a one- or two-year commitment. A review of the FBI's database of agents' skill sets, education, and training revealed that none who were suitable for or interested in undercover assignments had the necessary background. Ultimately, SCI helped us with all this.

FBI undercover operations sometimes involve ten or more agents and other times just three or four. All use a case agent, undercover agent (UCA), accountant and contact agent. The movies glamorize the agent in the undercover role, so the public *thinks* it knows what he or she does. I've been asked many times, "Is being undercover just like it is in the movies?" I usually say, "No. In real life I have to hum my own background music." I've heard other UCAs describe it as being long periods of mundane work, for the most part, with a few moments of stark terror. But for me, I enjoyed it almost all the time. The hours are incredibly long, and there is a level of anxiety associated with living a lie; however, it can be very invigorating. But you can't focus on the dangers of the work, or it will paralyze you. You have to occasionally step back and remember why you're doing it, and that the role is not who you are or want to be.

Behind the scenes of every successful UCO are several other agents and support personnel who are just as critical to the success or failure of the operation. Normally, the case agent handles all the details of the operation including all the administrative stuff, opening subfiles for subjects, and working out strategy with FBI management and the U.S. Attorney's office. The accountant obviously handles all the financial matters associated with the undercover operation. The contact agent makes sure the undercover agent remains sane—sometimes a challenge! Contact agents also need to be good listeners to the concerns of the undercover agent (UCA) and pick up on changes in attitudes or behavior that could signal a problem that needs to be addressed. The case agent brings you blank tapes, discusses personnel matters and happenings in the office, goes with you to occasional ball games or dinners, and makes sure you always remember who you really are. Often there are other agents permanently assigned to a case to assist in running down leads that come up over the course of the UCO, or those who assist on an ad hoc basis, such as surveillance specialists or technical specialists who can assist with the installation of cameras and recording equipment.

Finally, the decision was made and approvals secured to conduct a Class II undercover operation with me serving as the undercover agent *and* case agent *and* accountant. This was pretty unusual but certainly showed our commitment to keep this as low budget an operation as possible. I thought the FBI might ask me to be my own contact agent, too, but they assigned an agent on the squad in a part-time capacity. I took a crash course in mortuary science, two years worth of study condensed into about ten days focused on the basics of embalming. Then I went to work at one of the cooperating SCI-owned funeral homes with the cover name of Dave Bronson. If you think that sounds corny (using the last name of tough-guy actor Charles Bronson), well, my undercover name on my previous UCO was Dave East-wood. There was certainly some kind of macho name pattern going there. Prior to starting work, I got my undercover car, apartment and furnishings, credit cards, driver's license, and cover story.

Then we had to come up with a code name for the case. All FBI undercover operations have code names. For one thing, it makes it easier to refer to the case in conversation without saying anything that would identify it. First, we sent the Bureau the name "Night Shift," a takeoff on the funeral-home backdrop in the movie of the same name which starred Michael Keaton. It had already been used in a previous UCO; thus, it could never be used again. Then, we submitted "Grim Reaper," just something that sounded kind of creepy to us as tied to the mortuary theme. Again, it had been used before, apparently in a motorcycle-gang UCO. Finally, we submitted "Deadfall." The Bureau approved it but, interestingly, we almost had to change it when the U.S. Attorney's office objected to it. A "deadfall" is one of those traps that's constructed so that a weight falls on an animal or a box that traps the animal when the stick supporting the box is knocked out. They felt that the name implied that we would be "entrapping" cops to commit crimes. Of course, we told them we weren't going to and, by that time, I was tired of thinking up and submitting new names.

The Bureau usually sets up background stories for undercover agents, but I didn't think they always did a very good job of it. They weren't deep enough. If you're working against organized crime or police targets, who are very talented at seeing through or exposing phony stories, there is a good risk you'll be exposed if you have invented information without some link to reality. For example, the Bureau might give you a certificate to work in the funeral industry backdated two years, but if the certificate number is similar to ones being issued this month or is the same number issued to someone else, somebody might notice and question the validity of the license. That kind of carelessness concerned me.

So, I set up some of my own background myself. I'd learned some of the intricacies of phony IDs and cover stories from other UCAs and some from subjects I'd arrested. For example, I went to visit each of the colleges I claimed to have attended and asked the registrar to help me make up a complete "jacket" for me. If somebody went to that institution and looked up Dave Bronson's file, there would be a normal file just like any other students'.

Finally, I went to work in a funeral home on the far north side of Chicago. The new SCI area manager for Chicago knew who I was, as did a couple of senior SCI executives and their senior counsel in Texas, but nobody else locally was in on it. He helped me set up my role in the home so that I could start making payoffs and getting my hands dirty, literally.

What I quickly discovered was that a lot of the payoffs happened at odd hours. Old people who are ill often die in the middle of the night and are discovered very early in the morning. That meant I had to be at the funeral home very early. So, I usually came in early, but we just weren't getting as many police deliveries as we had expected. And I wasn't making many payoffs, either—only six or so during the first six months of the operation. I got good recordings of these payoffs, but the level of activity wasn't what we needed.

One of the first cops I paid off was a really nice, older guy who reminded me a lot of my former father-in-law.

I remember liking him a lot just during the first ten minutes or so after I'd met him. I determined that I wasn't going to give him the money unless he really pressed me for it. There was just something very "decent" about him that made me think he was probably a great cop otherwise, and I didn't want to see him get nailed. Maybe it wasn't up to me to "pick" who would go down or not, but I wanted him and his partner to get out of there without the cash. Unfortunately, he asked me for it insistently, so I paid him—just like every single cop over the course of the project. Not one refused the money. Ultimately, it cost the older cop even more than I thought. A short time after he was convicted in this case, he died of a heart attack. A few of the cops told me to my face that I was responsible for his death. And, for a while, I wrongly believed that I was.

In the meantime, I was getting acquainted with the funeral-home business, the financial aspects, embalming, selling funeral packages, wake duties ("saying prayers and consoling families"), etceteras. We decided to relocate the operation to another district, and I transferred to a funeral home SCI had just purchased. Within a few weeks after I was working there, I discovered that this particular home, almost uniquely among the three-hundred-plus funeral homes in the area, allegedly had been bought previously with mob money. The funeral home was connected, also allegedly, to Chicago's second-ranked outfit hoodlum Jack Cerone Sr. It was widely known that this home performed many of the Mafia's funerals.

I was concerned that my cover would be blown because I had previously met Jack Cerone Jr.—an attorney. I had met him during the trial phase of an earlier undercover operation. He had been the lawyer for several of the subjects of that case and he would easily recognize me if he visited his father at the funeral home. The funeral home was otherwise ideal for what we intended plus I'd already started working there; so, I quickly had to come up with some kind of disguise that wouldn't seem like a disguise to those I had already met there.

Normally I'm clean-shaven and wear my hair fairly short, but my hair was already longer than usual when I moved to the new home. So, I started to grow a beard and let my hair go. Within a couple of months, I got a perm—my first visit to a beauty salon—and I had to go in periodically to get my perm redone. I quickly became a big, furry ball. I started wearing glasses instead of my normal contact lenses. The transformation was complete. I figured nobody would ever recognize me, and nobody ever did.

Undertaker to the Mob

I started working at this new funeral home as the night manager. Though my hours were about 9 P.M. until 7 A.M., I'd come in early and leave late in order to assist with the embalmings and other duties. Some of the funeral directors were even a little suspicious of this guy who seemed to want to work so many hours, even without pay. But, I started making a lot more payoffs. And the recorded conversations with the officers got better. One admitted, "We're like Domino's Pizza. We deliver, but if you don't pay, you ain't gettin' your pizza." I wondered if the bereaved family would have appreciated the "pizzafication" of their dearly departed.

While I was there, we did the funerals for several mob figures. One of these was Joseph "Caesar" DiVarco, an imprisoned, aging mobster who died of natural causes just prior to testifying before the President's Commission on Organized Crime. He would roll over in his grave if he knew an undercover FBI agent helped embalm him.

Organized-crime bosses flew in from all over the country to make their appearances at the services held at this funeral home. Since the outfit knew that it was standard practice for the FBI and police to conduct surveillance at any gathering where La Cosa Nostra (LCN) members were expected, elaborate plans were made to foil these efforts. The outfit expected they would try to get a copy of the guest book and surveillance photos of attendees. Special arrangements were made for some of the funeral-home employees, including me, to assist with countersurveillance, transportation, and housing of these organized-crime figures and assuring the guest book was always closely guarded. Of course, these plans didn't prove to be very effective, and the FBI, amazingly, got all of the intelligence they wanted.

Shake and Bake

Embalming and preparing bodies for funerals turned out to be different than I expected. I had always envisioned the process as being a slit here, a slit there, stick in a tube, and drain out the fluids while the embalming fluid gets pumped in. No muss, no fuss. It is actually a very violent and invasive procedure in which the body is punctured several times by an instrument called "a trochar," which, in the simplest sense, sucks body fluids and spits embalming fluid at the same time. Every organ in the body must be penetrated by the trochar. More than once, I remember asking myself what in the hell I was doing. I had worked hard at becoming and was happy being a Special Agent of the FBI. What was I doing virtually living in funeral homes, dealing with grieving and, sometimes, wailing family members, and prodding needles into dead bodies while blood and shit and every other fluid poured out of them?

I've only wept a few times in my adult life, and once was after I helped embalm a two-year-old boy who had been killed in a traffic accident. My own son was about two at the time, and it affected me pretty hard. I'm not sure why. He was a dark-haired Mexican boy, and my son was pale-skinned with almost white hair, so it wasn't because they looked anything alike. Since he was being shipped to Mexico, we did a "shake and bake" on him— all his internal organs had been removed during an autopsy, and they were normally replaced into the chest cavity. You put the organs in a preservative powder, thoroughly coat them, then put them in a bag that is placed back inside the body—just like doing Shake & Bake chicken. Later, I took a long walk from the funeral home, down around Wrigley Field where the Cubs play baseball, and wept as I walked. Some people probably just thought I was a devoted Cub fan.

I also helped embalm a stillborn infant, a fairly rare event according to the other people in the business. I don't know why the family wanted to embalm and view a stillborn; most don't. We had to use syringe needles and improvised tools. Then, there was the tragic case of the teenage beauty queen who accidentally blew off part of her head while showing a rifle to a friend. I was very impressed with the team of expert funeral directors that came together, many working for free, to reconstruct her head for an open-casket funeral. They did some incredible work with putty and filler and she was beautiful, once more, before being laid to rest.

Wired for Sound

We moved the undercover operation again to get more cops from a different part of the city. I started actually living in the basement at the third and final funeral home I went to—and it was awful. This was at the beginning of what looked like was going to be year two of this UCO. Again, my thoughts were along the lines of, "What the hell am I doing here?" Well, one of the things I was doing was recording a lot of payoffs, and that meant I had to be wired up all the time. I wore a Nagra recorder twenty-four hours a day for up to a week at a time. I even slept with this thing taped to my body. There just wasn't any time when the doorbell rang in the middle of the night to get wired up, so I wore it constantly. Adhesive tape will do some amazing things to your skin after several months! The Nagra is a "small" recorder, unless you have to wear it on your body. Then it seems like you're trying to hide a boom-box in your pants. I usually wore it so the top of the recorder was about one inch above the buckle of my belt, and the bottom of it was just about as low as it can be without doing permanent damage to a guy. A "gir-dle" keeps it pretty snug. Then the wires (it's stereo) run up both sides of your torso to just above the nipples. I'd run an "on/off" switch into a hole in my pocket (of course, you can never carry change in that pocket again) and be ready for a recorded performance.

I was always concerned that a client or one of the other employees in the funeral homes would notice the thing, but they didn't. I usually dressed in clothes that helped hide it, but there are lots of times over the course of years of undercover work when it's more appropriate to wear slacks with a tucked-in shirt. Over the course of the UCO, some people would unintentionally bump into it. The possibility of being discovered was a constant concern, and, like all undercover agents, I worried about how I would handle the problem if the recorder was ever discovered by the cops. The first few months of this UCO, I carried a twenty-two magnum, two-shot derrin-ger. But, after awhile, the combination of having some-thing else to hide on your person and the rationalization that, if you're discovered, there's no way in hell you're going to be able to get to the gun in time to do you any good anyway, cause you to lose the gun.

Working at the second funeral home had produced many additional payoffs. We had taped over forty Chicago police officers taking money for body drops. I was ready to quit. We still didn't have a firm commitment from the U.S. Attorney regarding prosecution, and it just felt to me that we had as much information as we needed for the number of prosecutions that would ultimately be undertaken. It turned out that I was right, but some folks thought that if forty busted cops sounded good, then eighty would sound twice as good.

I didn't like the case anymore. It was proving difficult for me personally. I was starting to get some negative feedback about the case from other agents in Chicago, and I was physically tired. When you're undercover in a business, you have to work hard to make the business itself work (that's a full-time job), plus fulfill the object of the case (get close to the bad guys and get evidence), plus work with the other agents and the lawyers on strategy, evidence review, etcetera. Almost every meeting with government people would be during their normal business hours, but it was usually during the hours I would normally be sleeping. Doing essentially three jobs was tough since we each only get twenty-four hours to a day. It didn't leave much time for rest or for my family, and my wife was tired of my involvement in undercover operations for the previous seven years. I was gone a lot, tired a lot, and irritable a lot.

I had become less enthusiastic about the case itself. Many otherwise good cops, who never did anything more than take these occasional and traditional payoffs, got caught up in the sting operation. A mob guy that gets busted can do a few years in jail and then come back to what is for him a normal life. Everybody knows he's a wise guy; in fact, his family may even be proud of that and enjoy a certain status with some people because of it. But with cops, as I knew from previous cases, the price paid by each officer who gets arrested can be incredible. Even if they don't go to jail, the price is tremendously high. They lose their jobs and any chance to work in that career again; they lose their stature in the community, and, most importantly, their families lose faith in them. Their wives' and kids' friends say cruel things to their families or isolate them. It's awful! I was dreading what I knew would be a huge cost to the cops and also to the owners of some of the funeral homes who would be charged.

Quitting Time

You work very hard to get an undercover operation approved and authorized. It is fairly difficult to get one started. Then, in every case I have known, it is just as hard or harder to get out. We had originally intended to prosecute about ten police officers; now we had recorded payoffs to over forty officers and historical cases against many dozens more. It was time to quit, but the headquarters' supervisors and U.S. Attorney wanted more. Instead of quitting, I moved to still another funeral home in an area we hadn't recorded any cops in as yet. But we couldn't set up to get cops in every district in the city, or this case would go on for many more years.

I also impersonated a Chicago police officer to set up the owners or managers of the funeral homes, too. "Hello," I said, "this is Officer so-and-so. I have a dead body to deliver. I haven't been to your location before. Are you a member of "the club?""

"Oh, yeah, sure!" some would say.

Others would say, "The club? What do you mean?"

"Well, if I bring this body to you, am I gonna get something?"

The responses varied in degrees but certainly most said they always made the payoffs. If they said they normally paid $40, I'd ask for $60. Then we'd dicker for awhile about price, and they'd tell me how long they'd paid, what amounts, or how their decision not to pay had been catastrophic for their business. Some expressed an interest in "buying more bodies" and wondered if paying a lot more might help get them more than their current share. Based on the strength of those recordings, we decided which funeral-home owners to follow up on.

Another agent and I approached some of the owners of these homes and asked them to cooperate with us on the case. We got some of these people to "flip." We bluffed them with the RICO (Racketeer-Influenced and Corrupt Organization) statutes. RICO provides that if the government can prove just *two* violations of a list of about seven state crimes (and bribery is included), then they are guilty of a federal felony and can have their corrupt organization's assets (their funeral homes) seized by the government.

We said, "If you don't cooperate and we can prove just *two* of the hundreds of payoffs your home has paid over the years, we're gonna put you in jail, RICO your funeral home, and take it away from you!" I believed it was a bluff since I sincerely doubted that the U.S. Attorney's office would really seize a business for two payoffs. But, the owners bigger concern was, of course, the embarrassment to their families and loss of business that media coverage would bring.

Bluffing was a pretty effective technique. We installed surveillance cameras and recording equipment at one northwestside funeral home and worked out an agreement with the home that they'd continue paying off Chicago police officers as before. At another, on the near North Side, we did the same and I started working there as a manager.

Now, we were collecting evidence from even more police districts and had clearly demonstrated a pervasive pattern of corruption. An odd "political" problem developed as we neared the end of the case. The majority of the black-owned funeral homes in the city were on the South Side. Since our case had never operated at a South-Side funeral home, few of the funeral homes that we had gathered evidence of payoffs from were owned by blacks. It would have been virtually impossible for me to convincingly assume the same role I had in a "black-owned" funeral home.

In addition, only a handful of the officers recorded taking payoffs were black, a much smaller percentage than in the police department or the community generally. Since the mayor of the city, Harold Washington, and the Superintendent of Police, Fred Rice, were black, we anticipated that the appearance of reverse racism was a potential problem. This situation was almost the direct opposite of the problem sometimes encountered with disproportionately high statistics for black criminal conduct. In fact, in a previous case I had worked on the FBI took down six aldermen, and, since all were black, charges of prejudice resulted. This time the tables were turned, and it was still a problem.

During this last phase, I started getting involved a little more personally with some of the cops. I had heard about some of them being involved in the use and sale of cocaine, shakedowns, and home burglaries. For example, if somebody died alone at home and the cops knew the next of kin wouldn't be flying in until the next day, cops would go back and steal everything of value in the place. It was awful, and yet not surprising, how much disappeared from these homes. Who was to complain?

At the apartment of someone who had died just that morning, one cop stood, his whole body moving, as he shook and emptied a glass, ten-gallon jug filled with coins, mostly pennies and nickels. When asked, "Don't you have any pride at all?," he replied, with a grin, "Hey, it all spends!" People who do that sort of thing really should not be cops. Some of the cops I'd recorded were just not nice guys at all; a few were so psychotic that they shouldn't have been allowed to carry guns.

And so, by this time we had recorded payoffs to eighty-five different police officers, some as many as six times. I was told that was the most police officers ever recorded committing felonies in any investigation in U.S.

history. In addition, we would later seize records showing thousands of payoffs to hundreds of other officers.
We also had a lot of funeral-home operators on tape,
too. It was time to close the operation down.

Takedown Day

The day finally came to go overt. Weeks had been spent
writing lengthy interview questionnaires for funeral-
home owners, managers, other employees, and for the
cops themselves. We had about fifteen takedown teams,
each comprised of an FBI agent and a Chicago Police
Department Internal Affairs officer. Each team had the
names of officers to talk to, and each team was looking
for people who might "flip". We doubted anyone would
change voluntarily since we weren't going to tell them
that we had them on tape soliciting a bribe from an FBI
agent. But even if they didn't admit anything, we wanted
to get written denials from those that we already had on
tape to show that the payoffs weren't just considered
"tips". If that's what they thought they were, they
shouldn't lie to FBI agents, a felony punishable by five-
years imprisonment.

Many of these officers said, "Fuck you! I don't know
what you're talking about." Most lied and said the practice had ended many years before, and they had no
knowledge of anyone ever having accepted, or even
being offered, a payoff for a body. They admitted that
they knew it was a violation of law, thereby taking away
one of the defenses we anticipated they would use in
court. Surprisingly, we did get one older cop who admitted everything, laid it all out for us, even implicating his
former partners. I think the poor guy was a little senile
and didn't realize what he was doing. By that afternoon,
the Police Officer's Association had him hooked up with
a lawyer. Shortly after that, death threats were made

against him. If he didn't recant his story, he was going to be killed. His recollection changed shortly thereafter and he recanted.

Day Two sent teams around to funeral homes. We had search warrants—a lot of search warrants—and about sixty agents. These teams went to each home, seized business records, and interviewed the owner, managers, and other employees. We had a lot of success that day getting dozens of admissions about the long-standing payoff practice and historical records of thousands of previous payoffs to cops for bodies.

Then we indicted the first round of subjects. Thirty police officers and five funeral-home owners were charged. It was the lead story on every Chicago television station that evening. The press conference was led by the U.S. Attorney and his assistants, the FBI Special Agent in Charge, the Police Superintendent, Fred Rice, and the local area head of the IRS. We were charging tax violations against the cops for not reporting the income and against the funeral-home owners for illegal deductions taken on their taxes. Unbeknownst to the media, I watched as a spectator from the back of the large room. Months later, I told a reporter that, in the future, he should always look to the back of the room for the undercover agent(s) from a case, like arson investigators look to the crowds around a fire scene for possible suspects.

The assistant U.S. Attorneys working on the case and I met with every officer who had been charged and their lawyers, informing them that I had been an undercover FBI agent and played the video or audio tapes of the payoffs. We had a lot of very ugly interviews. Shortly after the indictments came down, the wife of one officer came into their living room. "You think you've got problems now?" she asked her husband. "Watch this!" She lifted his service revolver, put it in her mouth, and pulled the trigger. Both the officer and his wife were, allegedly, habitual cocaine users and had other problems, too. Even so, three Chicago police officers told me that her blood was on my hands and that I was responsible for her death. Like the case of the cop who died of the heart attack, I assumed the guilt for many years.

In From the Cold, Into the Fire

Coming in from an extended undercover assignment is always weird. You come back to the office and find many people have transferred out and new people you don't know have transferred in. Sometimes it can feel a bit like being a star athlete—you walk down the hallway and know that some are talking about your "heroic" exploit. Normally, other agents are proud and pleased and congratulate you for your sacrifice and success. But not this time.

This time, it sometimes felt that if I had a finger pointed at me, it was the middle finger. Much of the talk in the Chicago FBI office criticized this case, and said how it was going to ruin relationships between the FBI and the Chicago Police Department. And for a while perhaps it did. Normally if an FBI agent or any cop gets pulled over for a traffic violation, you just flash your badge or credentials and you drive away. I was told that for a while after this case broke, FBI agents in Chicago got traffic tickets instead of a friendly smile.

One of the agents in my office told me, "You're a bullshit agent on a bullshit case!" Another one of my FBI colleagues told me confidentially that he had taken the same kind of payoffs during his time as a Chicago police officer. That is a huge admission for an FBI agent. "There's just no way to avoid it," he told me. "If you don't take the money, you're saying you're better than everybody else, or that they're bad cops." The emotional consequences of the operation were high for everybody involved with the case, on both sides.

During the prosecution phase, several unfortunate things happened. All but two of the funeral-home operators who played hardball with us, the ones who refused to cooperate, and whom we threatened with heavy prosecution, actually got a pass from the U.S. Attorney. Those unfortunate two later pleaded to felonies. The funeral homes that helped out and cooperated with us, the ones we promised light treatment if they cooperated, were also indicted and ultimately had to plead guilty to misdemeanors. I hated that, but that's what happened.

Of the thirty policemen we charged, all were allowed to plead guilty to two misdemeanor counts each. In exchange, they got no jail time. They were also subject to internal disciplinary proceedings by the police department. We expected that meant these officers would be fired, but two years after the conclusion of the case (when I left the Bureau to work in private industry), the cases were still open and nothing had been done with these cops. The other fifty-five officers who had been taped taking payoffs, and the hundreds of others implicated by the records seized from the funeral homes were never even reprimanded or counseled. I have always believed some high-level deals were made to get this thing behind the police department. And, perhaps, that was appropriate. One of the positive results of the case, though, was that the Superintendent of Police put a stop to the practice of body deliveries being made by the police. And today to my knowledge, Chicago cops are neither delivering bodies nor getting paid cash for doing so.

There were reports that one of the cooperating witnesses, a funeral-home manager, and I had death threats made against us by cops. I had become close friends with the manager and his wife during the case and knew they were scared. He knew several of the cops well, and he knew a few were really bad actors, very capable of carrying out these threats. He didn't want to enter the Witness Protection Program, so several other agents and I got together and moved him out of state. We set him up in a new business far from Chicago, and today he's very happy and successful, making more money than he would have otherwise. He and I still talk once a year or so by phone. And he and his wife assured me that the only reason their child isn't named David is because she was born a girl.

Due to the threats against me, I requested, and the Chicago SAC supported, a transfer to another FBI office. The Bureau declined to move me, stating they didn't place enough "credence" in the threats (though they had moved the cooperating witness based on the same threats) and were being very sensitive to complaints that headquarters was "rewarding" undercover agents with plum transfers. We resubmitted the request citing recent cases where Chicago police officers charged with crimes had hurt or killed witnesses or family members. One had occurred just a few months before "Deadfall" went overt. A different case of police misconduct had surfaced involving a ring of cops who were doing burglaries until the FBI broke it up. One of the cops cooperated, and the night before that lone cop who flipped was to testify, his seventy-year-old father was beaten to death.

The Bureau reconsidered and advised that I would be transferred but, to avoid the appearance of it being some type of reward, I would go to a Top Twelve office. The Top Twelve are the largest offices and included many locations, particularly New York and Newark, where I had no interest in moving. "No fair! That's a penalty," I told them. They countered with, "We will give you a list of three Top Twelve offices, and you can pick one from those." "No way," I said, "I decline. Forget the transfer request; I'll think of something else". Then came the ironic kicker from the Bureau: "We can't let you decline because of the death threats; you are at risk." Finally, a compromise was worked out that I would continue to work out of the Chicago office, but I would move myself and family out of state (to Wisconsin), at my own expense.

I got a $2,000 incentive award for the case. For all that time undercover, that might sound like an insult and not much of an incentive, but by FBI standards it wasn't bad. Joe Pistone, the agent whose undercover work was the subject of the movie *Donnie Brasco* and who came the closest of any law enforcement agent to becoming a made member of the Mafia, only got a check for $500 a few years earlier. Undercover work is just not rewarded very well in the Bureau, and perhaps it shouldn't be. Sure, only a small minority of agents can do it well, but only a minority of agents have certain language skills, or superior forensic-audit skills, or other specialties, and they are not necessarily rewarded for their work beyond their normal salaries. I think that most undercover agents would seek those types of assignments anyway. You get to manage real businesses, and many UCAs are really entrepreneurs who just don't have their own bankroll. Others enjoy being actors. The problem is that with this kind of acting you can never afford to get a bad review. The case can fold, or you can get dead.

My next assignment was working on a joint DEA–FBI squad working Colombian drug intelligence and coordinating the Chicago division's asset-seizure and forfeiture program. I worked for the Bureau for another year and a half after "Deadfall" ended. Then, after serving as a special agent for ten years, I left the Bureau for a corporate-security position with a major corporation which afforded more autonomy and better pay. I have the fondest of memories of the FBI and its people. I have oftentimes thought back on the undercover operations I have worked on and thought of writing a book or a screenplay. I always figured I'd just need to add a little extra sex and violence to the story and that baby would sell! Of all those cases, "Deadfall" certainly wasn't the most enjoyable or satisfying operation, but it may have been the strangest.

Madam Commissioner

Bonni Tischler is currently Assistant Commissioner for Investigations, U.S. Customs Service, but she started her career in 1971 as a young "sky marshal" and was one of the very first women in federal service to carry a gun. She became a Customs Agent in 1977 and has been a trailblazing hardcharger ever since. She now presides over one of the largest, most aggressive, and successful federal law-enforcement investigative operations, but she hasn't forgotten what it is like to work undercover in the field—including a role as the "madam" in a call-girl operation.

In the 1970s and '80s it was rare for a woman to carry a gun as a federal agent—for the most part, our role seemed to be as secretaries and supporting players in any of the federal law-enforcement agencies. It took a while for us to move into leadership roles, so at the beginning of my career I had some bit parts in some fairly big operations. I was pretty much the first woman to do a lot of things, before I eventually ended up being in charge.

Operation Greenback

Back in 1980, I was assigned with some other agents
to Operation "Greenback" down in Miami. This was a
prototype operation against money-laundering activities,
and it became the foundation for the Money Laundering
Control Act of 1986. We worked regular cases as well
as occasional undercover roles. I had done undercover
work on one of these, and it had been quite successful,
so another agent approached me and said, "Look, we've
got another chance to work on some attorneys who appear to be laundering money—and they're involved in a
call-girl business."

"Ummm . . . okay, but what exactly did you want *me*
to do?" I said, wondering where this request was going.

"We want you to work for one of the principals. According to our informant, he's running several brothels,
and we want you to be his partner."

"Now, did you have me in mind for an *executive* role,
or am I supposed to be one of the 'girls'?" I asked him.

"No, we want you to be the madam of one of the call-
girl operations," he said, and that role was okay with me.

Now, back in 1982 I was an attractive young thing, and
it was very rare for women to be involved in undercover
operations, both factors that I thought would be advan-
tages for my role. So we showed up for a meeting with
these guys. The informant was there, and he played his
role of a low-life quite well. Our story was that I had a
call-girl business, and we needed to launder the money
the business generated.

While these guys seemed interested in doing the deal,
it was obvious that we didn't yet have the rapport necessary to complete it. In any undercover operation, you
have to establish a personal relationship. They have to
accept you in your role, and they have to trust you. And
I wasn't getting *anywhere* with these guys.

Well, I was supposed to be a madam, and that suggests
some sexiness. I wore a very nice long leather skirt to

the meeting, with snaps up the front. I started discreetly unsnapping a few of these fasteners, showing a little more leg, and smiling winsomely. There was no reaction from the guy, at all! We were negotiating a deal, but there was none of the necessary rapport you like to have in any sting operation.

They wanted to know all about the business—how many girls we employed, how much they charged, how much we paid them, how much money needed to be laundered. I had answers for everything. I also told them that I really wanted the money to be taken out of the country and gave them all sorts of other details. The attorney took this all in, but he still wouldn't talk to me. He was only talking to our informant, and not dealing with me as a person. I laid on all the sex appeal I could, and it just wasn't working. There was no reaction at all. We wrapped up this preliminary meeting and left.

Back at the office I went to see the Senior Agent in Charge and told him, "Listen, I know I was really successful with our previous operation, but this role just isn't working for me! This guy just isn't connecting with me, and he isn't going to tell us anything unless you have somebody else in there."

He agreed, and we sent in another agent posing as an "enforcer." This guy worked, and we made the case, arrested the attorney and some other people, and got them convicted. About a year later, as it was all winding up, I got a call from the Senior Agent in Charge.

"I just thought I would let you know," he said, "why you weren't connecting with that attorney, and why he wasn't influenced by your wiles. Both he and the other guy were gay."

Not long after that, in 1981, I played an important role in a larger operation, and it was reportedly the first time that a woman agent played a key role in a major undercover investigation. My job was, essentially, to be the First Vice President for Finance of a narcotics organization. Prior to this operation, women had been support players, but here was a chance to be a principal and it worked out quite well. For one thing, I found it a lot easier to be a "high-roller" than a sleazy madam!

Back in the 1980s, we weren't very well "back-stopped". We didn't have the Rolex watches, the expensive cars, and all the props and costumes required for somebody playing the role of a kingpin in a narcotics organization. Undercover work really wasn't well thought out, and there was a lot of suspicion within the agency that if you, as an agent, started living the part of a very wealthy, fast-living person, you could get seduced by it and maybe go over to the other side. As a result, we didn't have the clothes, the props, the cars, or the cash appropriate to the people we were pretending to be—and that increased the risk to us, and that made us all uncomfortable. So I went into the role with my own clothes, which weren't too bad, but without the Rolex and the Mercedes.

We were investigating an old guy down in Tampa, Florida, who owned a small airport and flying service. With the flying service as a cover, he was moving narcotics into the country and sending cash out to the Bahamas for laundering.

We met with the old guy, and he turned out to be a really dirty old man. He was all over me! He was quite a bit older than me, and he apparently thought of himself as quite a lover. I had a hard time staying out of his clutches!

The operation proceeded pretty successfully, and we started collecting information, some recorded and some not. One day he took us to his airport and gave us a tour of the place, showing us all his aircraft and explaining how he used them for smuggling narcotics.

Well, we weren't taping the meeting, and I wasn't an aircraft expert, and we were trying to memorize all the registration numbers for the aircraft—but there were too many of them. Later, when we went to a judge for the search warrant, all I could say to identify the individual airplanes was that one was a short, fat one, and another was longer and somewhat skinny. I remember the judge looking at me and asking something to the effect of "What kind of undercover agent are you, anyway?"

Anyway, it was time to wrap up the investigation and make arrests. We concocted a deal that involved me delivering $250,000 to him. He was supposed to take the money offshore, to the Bahamas for laundering, and he expected us to ride with him.

Now, $250,000 doesn't sound like a lot of money these days, but back then it was a really big deal. Today we'd be working with millions of dollars. We went to the Federal Reserve and "checked out" a quarter of a million dollars in cash—on my signature—and off we went to Tampa.

We couldn't actually allow ourselves to be flown out of the country, as our "target" thought we would. We planned to hand over the cash, go out to the aircraft, establish that the money was going to be taken illegally out of the United States, and then make the arrests.

During the night, our agents had infiltrated the airfield and set up observation positions, waiting for us to show up. The actual arrests would be made by teams of agents in two Huey helicopters, orbiting the field out of sight. When the observation team saw us approach the aircraft with our "target," they were supposed to call up the helicopters on the radio and tell them it was time to pounce. As a fallback position, we were supposed to call the office and tell them we were leaving about twenty minutes prior to departure from the airport.

I handed over the target's cut, about $25,000, at the guy's airport office. After calling our office to alert them, and to cue the arrest teams, we headed for the airport.

The only problem was that the person who took the call didn't know anything about the operation and didn't pass the word! Consequently, the helicopters never got the call alerting them that the show was about to begin.

Then, the observation team out in the weeds kept trying to make radio contact with the helicopters, but the team couldn't get through because the helicopters were out of range. I didn't know about all that until later.

Anyway, my partner and I took our little briefcase full of money and headed for the runway. My partner was going to ride with the principal and his chief pilot in one aircraft while I was supposed to ride with his associate, a guy named Rudy, and another pilot in a second aircraft. Both aircraft were Piper Navajos, twin-engine aircraft with the range for the flight to Nassau.

We get into the airplanes, and they start the engines and we start taxiing out and I'm thinking, *Where are those damned helicopters, anyway?* The operation was supposed to be stopped right on the runway. We were *not* supposed to take off! I didn't know what to do and was trying to figure out a plan on the spot. *Maybe I should tell them I need to go to the bathroom,* I thought.

While I was trying to come up with some stall tactics, I looked out the window and noticed the first aircraft has stopped and shut down its engines. Rudy, the guy escorting me and the money, sees the other aircraft shut down, too, and turns to me and says, "I don't know what's wrong. We'll take off anyway and go on alone."

"You will not!" I told him. "Just taxi this airplane over there and find out what's going on!"

So the pilot taxied over and shut down the engines. I was scanning the sky for any sign of inbound helicopters, but there was still nothing in view. My partner and the two bad guys were already out of their aircraft. Just as we were climbing down out of our plane, my partner comes over, whips out his pistol, and yells, "Federal agent! Get out of the airplane! Everybody's under arrest!" Well, my heart stopped—that scared me to death! That was *not* what he was supposed to do!

"Everybody put your hands on the aircraft!" he ordered, and he wasn't making exceptions for me. I figured he didn't want me to break cover and to see if perhaps I could get some more information from them later. He starts patting everybody down, then putting the suspects in kneeling positions on the ground. It was really hot and nasty, and the operation was not going as planned. I was getting crabby about it.

Just about the time he starts patting me down, the helicopters pop up over the trees with the arrest teams standing in the door ready for action. One of them almost fell out as the helicopter flared up to land. The rotor wash kicked up a big cloud of dust and dirt. I start to have an asthma attack while everybody else is swearing and yelling and carrying on generally.

The whole thing was extremely bizarre. One of the helicopters took off and was attacked in the process by a huge German shepherd that came out of the weeds with one of the surveillance agents. While this dog is doing its best to take a big bite out of the helicopter, the arrest team charges over to take control of the situation.

One of them yells at me, "Okay, bitch, up against the airplane!" He threw me up against the plane, messing up the nice, white suit I was wearing, and leaving a big bruise about twelve inches long on my back.

There was a good reason for all this, it turned out. We had already given the old guy $25,000, ten percent of the total $250,000 as his fee for laundering the cash. But we didn't know where that $25,000 was, and the other agents were hoping somebody would say something in my presence revealing its location. So the agents handcuffed us all and put us all on the ground.

Finally we all got dragged off to jail—except that I was actually going to see the grand jury in my bedraggled state. First, though, I had to sign off on a search warrant so we could inspect the guy's records and look for the money in his office and in his home. All I could think of was the missing $25,000 that I was responsible for.

Well, we looked everywhere for that money, and nobody could find it anywhere! The agents turned his house upside down while I appeared before the grand jury in my formerly clean, white suit that was now dusty and dirty.

The cash finally showed up a day and a half later, after much frantic searching; it had been casually tossed in a file drawer in his office instead of carefully hidden or secured in his safe, as we expected. The search of the guy's home came up with some interesting stuff, though—the world's largest collection of pornography!

The principal in this case was an important figure, and the Customs Service wanted to have me work with him again. He seemed really attracted to me, and we seemed to have good rapport. But that was not to be. He must have made somebody mad at him because he was killed shortly after the arrest and the body found about forty-five days later. As the U.S. Attorney said at the time, he was found with a fourteen-inch rope around his seventeen-inch neck, partly mummified and partly eaten by animals. It was a fitting end for the old guy.

Police Harassment

Things have changed a lot since I became a federal agent. To give you an example, let me tell you about an operation we conducted against an aircraft manufacturing company back in the late 1970s. We had information indicating the company was illegally selling aircraft to Iran and Customs got a search warrant to go in and look at their records.

But we didn't know exactly where in the building the appropriate records were located and we wanted to get control of them immediately, before anybody could remove them. That was my job, to case the joint. I applied for work with the company as a secretary. I took their tests, was interviewed, and got the information we needed about the location of the files. We then executed the search warrant.

Normally we don't send somebody who's already played an undercover role along as part of the team executing the warrant, There's something about an ex-employee showing up wearing an agents badge that just annoys the hell out of folks, and they tend to get crabby about it. But because it was a small Customs office and for other reasons as well, I was elected to go along on the search.

My part of the search involved looking through files of correspondence with members of Congress, and while I was looking through the files, the woman who had once interviewed me showed up with the local vice president. The two of them started harassing me. Well, in the movies nobody ever harasses a federal agent, but this was real life and 1978.

Part of the problem was that we were serving a document warrant, so finding the right documents was a logistics problem, particularly for the employees of the company. The two of them appeared in the office every few minutes and started berating me. Finally, I told the woman, "Get out of here and stop harassing me!"

"Well, that just shows what a blue-collar jerk *you* are! It isn't 'har-ASS', it's 'HAR-ass'!" she said, trying to correct my pronunciation.

"I don't care what it is," I replied. "Get out of my face! If you don't leave here immediately I will have somebody take you down the hall and handcuff you to a chair." Today, of course, we would never let somebody stand around and watch while we conduct a search, but back then the Customs agents were more touchy-feely.

Agents today are involved in some very stressful undercover operations, and as a manager I can tell you it's a bit like being Wendy and Peter Pan. When we have people undercover, or out on a raid, or anything related to enforcement, I don't rest easy when these things are under way!

People really don't know much about what Customs

does. Our major enforcement efforts are in money laundering, narcotics trafficking, fraud, and what we call "strategic investigations"—high technology and weapons of mass destruction being shipped out of the United States. The kinds of people you deal with in some of these cases tend to be very dangerous.

Sex, Drugs, and Rock
and Roll

Jim Lilley is a retired sergeant formerly in charge of the Street Drug unit for the Howard County, Maryland, Police Department. His unit normally operated undercover or in plainclothes and was extremely active in going after street-level drug dealers by any means.

Working undercover requires a special person and not every officer can do it. For one thing, you have to be a great actor. You have to give an Oscar-winning performance every day, or you might not be around tomorrow to continue the act. You have to be quick, sly, and able to react convincingly—and in character. It can be very taxing physically because of the scheduling; you can be doing routine police work one minute then be deep undercover the next. You have to be able to think at high speed while your body is working in slow motion. There is always the chance that the "Monday-morning quarterbacks" will second-guess everything you do. Above all, you have to have the courage "to dance in the arms of the devil." But we made more arrests in four years—over 2,000—than many officers make in a career, and we had fun doing it!

Undercover operations get mixed into everything else.

For example, in September 1991, we were down in an area called North Laurel, in Howard County, Maryland, trying to serve an arrest warrant in a narcotics-distribution case. While waiting outside an apartment building, preparing to serve the warrant, we kept noticing a woman standing at the curb, hailing cars on Route 1. It didn't take long before she had one stop; she then climbed in and they disappeared around the corner.

Ace detectives that we are, we conclude that she is a working girl engaged in prostitution. We follow at a discreet distance, find the car, and sneak up just in time to overhear the girl and the guy in the car concluding a financial transaction for sexual services. We arrest both.

While she's in the back of the car getting ready to go to jail, she says, "Look, I can't afford to go to jail. I'll set something up for you if you'll let me go."

So we start talking to her about setting up a drug buy. But before we get far with this conversation, a pickup truck comes screaming into the parking lot. It screeches to a halt and out pops a naked woman! There is a lot of screaming between this lady and the male driver of the truck. Negotiations for sexual services seem to be the subject, but apparently this time the two parties don't agree. "Screw you!" the driver yells, although he doesn't seem to really want to, and then he takes off. All this provided quite a show and was very entertaining. We all paid close attention.

Well, the girl's clothes are still in the truck. She grabs the pickup as it takes off and she hangs on. The driver takes off, gets back on Route 1, and moves out at high speed with his headlights off. We took off right behind him.

He soon gets off the highway and onto a beat-up secondary road full of potholes with the woman attached like a leech and with us in hot pursuit. After a couple of miles, we pulled the guy over. After a brief chat, we discovered that he objected to her prices, and that's what the fight was all about. He was charged with reckless endangerment, reckless driving, and a bunch of other charges. She was charged with prostitution. Then we went back to the apartment complex and used the first hooker to help make another drug arrest. As a result of the drug case, we took the guy's Audi, a nice new car at the time. That was how we got our vehicles in the drug unit, as seizures and forfeitures.

Our prostitute friend set us up for a buy from a dealer who showed up with an even nicer car, a bright red Nissan 300ZX. The guy offered us fifteen rocks of crack cocaine, and we busted him.

Instead of calling a tow truck, we decided to take his car. Detective Mike Ensko hopped in and fired it up. "What are you doing with my car!" the suspect wailed.

"Is it paid for?" I asked him.

"Sure!" he replied.

"Do you *really* like that car?" I asked again.

"Oh, yeah, I love that car, man!" he said.

"Well, then, I suggest you go over and kiss it goodbye because this is the last damn time you're ever going to see it!"

Mike popped the clutch and did a fast, gravel-spraying circle of us in the parking lot and took off with his shiny new toy, much to the dismay of the drug dealer. The car went to the impound lot and, not long after, was forfeited. We had another new set of wheels.

The Unbearable Dan Coon

Drug sellers can get pretty brazen sometimes, and some of them virtually dared us to catch them. Naturally, we planned an operation against them, and it kicked off one cold December night. Dan Coon is a playful officer who likes to have a good time on such operations, and he likes to dress comfortably at the same time. Dan dressed for the operation in black "cammies" (camouflage out-

fits) and the head, hands, and feet from a bear costume.
Now, actually, the head is a kind of hat rather than a
full-head shape, but it is quite convincing, particularly
on a cold, dark, damp night.

Our first tactical problem was just getting into the
neighborhood. We couldn't drive up without being noticed—especially Dan—so we decided to create a diversion. I called the patrol division and asked them to send
two cruisers into the apartment complex with red lights
on, at high speed, and have them screech to a stop. This
ought to get some attention, and it did.

While most of the residents were trying to figure out
who was being arrested this time, we sneaked in the
back way. Dan ambled out of our car, across the parking
lot, and climbed up a pine tree—a bear with handpack
radio and binoculars. He climbs up to the level of about
the third story of the building. The rest of us are also in
black cammies—including shirts with "POLICE" on the
back and "IF YOU'RE CLOSE ENOUGH TO READ
THIS YOU'VE BEEN BUSTED BY THE STREET
DRUG UNIT" on the front—but without the furry
parts, and we set up observation points around the
complex.

Dan perched in that tree for several hours, reporting
on drug sales, while people walked by under his tree.
We were watching a particular drug dealer pacing back
and forth on the sidewalk between two apartment buildings. Dan called on the radio, "He is definitely making
drug sales."

I had two members of the Tactical unit in position.
"When I give the word, snatch the dealer and get him
out of there," I told them on the radio. They moved
stealthily into position, within just a few feet of the guy
but totally invisible to him, since they were covered in
black from head to foot. "NOW!" I called, and they
pounced on this dealer. They swept him right off his feet
and carried him away on their shoulders. He shit himself

in fright, and was dragged off, cuffed, and taken to booking.

Dan came down, and we shifted to another area where we had been getting complaints. We raided the place. The woman who owned the place looked at the message on the front of my shirt and said, "I've seen that before, motherfucker!"

"You are going to see it again, bitch!" I told her.

A week later she and her friends were all out of jail. We received a complaint from a neighbor that they were back at it again. She hadn't learned a thing. We got another search warrant and raided the place again. The Tac unit went in, but this time the people are dispersed throughout the place. Dan Coon and Mike Ensko go upstairs to the master bedroom, the double doors are locked. Dan is about six-foot-three and plants a size fourteen boot on the door. The whole double door, frame and all, pops out and falls inward. Dan and Mike go charging in over the door.

Once inside, they find the place apparently empty except that the wreckage of the door on the floor is moving around a little. They lift up the broken lumber to discover the inert form of one of the suspects. He'd been cowering behind the door during the raid, and the whole thing came down on top of him. Ricky and Mike had just trampled over the guy.

We packed them all up and loaded them in the prisoner van to be taken down to booking. But before we go, the phone rings. I answered.

"Hi, is Judy there?" somebody asked.

"She's here, but she's . . . um, tied up right now," I told him.

"Well, I need to get something from her."

"Oh, I can take your order," I said. "What do you need?"

"I'd like to get a half ounce of coke," he said.

"That's no problem. It's right here. Stop by if you want to pick it up."

"Okay, I can be there in about fifteen minutes."

"Good. We'll wait for you," I said.

We took the prisoner van around the corner and hid it, still full of suspects. Sure enough, about fifteen minutes later the guy shows up. He knocks on the door and when he opens it, he recognizes all of us from previous arrests, and we all recognize him. "What the hell?" he says. We snatched him, dragged him inside, collect his paraphernalia and drug money, and slap him in irons. Soon he is in the van with the rest of them.

Dan Coon is still providing surveillance outside, and he is getting cold and bored. He collects his bear hat from his vehicle and starts patrolling out in front of the house in his black outfit with bear hat, feet, and paws. Even this was too dull for Dan, who sneaked over to the prisoner van.

Dan started banging on the side of the van and growling somewhat like a black bear. Then he started sneaking his big, hairy paws up to the windows and started scratching the glass like he wanted to get at what was inside. The prisoners start screaming, "HELP! PO-LICE!" Then he very slowly starts raising his head up. From the inside it must have looked like a real bear was about to peel the van open and start chewing on the contents.

Dan finally got bored with scaring the dealers and sneaked away, leaving our prisoners happy to be inside the van.

We collected a few more buyers, loaded them up, and carted the lot off to jail. Dan was perfectly comfortable in his new uniform and didn't bother to take any of it off at the office. After the raid, he kicked back for a few minutes with his bear feet up on his desk, his bear paws behind his head, his bear hat still in place. Two detectives from another agency happened by. Both looked at Dan, shook their heads in amazement, and scurried back to their dull, quiet, normal jurisdiction at the first chance.

Dan wasn't through, though. He thought he'd go down to booking and see how the prisoners were doing. They were doing fine, although somewhat annoyed, and didn't think Dan was funny at all. Neither did a drunk who had been hauled in for some transgression. Dan popped around the corner and scared the poor guy so badly that the drunk urinated all over himself.

Truck-Stop Follies

There was a lot of drug traffic and prostitution at a truck stop within our jurisdiction, and we decided to set up an operation against it. The idea of "stoned" drivers operating these big rigs down the highway is pretty scary, and we wanted to put a lid on the practice as much as we could.

Our plan was to go down to this truck stop and conduct what is called a "reversal" sting operation, with us offering the drugs and prostitution services for sale instead of offering to buy them. Of course we can't solicit unless somebody tells us first that they're interested in buying something, so we were careful about what we said. Even so, it was usually pretty easy to snag them.

I had spent enough time listening to these guys on the CB radio to know their codes. "Does anybody have one to burn?" is a request to buy marijuana. "Anybody got some 'go fast?' " is an offer to buy "speed" or methamphetamine. "Nose candy" is cocaine. Prostitutes are known as "lot lizards," and you hear calls asking for them, too. And there are lots of other expressions in common use by these guys.

So I took my CB radio and some of the guys from my squad down to the truck stop and set up shop one evening. There were four of us—Ricky Lee, Paige Christis, Linda Reimer, and me. I turned on the radio and almost immediately heard a guy call, "I'm looking for some 'smoke' " another expression for marijuana. I radioed back that I could help him out. We met in the parking lot and I sold him some. My signal to the bust team listening to the transaction on a "wire" was, "It's been nice doing business with you." Then we busted him. Within five minutes we had our first guy in custody.

The place turned out to be a gold mine. We were busting people quite often for all kinds of crimes.

Dan Coon was working the CB one day while I was doing sergeant work. Dan called me up on the radio and asked indignantly, "Did you hear what that guy just said to me on the CB?"

"No, I was talking to somebody else on Channel 19."

"Well, this guy called me on Channel 3 and says he wants a blow job! And he says he's willing to pay the standard price!"

"Did you ask him what the standard price is?"

"Yeah, he said it's $20."

"Well, let's go ahead and meet him and see if he'll make the solicitation again. We really don't need to have him repeat the offer to convict, but it would be a good idea just to make sure. We don't have time to set you up with a body wire, so we'll watch you. Signal us to make the bust by raising your ball cap if he makes the solicitation again."

They agreed to meet near the fuel pumps and we all moved our vehicles over to that vicinity. Dan found the customer and we could see the two of them talk beside the vehicle (a step van, not a semi) for a few moments; then Dan returned to his car. He called on his handpack, "Now the guy doesn't want to pay. He wants the blow job for free. What shall I do?"

"Well, technically, we can bust him. He made the solicitation for money the first time. It's a violation and we can take him. Go up and stand in the doorway to the lounge. We know he went in there. If he comes out and propositions you again, use the hat signal and we'll take him."

We could all see Dan and the entrance clearly. I sent Ricky and Paige over to wait by the stairwell, and Linda and I waited in my vehicle. It was Ricky's job to take the trucker into custody and do the preliminary pat-down search. "Well, okay, but I am *not* touching this cocksucker under any circumstances!" Ricky says, and he goes to his car to retrieve a pair of bright blue rubber gloves that we normally wear while handling people who are bleeding (or worse).

It was at about this point that I began to lose my composure. The sight of big Ricky Lee, our muscular and fearless detective, so upset about the possibility of contact with this guy that he first put on rubber trauma gloves had me starting to giggle.

It wasn't long before the trucker comes back out of the lounge. We could see him approach Dan, and the two of them begin to talk. Linda is starting to get nervous, but I am still trying to suppress giggles. Then Dan and the trucker start to walk toward the truck, and then I notice it is a *fruit* truck, at which point I lose it completely.

Linda doesn't see the humor in this at all. "What if we can't see Dan give the signal?" she asks.

"Well, I hope Dan's ready to come across," I told her.

"How can you say that!" she says.

"Don't worry. Dan's a big boy and everything will be fine."

We are close enough so that we can clearly see both Dan and the trucker. They sit in the cab and talk; then we see some movement in the truck, on the driver's side; then the door on the passenger side flies open and Dan pops out. His right arm is working that ball cap up and down like a piston! He's waving to us! Then Ricky and Paige run over, and I can't move because I am laughing so hard! He must have popped that damn hat on and off his head twenty-five or thirty times in the few seconds it took Ricky and Paige to run over. Linda went to help out, but I was out of action. The whole scene with the blue gloves and that hat popping up and down was just too funny.

Later I asked Dan what happened. "Well, we were talking in the truck, and the guy starts to unzip his pants and pull out his cock. 'I guess this won't take too long,' he said."

"Why didn't you just take off your hat in the cab instead of jumping out like that?" I asked him.

"Because I wanted to make DAMN SURE you guys got over there in a hurry. That's why!" he said.

A few months later, at a party for the unit at my house, we discovered that Dan hadn't bothered to tell his wife about this incident. Naturally, we filled her in on Dan's "truck stop buddy." Now she likes to tell him that she knows somebody else has eyes for him. He will never live that one down!

Good Loving Gone Bad

When something happened in our unit, we stayed with it until it was finished. That could sometimes mean long hours and no chance to call home to report your where-abouts or schedule to your spouse. For most of us this was not a problem. My wife was also a police officer, and the same was true for many of the other members of my unit.

We had a case start one Thursday night about 11 P.M. We set up a surveillance on some people in the Cedar Motel, a notorious flea-bag resort. It was the kind of place where you had to fight with the cockroaches to get into the room. Two drug dealers from Baltimore were supposed to make a delivery to several people at this motel, and we wanted to catch them all. We already had three in custody and were waiting for a couple of others to show up. Other units were keeping an eye on them and reports came in over the radio: "They're in Anne Arundel County; they should be at your location soon."

The surveillance dragged on all night, through Friday, and on into Friday night. At the time, I was the only member of the team with a cell phone, and Dan called on his radio from his surveillance location. "Jim, would you call my wife and let her know that I'm tied up and can't get home?"

"No problem, Dan. I'll be *happy* to tell her that for you, buddy!" I had been Dan's supervisor for only a couple of months at that time and didn't really know his wife as yet.

I called and his wife, Cindy, was less than thrilled about Dan's disappearance, even before I talked to her. "Hi, this is Sergeant Lilley, Dan's supervisor . . ."

"Well, where is he?" she demanded.

"We're on a surveillance right now, and he's kind of tied up . . ."

"I want to know where he is!" she said.

"He's in a motel room," I told her.

"A motel room? With who?"

"With Linda."

She was livid. "Are you sure it's a surveillance?" she wanted to know.

I was able to reassure her a bit, but she still reminds him that he's gone off to cheap motels with other women while on duty. I pointed out to her that he's done the same thing with Ricky Lee, too, and so Cindy has a lot of blackmail material to use on Dan whenever he gets out of line.

Freedom Bridge

We picked up a couple of kids smoking dope, and both were quite nervous and very upset about being arrested. All we got off one of the kids was a couple of joints, but they were still quite worried about what would happen to them. "If I give up my source, will you drop the charges?" one wanted to know. We made a deal with the kid.

A couple of days later the kid calls. "The guy who sells to me is down on Main Street in Ellicot City right now, and he's dealing." We hopped in our vehicles and bop on down there. We find the dealer, and he sells us two ounces of marijuana. As soon as he makes the sale to Dan, we bust him.

The dealer, like the kid before him, goes into a real panic. "I can't afford to be arrested," he says. He has spent time in jail and doesn't want to do it again.

"Okay," I tell him, "we can take care of that, but you're going to have to do something for us in return. We want your supplier." He agreed that he'd try to set something up. Charges were filed against him, and his trial date was set for a few months in the future. We didn't hear from him right away, so I called a couple of times to remind him, "Listen, buddy, your trial date is coming up pretty soon. You better shit a brick real soon, or we're going to hang your ass out to dry as a major dealer."

This seemed to get the desired results, and the man arranged to set us up with his supplier. Since Dan had made the original contact and this was essentially his case, we did the observation while he did the buying. The first deal was for four ounces of marijuana. "Look," Dan tells the dealer, "I'm interested in doing some major business."

"Well, maybe I can get you some larger quantities. Let's get together next week, and I will try to bring you a pound." They set up a meet time for a week later, and Dan bought a pound of marijuana. At the same time, Dan tells the guy, "I want to get into a higher volume business. How much can you get me?"

"How much do you want?" the dealer asked.

"Can you get me five pounds?" Dan said, and the dealer didn't blink. "Sure," he said, "not a problem. I want $7,500 for it, up front."

The dealer was a very slick operator. We weren't sure just how far we'd have to travel to make this buy, so we got statewide jurisdiction. The dealer had license tags listed to a home address he never visited.

The only way we could find out anything about where this guy lived was to tail him. We assigned five undercover cars and officers to the chase, and we followed him down dirt roads, around the beltway, through town. He made stops frequently, doubled back on his trail, making life difficult for us, but we managed to keep him in sight. It took a couple of days, but we finally located the apartment where he normally stayed.

At the same time, we were in contact with him by phone. "Where do you want to meet?" Dan asked.

"Let's meet at the bar on Woodstock Road," he said. The meeting was all set.

We wired up Dan and started planning the details of the operation. Chuck Jacobs and Mike Ensko joined my unit that day, and I put the two of them in a vehicle overlooking the bar at the top of a small hill. I put Linda in a surveillance vehicle. Paige is sent in another vehicle to watch the guy's apartment over in Baltimore County.

Ricky and I hopped in my GMC Jimmy. We put on reflectorized vests, hard hats, jeans, work boots, a hundred-foot tape measure, our police radios, and—looking just like surveyors—we went to work on the bridge just outside the parking lot for the bar.

Paige called to report that the guy was en route, and then she called again to say he was approaching our location. Pretty soon he rolled into the parking lot, walks into the bar, and then we can hear him greeting Dan at the bar. "So—got the money?" he wants to know.

"Sure," Dan says, "but I'm not going to show it to you in here. I'll show it to you outside."

They drink a beer and then go out to Dan's car. He pulls out the cash and the dealer counts it out. "Okay," the dealer says, "wait here and I will be right back with the stuff."

The guy takes off and drives right past Ricky and me, measuring that bridge and writing things down on the clipboard. I called Paige on the radio: "He's headed back your way, hopefully to get the stuff."

Paige acknowledged the call, then silence. Was the guy getting the dope from some other location? We waited a long time, then my pager went off. I looked at the display and it read "1076" which means "enroute" followed by three numerals that I recognized as the dealer's last three license plate numbers. Paige's radio battery died, and she used her cell phone to call my pager with the information. And soon enough, the dealer comes zooming down the road past us again, paying us no attention, and skids into the parking lot.

Dan keys his radio and reports, without the guy noticing, "He's got the package on the seat." Ricky and I get in the GMC, drive into the lot, and block the guy's vehicle. The dealer looks up at Ricky looming over him, looking authoritative, and he suddenly realizes "Holy shit! This is *not* a construction worker!" The dealer takes off on foot with Ricky right behind him while I radio Mike and Chuck up on the hill, "Get down here. We have a foot pursuit!" They arrived in a flash and screech to a stop on the far side of the dirt parking lot.

It was really kind of fun to watch. Ricky was closing on this poor guy like a freight train. The dealer was picking 'em up and putting 'em down like an Olympic sprinter running for his life. Mike and Chuck run for the guy, too, from the other direction, and suddenly I see what must inevitably happen. All four of these guys going full tilt crash into each other, then ricochet off the side of the surveillance truck. The truck rocked from the impact, and the noise was just like two cars colliding.

All I could see at first were three pistols flying through the air. Then I saw the crook. They hit him so hard he was knocked right out of his shoes! Even so, he recovers enough to get up and start running again.

It is about 5:30 in the afternoon, and traffic out on Woodstock Road is getting heavy. It doesn't faze this guy at all. He runs right down the middle of the road on the double yellow line. He is headed for the bridge!

Ricky, Mike, and Chuck dust themselves off and take off after him again while I am left to wander around the scene of the collision and pick up pistols.

The dealer finally gets to the bridge and stops on the far side. "You can't touch me!" he yells, "You can't touch me!" He should have added, *nyaa, nyaa, nyaa!* The three detectives crash into him again, leveling him this time for keeps. Later we determined that he thought that if he made it across the bridge, out of Howard County and into Baltimore County, he would be out of our jurisdiction. Of course, that wouldn't have been true in any case, but your normal criminal really is dumber than dirt. Ever since, that bridge has been known as "Freedom Bridge" within our department.

Anyway, we took the guy in, and he wants to play hardball. He won't tell us a thing. "Okay," I whispered in his ear, "we know where you live. Guess where we're going next? We're going to go pay your wife a visit." At this point he becomes quite upset and it turned out, with good reason.

The Baltimore County Vice and Narcotics unit went with us on the raid. We all hit this dealer's house and come up with another kilo—over two pounds—of marijuana, a hundred tabs of LSD, a large quantity of hallucinogenic mushrooms, and $1,200 in cash. We seize all this, plus his two cars, much to the guy's dismay.

While searching the place, we find identification in several names. After investigating further, we find this same dealer has several bank accounts and safe deposit boxes in different names. We check out the safe deposit boxes and discover even more IDs, with addresses in

Florida, Mexico, New Mexico, California, Oregon, and Illinois.

A call to the Oregon State Police produced the information that they'd been watching for him out there. We did a cooperative "buy" from an Oregon source; the drugs were shipped by overnight express to us in Maryland. That was all the Oregon State Police needed to raid the Oregon place, which they did.

Inside they found 2,000 tabs of LSD, a large indoor marijuana-growing operation with the best hybrid plants, along with everything needed for a major drug distribution business.

The DEA called us from Oregon shortly thereafter to report that the accounting records we seized in the raid on the dealer's house were instrumental in taking down a major kingpin in the manufacture and distribution of LSD. The Oregon police also made another raid, as a result of our work, that resulted in the seizure of 116,000 doses of LSD.

All this was the direct result of Ricky and Dan arresting two guys smoking a joint in a car—plus ten months of dedicated, undercover detective work.

Baby-Sitting Blues

One sad part of this business is that we frequently come into contact with children who are unwitting victims of the drug trade. These are the children of the drug dealers and drug users, and what happens to the kids can be heartbreaking.

We set up a drug buy from a guy known to us as a dealer. The deal went down in a motel, and we nailed the guy with five grams of crack cocaine. Two other people were with him, one of whom had a four-year-old child with her.

While we were going through the arrest procedures

with these adults, the little girl reached up and grabbed the hand of one of my detectives to get his attention. She told the detective that she knew her uncle, the guy we just arrested, brought a load of crack to the motel. This detective couldn't believe a child so young would know about crack, but as he talked to her further, it was obvious that the little girl knew precisely what the stuff was. She also said that there was a lot more at her mother and father's house, and it was there right now. She told us that they sat at the kitchen table cutting it up, and that people would come to the house to get the crack.

We got a search warrant for the place immediately, based on what the child had said, and raided the residence right then. Once inside, the odor of marijuana was intense, and two people are sitting at the kitchen table rolling joints. Another woman was found in a bedroom, high on crack cocaine, with drugs and drug paraphernalia all around the room.

There were two more children in the apartment, both asleep. Social Services was called but they couldn't respond, so we had to care for the kids on our own. They were placed with grandparents.

Another time we raided a residence, and just as we were about to bust down the door, the guy we were after walks around the corner, headed home. "Hey," he said, "what's going on?"

"Police!" we said, and he was soon flat on the ground with a pistol in his ear.

We entered the apartment and found two children, one and two years old, alone. The guy and his girlfriend had both gone out to buy more crack.

The youngest child was in a crib with just a bottle of water. The sheets on the crib are filthy. The baby's diaper hasn't been changed, and the baby is filthy. The two year old is wandering around the apartment in filthy clothes. Cocaine is visible everywhere in the place—on counters, mirrors, on the coffee table, in the kitchen, upstairs, downstairs.

We started looking around for diapers and food for these neglected kids; taking care of them suddenly became, after we secured the place, a high priority. There wasn't food of any kind for these little kids—no milk, no baby food, nothing at all for a baby. So we each kicked in a couple of bucks and sent one of the uniformed officers out to an all-night supermarket with a shopping list.

The two policewomen in my unit, Linda and Paige, took the kids to separate bathrooms and bathed them, put clean clothes on each, and started feeding them when the officer returned with the groceries. Both ate like they hadn't been fed in a month.

All this makes me *very* angry. I am ready to punch the people responsible for this neglect—and then, right on cue, in walks mom. "What's going on?" she demands. "Where are my babies?" The officer explains the situation and informs her that Social Services will be over momentarily to take the children as a result of her neglect. "YOU CAN'T DO THIS!" she screams. "I demand an explanation!"

At that, I roared down the hallway and pounced on her, with my fist in her face. "Let me tell you something, you fucking worthless bitch . . ." I began, at which point Dan peeled me off her. "Sarge." he said, "why don't you go someplace and cool off?" And it was close. I very nearly punched that woman.

I went outside for a few minutes, then came back in. It was time to start moving the adults down to jail and the kids to the county shelter. The prospect of losing her kids inspired the mother to start singing like a canary. She offered to take us down and do a buy from her supplier for us if only we wouldn't take her kids. We accepted her offer but took the kids anyway.

Even though we took a lot of drugs off the street with that operation, it is very upsetting to see these little children get involved. Their parents waste all their money on drugs while the kids don't get anything, not even food or clean clothes.

Trick or Treat

While the operations involving children could sometimes be depressing, the other ops involving childishness were lots of fun. For example, we were scheduled to do some raids on October 31, Halloween. My unit never passed up a chance like that, so we all bought masks. Ricky had a death mask, I went as a werewolf, Mike went as a gorilla, Dan was a space alien, and Paige had some weird mask I couldn't identify.

A Montgomery County, Maryland, officer called asking us to pick up some folks on a felony warrant who were known to be staying at a motel in our jurisdiction. "No problem," I told him, "come on over and let's go get them."

The officers from Montgomery County showed up. "How are you planning to get in the room?" one asked as we arrived at the motel. We put on our masks and smiled sweetly. "Oh, no," he said.

I sent Chuck Jacobs in first. He pounds on the door and yells, "Trick or Treat! It's party time!"

The door opens. "Hi, come on in," somebody says. We all troop inside, my people in their masks in the lead. As soon as we're inside we can see all sorts of drugs and drug paraphernalia lying around in plain view. The occupants are standing around, obviously wondering who we are.

About that time, the badges and guns start coming out, and the felons realized they've been had. "Aw, shit!" one says.

"The party is now over," I said, "and everybody here is under arrest."

The masks were so successful that we spent the rest of the evening cruising for drug dealers. Ordinarily they'd be wary of us, but with the masks on, they ignored us entirely, thinking we were just out partying. We busted a lot of them that night.

And that was pretty typical of the way my unit operated. We were notorious for doing things a little differently from everybody else and making up things as we went along.

The Great Ebonics Debate—Anonymous Federal Agent

The use of the "N" word has, as we all know from the O. J. Simpson trial, become the most obscene term in the English language. Curiously, that doesn't seem to apply to its use by black people, some of whom use the expression quite often. It is a sad fact of life that black Americans are very disproportionately involved in the drug trade, as dealers and as customers, and this story is about some of those cultural curiosities. And while everybody in law enforcement—black, white, and every color in between—know about these cultural attitudes and behaviors, it is politically incorrect (and a career-ending maneuver) to speak about them in public. The source for this story, then, insists it not be attributed to him.

I look like every Irish cop you've ever seen on every New York street corner—I'm tall, dark-haired, rather muscular. I am of French heritage, however, with some Scots-Irish in the background. This makes it very difficult for me to do undercover work in places like Harlem even though that used to be part of my assignment.

But I grew up in the French Quarter of New Orleans, in a largely black neighborhood, with black neighbors. Most of my friends growing up were black, and we all spoke a dialect you'd call "Ebonics" today. As a result, I speak better black English slang than most black people.

I grew up in a community where I saw people injecting heroin before I was in kindergarten; I saw my first murder when I was eight. But it was *my* 'hood, and those black people are *my* people as surely as any white people. They are the victims of the people selling and using drugs. I am the polar opposite of a racist, but because of the way things can be twisted, I prefer not to be identified for this story.

Well, we'd arrest somebody, and she'd identify her source but refuse to do a buy for us by saying, "I'm terrified of this guy. He's so dangerous he'll kill me if he knows I gave you any information," or words to that effect. So I would get the guy's phone number and speak to him in black dialect and have him actually deliver drugs to the building where we had our offices!

I'd tell him, "Hey, baby, 'dis is Bobby! How you doin' man? My ride *(car)* down an' I need an O Z *(ounce of heroin)*. Can you he'p me, brother?"

We'd have a nice long chat, and we'd talk about subjects common within the black community. "How's yo' momma's sugar?" I might ask him, knowing that diabetes is common among older people in Harlem. I told him that my old lady had a job downtown and that she was going to steal the money for these drugs from her boss's safe. I told him to meet me near the building where my "old lady" worked.

At this point the guy would get in his little car with his little package, and drive on down to our place, and wait for Bobby to show up, figuring that he'd know Bobby when he saw him. When I approached his car with my badge and gun saying, "Federal agent. You're under arrest," it was typically quite a disappointment.

One of these defendants was furious about the way I caught him and felt entrapped by my portraying myself as a black man. Of course, that's not entrapment, but he thought it was and when he got to trial he was steaming.

The whole time I was on the witness stand, this guy was nudging his attorney, insisting that the attorney say something about the "entrapment." The attorney was telling him to shut up, warning him that he was digging himself in deeper.

On the stand, I identify myself, describe the buy, and answer all the questions, sounding just like a big Irish New York cop. Then they play the tape of the telephone conversation, and you hear "Hey, baby, 'dis is Bobby. How you doin' man? . . ."

The judge and jury were nearly all black. All of them looked at me in total amazement; the voice just didn't match the person. None of them had ever heard a white person speak that way.

But all this was just too much for the poor defendant. He jumped up and yelled, "It ain't fair, yo' honor! *He sound mor' like a nigger than a nigger!*"

The judge (also a black man) put his head down and laughed so hard that the whole bench jiggled. The black lady who became foreman of the jury put her head down and laughed, too. They all did! The U.S. Attorney (an Italian with a rather prominent nose) dropped his head down on the table so hard that the impact of that nose sounded like a gun going off. Everybody thought that was funny, except the defendant—who was convicted.

The Dealer's an Idiot

We had a case involving a fairly major black New York drug dealer. He operated out of a fifth-floor walk-up flat and sold to both black and white customers, normally in large-quantity buys.

I went to the guy's apartment and started negotiating with him for a deal. He had a bodyguard with him, and this guard is standing in the background looking like he'd like to kill somebody just for fun.

While we're negotiating, the dealer says to me, "You ain't wearing one of them microphones, is ya?"

"I don't know what you're talking about," I said.

"Well, I read about the cops wearing these microphones and recording conversations." In fact, I had a Kel set (transmitter) on and I was thinking *Oh, shit!* The guys in the car, a block or more away and listening to this conversation, were thinking *Oh, shit!* too.

"Take off your shirt!" the dealer says. I took off my shirt.

The antenna for the transmitter is in a clear plastic tube running up my chest, taped to my pectoral muscle.

"What's that?" the dealer demands.

My backup guys are hearing all this and are charging to the rescue. They are already coming up the stairs, although I didn't know that then. Fortunately, one of the agents kept his ear-piece in and could hear the rest of the conversation.

"This thing?" I asked. "This is a pacemaker."

"What's a pacemaker?" he wanted to know.

"It keeps my heart going. If I took this off, I'd be dead in ten minutes."

"No shit!" he said. "Okay, put your shirt back on."

The guy listening to this, coming up the stairs, told the other agents, "Stop! The dealer's an idiot!" They went back to the cars, I made my buy, and we nailed the guy later on according to plan.

That's the kind of thing you have to be able to do as an undercover agent at times. My backup might not have been able to get there in time to rescue me, and the dealer might not have actually had me killed, but those are things I wasn't interested in finding out at the time.

There were some fun moments in these operations. The normal procedure for large drug buys was that the dealer would first have to show the drugs, then the buyer would show the cash. Since there was typically a *lot* of cash, it was normal to have it in the trunk of a car. So the dealer would be led down the street to a car where the undercover agent would put the key in the lock, open it up, and out I would pop, with a shotgun and badge, saying, "Hi! Federal agent. You're under arrest!"

The reactions you'd get from these guys were somewhat unpredictable. Some would take off running down the street. Some thought they were being ripped off by another bad guy. Some would release their bladders.

We stopped doing that when one dealer heard about the technique. He walked up to the car and said, "Excuse me. I'll pay for the damage," and fired a couple of pistol rounds into the trunk of the car. Happily, there wasn't anybody inside that time, and we changed our routine after that.

Making an Entrance

A group of drug traffickers in New York hired a number of poor, fat, older women addicts to come in and cut the heroin they were selling. Since these women were all addicts, the dealers took precautions to keep the women from stealing the drugs. The women sat at tables wearing hairnets, surgical masks (to keep them from breathing the heroin which would get them goofy), and nothing else at all. So here you had a group of big fat women sitting around a table cutting heroin, in the nude.

We got a warrant to go into the place. Our information indicated that the front door was heavily locked, and the chances of getting in that way were nil. The walls were brick, and there wasn't much chance of going in that way, either. But there was a large picture window on the back side of the house, and that seemed to be the easiest way in.

This block was all row houses, and normally that would make entry difficult. But we went in through one of the neighboring houses to the back of the target residence.

Our unit had an old, long overcoat that we used on undercover and surveillance operations. It was filthy and stank. We put our feet in the sleeves and walked around with it on the ground to get it *really* dirty and funky.

This overcoat was along on the raid, and the agent in charge took the coat, wrapped himself up in it to protect against flying glass, and took a dive through the picture window.

The window broke on cue, but some of the glass landed on the floor inside. The agent landed with his feet on the glass and slid at high speed into the room, crashing to a stop underneath the table at which all these fat, naked women were sitting.

There was a brief delay before the rest of the team followed the agent inside; we were laughing too hard to move very fast. The women were shrieking.

The agent in charge pulled himself up from under the table, pointed his gun at all the women, and said, "Nobody move." Then he turned around and yelled to the rest of us, laughing ourselves sick, *"Get your asses in here!"* And we did.

Making entries can be dangerous in various ways. One time in New Orleans, I kicked in the door at a cheap hotel. The door, the door frame, and half the walls on both sides fell down inside. We were raiding a Cuban heroin dealer, a dangerous guy, and he had heard us coming. He flushed half of his dope down the toilet before we got to the door and was coming back for the rest when the door came down. I lost my balance when the door collapsed, got turned around, and fell into the apartment backwards, at a high rate of speed. I fell toward the dealer.

As we made entry, the dealer dropped the dope and reached for his pistol, a nine-millimeter Browning Hi-Power. He actually had his hand on it and was bringing it up to fire. The agent behind me had been a track star in college and passed me. He was flying! He jammed his gun into the dealer's mouth, breaking a couple of teeth.

"Don't move," he said, and the Cuban dealer froze with his hand on the gun.

Another time we went to get a guy who was more of a killer than a dealer. He really liked killing people, and he had killed a lot of them while ripping them off.

We figured that if we just busted into the place, or if he had a chance to react, there would certainly be a shoot-out. The guy was always armed. Well, this was back in the days of the "no-knock" warrant, when federal agents could go in unannounced; so, we decided to go in quietly.

An informant provided us with a floor plan of the apartment. We knew where everything was located. We had a guy on the squad who knew how to pick locks extremely well. He could get in most doors faster with a pick than I could with a key.

We went in late at night. The lock and door hinges were sprayed with lubricant to keep them quiet. The lock was picked silently. The door was slowly opened. Then we low-crawled into the apartment and over to this guy's bed. I rose up, threw my leg over the guy in bed, stuck my gun in his face, and said, "Hi, my name's 'Bob.' " He thought he was dead. He'd killed a lot of people and expected revenge. He wet the bed, but there wasn't a shoot-out, and nobody got hurt.

Criminal-Family Values

Tom McCready recently retired from a thirty-year career as a patrol officer and detective. During that career, he worked vice and auto-theft details that occasionally required impromptu undercover techniques—the kind of imaginative, innovative skills that make for good police work.

One thing about law enforcement, you get to know the same people pretty well. During my thirty years as a cop, I arrested the same people over and over. I put one guy in jail three times, each for long stretches. The first time was in 1974 for burglary, robbery, and kidnapping; then again, just a month after he got out in 1979; and again not long before I retired.

During the course of thirty years as a cop, I had occasion to arrest members of three generations of a single family—a father, son, and grandfather—and *all* of them went to state prison! I was in court for the trial of the grandson when a vaguely familiar face walked up and introduced himself. It was the kid's grandfather, and I had sent him to prison long ago. We got to talking, catching up on old times. "He's still doing it," the old man said, pointing to the kid's father in the group in the hall—another vaguely familiar face, another member of the family I sent to prison.

"How do you always have such good cases against us?" he wanted to know.

"Genetics," I told him. "Your whole family just naturally gives them to me."

Another time, while I was riding "motors," I pulled a gal over for running a red light. I cited her but didn't feel good about her story. She didn't have ID, and in those days you didn't always take people in and book them if they didn't have a license, particularly a female late at night. I noticed she had a distinctive triangular birthmark on her knee, wrote her ticket, and turned her loose.

Back at the office, I ran the information she'd given me. Damn, it didn't match the photo that came back on the computer. She gave me information for somebody else in her family. I started doing some research and finally found a photo that matched; then I pulled up the booking sheet for the gal, whose real name was Irene, and it indicated a triangular birthmark on the left knee. So I wrote up a report for the incident, "false impersonation of an individual" and "giving false information to a police officer." I got a warrant for her and started wondering how I was going to catch her.

Well, it was almost Easter, and people in East San Jose like to have big family Easter dinners, so we decided to drop by the house on Easter Sunday. The day arrived, we pulled in some extra officers, the beat officers, and swung by Irene's place.

I knocked on the door. "Hi, is Irene here?" I asked.

Everybody in that entire family, from age fifteen to sixty, bailed out of that house on the run! They went over fences, were hiding under bushes, and went running down the street! We arrested Irene for the false-information charge, but we also arrested two or three kids who were escapees from the Boy's Ranch, plus adults wanted for probation or parole violations. The whole family was involved with the criminal justice system. We took *every-*

body to jail except grandma, grandpa, the youngest kids, and the turkey.

A Tool for Every Job

I was working the auto-theft detail when my partner and I were checking out a vehicle that had just been recovered. We dusted for prints and were inventorying the vehicle when I found a notebook with a sketch inside. The sketch strongly suggested to me the layout of a bank, complete with tellers' windows, parking lot, adjacent intersection, and hamburger place across the street. We processed the sketch for latent prints and put it all aside.

About a month later, I got a report about two cars stolen from a dealer's lot. One was recovered. Being an inquisitive guy, I drove down to the towyard to look at the car. I like to actually *look* at something when I am trying to understand what's happening. Well, it was a brand-new, white, high-end American car, and it hadn't been dusted for prints.

I used to run the fingerprint unit, and over the years I have made tons of cases with fingerprints. It is a very easy way to sneak up on a guy! So I dusted the car, popped the trunk, and found a set of license plates! I dusted the plates and ran the numbers on them. The plates came back to an unrecovered, stolen minivan taken from the area around City College.

I called the dealership and got some more information about the recovered car and the other missing car, another high-end luxury model; this one was black. Then I drove around to the apartment complex where the minivan was taken, thinking there might be some connection. And, lo and to say nothing of behold, while driving around the complex, there was a big, black car hidden mostly under a car cover. I stopped, lifted the cover to check the plate, and went back to my car. I ran the plate, and it comes back assigned to a very different vehicle, which was another unrecovered minivan also stolen from this same complex!

I pulled the cover up around the windshield to check the VIN (the vehicle identification number) and discovered that somebody had covered the data plate with a candy wrapper. Hmmm I now have all sorts of details that are suddenly beginning to match up. I remove the car cover, call for a tow, and call for a backup since I didn't know if I had a suspect in the area. I dusted the car for prints and then the stolen plate for prints. I got a real good, juicy print on the plate. Obviously, the car has been stolen for only a few days as the print is very fresh. Back at the office I had the prints run and went home.

The next morning, one of my guys came over and said, "Mac, I got a hit from the automated fingerprint system. The prints match those from a guy who stole a Jeep Cherokee from the vicinity of City College." He gave me the guy's name and his two addresses, one of which is the apartment building where I found the black stolen luxury car! The more we looked at this thing, the more connections there were to this apartment building.

We went down to "Fingerprints" and asked them to run "Johnny Jones." He matched on the thumbprint I got from the black car, but then we checked him against the prints found on the sketch book, the white car, the first-recovered vehicle, and the Jeep Cherokee.

We went out to the apartment, talked to the manager, and found another vehicle that matched the same pattern right down to the candy wrapper on the VIN. We called the vehicle in and it came back stolen, too. But we were still missing two minivans that ought to be related to this same basic pattern—the one whose plate was found in the trunk of the white car, and the other whose plates were found attached to the black car.

While pondering all this, my radio announced "a 211 (robbery) in progress" at the bank described in the sketch. The description of the suspect matched Johnny

Jones perfectly. And even better, a witness reported that he and another guy fled in a minivan matching the description of one of the two stolen vehicles!

Now, I had already told the robbery detail that I was sure somebody was planning to hit that particular branch. It hadn't been robbed in at least six months, the sketch matched perfectly, and everything lined up. It had just been hit, and I thought I knew who had done it and, if we were lucky, they'd be headed home.

We called in some other unmarked cars, set up a loose perimeter on the apartment complex, and settled in to wait. No sooner than we found a good spot to watch the apartment than the radio reported that one of the stolen minivans had just been recovered with the engine still running! I radioed the other units to look for another one just like it, and within minutes they had that one, too! Both had been left at the curb, empty, but with the engines still running.

"Doug," I said to my partner, "maybe they aren't headed back here after all."

Just then a guy jogged into the parking lot. He was wearing a flop hat and clothes that weren't appropriate for the weather or for jogging, and he was carrying a workout bag. "That's one of them! Let's go!" I told Doug, and we bailed out of the car.

The suspect had a good head start on us, but just as we exit the vehicle, the other guy comes running into the lot. We essentially ran into him and took him down on the spot. He had a gun and money in his workout bag. We called in the beat units to secure him, and we called in the others to isolate the apartment where the first guy was headed. One patrol officer hid in the bushes on the back side of the building in case the guy jumped off the balcony. But we didn't have a way to cover the front.

Well, I was dressed *quite* casually, flannel shirt, jeans, working attire generally. So I took out my Leatherman combination tool, a knife, pliers, screwdriver, and more all in one. It looked a little like pruning shears, if you didn't inspect it too closely. I started pruning some of the shrubbery at the foot of the stairs leading from the apartment.

After about five minutes of clipping, my guy appeared on the steps. He was dressed in a business suit now, and he matched perfectly the booking photos we'd been looking at earlier in the day. He passed me, and I whispered a warning over the radio to my partner, "Look out! He's coming your way!"

Then I called to him, "Freeze! Police!" The robber turned around to look at me; I had my radio in one hand and that Leatherman tool in the other. He took off running. He ran right into the uniformed officer waiting around the corner. Inside his clothes was a lot of cash stuffed into all available pockets.

The detectives questioned him and put the whole story together. He and his partner had a string of cars they stole to use in stickups just like this one, stacked up everywhere. They used them like the Pony Express, changing them often to throw off anybody looking for them. When the "defectives" were finished, the robber had a question for them, "Who was that old guy," he wanted to know, "who was pruning the bushes?"

Working Hookers

Early in my career, a long time ago, I was assigned to the Vice unit and "working hookers" downtown. My partner, "Squeaky," was a master at picking up prostitutes! He was totally unassuming, with thinning hair, a high, squeaky voice, and was kind of grubby like a working man. He looked like anybody *except* a cop. Since he was so good at picking up hookers, he'd do the "trolling," and I or the sergeant would provide cover and do the bust.

We were sitting in a bar in downtown San Jose. A girl came in, hooking, and my partner Squeaky picked her up, developed the elements required for a case, and we busted her. Off she went to jail.

A couple of weeks later the two of us are sitting in another bar downtown. The same gal we'd arrested previously strolls in and starts working her way down the bar, hitting on all the guys. Squeaky recognized her and called, "Hey, Sally, come on over here!"

She looked over at us with a big, sweet smile; then she recognized the two of us from her last encounter. *"Oh, no,"* she says, "I'm not going to have anything to do with *you* guys! You're cops!"

"Sally," he says, sounding offended, "of *course* we're cops, but *we're off duty!* And we got *urges,* just like any other guy!"

"Go on!" Sally retorts, not really convinced but starting to weaken to Squeaky's famous charm.

"Would I kid you?" Squeaky says. "Now, you *already* know I'm a cop, I've *told* you I'm off duty, but I still think you're really cute, and I want to have sex with you!"

"Well . . . okay, but after what you did to me before, *it's going to cost you $50 instead of $25!"*

"Great! Now, my friend here (he indicates me), he doesn't want to have sex with you. He's gay, but he does like to watch. Is that okay?"

"Okay, but that will be another $10," Sally said.

So we all went out of the bar, and we arrested Sally for the second time in two weeks.

That line worked with men, too. We trolled for gay prostitutes and picked up the same preacher twice within a few months. It is a fundamental in police work, no matter if you're trolling for prostitutes, overt homosexual acts, burglars, or whatever that your typical crook is dumber than dirt.

"We All Carry Guns in Here!"

I *hate* working hookers and I *hate* working bars, but that's part of the assignment. And you don't go to the nice bars, either, but the worst in town. One time we were sitting in a really low-class Mexican bar, looking for people playing a gambling game called "Punch." You pay a buck and get to punch out a spot on a card; if you get the right one, you win.

So we're sitting in this bar, the only two gringos in the place. We had a beer. Nothing happened. We shot a game of pool. Nothing happened. We had another round, and I pulled out my wallet to pay for the beers, and my little twenty-five-caliber Beretta automatic backup gun came out with the wallet and goes scooting across the floor! It stopped underneath the pool table.

"Cover me," I told my partner and sheepishly went over to collect my wayward little pistol.

As I returned to my bar stool and picked up my beer, the bartender leaned over and said, "Hey, man, don't worry 'bout it. *We're all carrying guns in here.*"

My Last Day on the Force

It was my last day as a cop. After thirty years as a San Jose police officer, I was going to retire at the end of my shift, but it was a normal shift on the auto-theft detail just the same. My partner and I were in plainclothes, sitting in an unmarked pickup truck, looking for some suspects or vehicles associated with a car-theft operation.

We had found one of the vehicles and were sitting there, smoking ceremonial Honduran last-day cigars, polluting our lungs, and discussing if we ought to have the vehicle towed. It was about 4:15 in the afternoon, almost time to head back, the end of the shift and the end my career.

A woman screamed somewhere behind our car. We turned and looked. A young guy was stealing the lady's purse, trying to tear it away from her. While we were reacting, he succeeded and took off, running across a park and school yard.

We bailed out of the vehicle and took off after him. He jumped a little fence. We climbed over the little fence. He kept running. We kept running, me with my cigar still in my mouth. Well, both my partner and I were a bit outclassed in this race. We were both over forty, both had been smoking cigars, and neither of us were gaining on the kid. The whole maneuver didn't seem like real smart police work; so I told him, "Get the truck!" Now, my partner had a hand-pack radio, but I didn't bring one. It was, after all, my last day at work. I didn't have my handcuffs, either! I did have my gun and my badge, both in a little belly pack. "*You* get the truck," he huffed, and I turned back for it.

On the way back, after climbing the fence, I finally tossed the cigar, regretfully. It was an expensive one and good, too!

I drove around the school yard just about the time the suspect emerged, still running. He cut in front of the truck and I yelled at him, "Police! Freeze!"

He didn't quite freeze, but he stopped for long enough to go through the purse, grab some money, and then threw it down saying, "Okay, if you want the purse, here it is!" He took off running again, but I could tell he was getting winded. He wasn't moving so fast, and I trailed him with the truck. Once I got to a position where I figured I could trap the guy between the truck, my partner, and me, I stopped and bailed out of the pickup.

This belly pack is designed to hold a pistol. There are zippers across the top and a quick release. I undid the zippers as I got out of the truck, but the pistol was in the pack, and it was starting to flop around.

As I started fighting with this guy, the gun wasn't really secure. I footsweep the kid, taking him to the ground; then I try to secure the gun. The kid starts to get up. I don't want to have the gun in my hand, but I can't really get the pack secured. While trying to close it, I have to keep knocking this kid back down, and I am about twenty years older than he is. It's hard work!

My partner is still nowhere to be seen. I am fighting with one hand while trying to secure the pistol with the other, and the kid keeps trying to pull himself up while grabbing my shirt. I finally got him in a "C-clamp" hold, one hand on the throat squeezing his larynx, and tried to shut off his air supply. Now, remember, this is a purely *defensive* tactic! Really!

Anyway, we continue thrashing around, and he keeps getting closer to grabbing the pistol. I continue footsweeping him, continue to try the C-clamp, and continue to try to do about eight different things all at once by myself. Finally, I pull the pistol out to keep it away from him. It is pointed down at the ground, on my off side. I am not going to "cap" a guy who doesn't have a gun, except as a very last resort, but while we were struggling, the gun discharged right into the ground!

Well, the discharge didn't phase this guy a bit. My partner just rounded the corner, and he came flying into that guy, taking him down. The kid was, it turned out, on drugs and alcohol and was difficult to handle. We held him down until the "fill" units arrived, and he was cuffed and taken into custody.

Now, our department takes every weapon discharge *very* seriously. So we had to call out the shift sergeant and the lieutenant, too. Pretty soon the place would be swarming with cops to investigate the discharge.

I looked at my watch. It was 4:24 and I was due to go off duty for the last time at 5:30 P.M. An hour and six minutes short of thirty years as a cop, and I fire my first and last shot on duty, other than at the range!

The guys come out and dig the slug out of the ground, document everything, take statements, and we finally get to go in. The captain and lieutenant were waiting for me.

"You have to write a memo to the chief about this shooting," they told me, "and you need to get your weapon's trigger pull tested at the range, too." They wanted me to do a lot of paperwork.

By then it was 6:30. I had already turned in my time

sheet and was officially no longer a police officer. "I don't have to do *nuthin',*" I told them. "I've been a civilian for an hour and fifteen minutes! You guys are 'Prop 115' (a provision of California law that permits officers with over five years experience to take testimony and write it up), and *you* can write the damn report!" But they insisted.

"Okay," I said, "I'll write it." I wrote, "Dear Chief: While chasing a purse-snatch suspect, I accidentally discharged my weapon. Aw, shit. Sincerely yours. . . ."

After toying with the two of them for a while, I wrote up a real memo and never heard anything more about it. Normally, anybody in our department who has an unintentional discharge automatically gets ten hours of unpaid leave, no matter what the circumstances, but I guess it was too late for that.

While recovering from all the excitement, I discovered that my badge had gone astray during the pursuit. It had been attached to my belt but got knocked off during the chase. We checked the truck and called the units still on the scene, asking them to look for it—no luck.

I was done with everything by 9:30 P.M. and headed back out to see if I could find my badge. I drove along until I found a special landmark I was looking for, that cigar I tossed away. That's where the chase began. There was the butt smashed on the ground. I parked my vehicle, got out, and walked to the chain-link fence. And there it was. That was my personal badge, not a city-issued one, a silver one I had custom made, and I wanted to keep it. Now I had it again thanks to a dollar-and-eighteen-cent cigar. And that was the last day of my thirty-year career as a cop.

Joe Undercover and the Look of Love

Officer Anonymous is known among other cops in his department as a "super cop," one of those guys who likes working double shifts and dreams at night about new and innovative ways to make arrests. One great place for a hard-charging, young officer who likes to make busts is in the Street Crimes and Vice units, and that's where he began his career.

I was hired on as a San Jose police officer in 1978 then hit the streets in 1979. At the time, San Jose was having the same kinds of problems experienced by other major cities in the United States. There was a downtown "combat zone" with a lot of bars, a few low-class restaurants, and a lot of prostitutes. I went right out of the academy into street crimes and worked undercover for virtually the whole first two years of my career as a police officer. I worked those years with long hair and a beard, looking rather dirty and decrepit. A team of five of us would hit the streets, and it wasn't uncommon for me to average from six to eight prostitution arrests every day. Although we were on the day shift, we occasionally worked nights, too.

My Sergeant, the Deviate

We were having a problem back then with a few of the girls in the zone. They knew who the cops were and how to avoid them. Sometimes these girls would want to inspect your dick. Well, you can't show them that; it's a violation of the law. They'd try every trick they could think of to discover a cop, and they'd look everywhere to find evidence that you were an undercover officer. Asking you to show your dick was one sure method.

I was a rookie, one of the new guys, a hot dog. I was teamed up with veterans, guys who'd been doing this for twenty years. I was trying to arrest these hardcore girls and was complaining to the sergeant about the problem of these wise girls.

The sergeant was a real deviate! "I'll figure something out," he said. So he got a pair of panty hose, a frigging dildo, and some steel wool! "Okay," he said, "here's what we'll do. We'll have the undercover officers put these things on at night, with the steel wool and dildo under their jeans. That way the girls can unzip you and see something, but they'll never see any actual flesh!" Everybody on the team laughed; we thought he was putting us on.

"I'm going to run it past the lieutenant," he said. Well, we had a kind of meek lieutenant back then, a very religious guy, a member of the school board, a nice man, but not somebody with a lot of "command bearing." The sergeant showed him the dildo invention.

"Let me take it to the staff," he said.

The lieutenant took this stuff to the staff meeting, the chief and all his cohorts, and you could hear the hoots and howls of laughter through the whole building! Those guys were crying and falling on the floor; they thought it was so funny! He got laughed right out of the meeting, and we weren't wearing any dildoes after that.

Joe Undercover

Some guys weren't too good at being "Joe Undercover." They'd carry their regular wallet with the imprint of our star-shaped badge still in the leather, or they'd have their ID in a pocket where the girl would find it—and they always wondered why they couldn't pick up a girl.

I had some fake ID put together and made out some booking sheets for myself in that identity, to make it look like I had been arrested, and that went in the wallet. I had copies of a couple of citations in there, too. When you're working undercover, you have to assume somebody else's identity, and that identity has to be the opposite of a police officer.

Walk and Talk

My first couple of tries to pick up hookers as an undercover officer didn't work too well. I didn't have my walk and talk down right. The gals would hop in and say, "Hi, baby, what do you want?" and I'd get all cotton-mouthed and not know what to say. "Oops, I just remembered my mom is baking cookies and needs my help. I'm outta here," she'd say, closing the door behind her. I looked like a complete fucking chump on the first half-dozen attempts.

Now, if you really wanted to behave just like the perverts who are the prostitute's normal customers, you'd drive down the street with your dick hanging out, jacking off, and drinking beer. The girl hops in the car, they go to some secluded spot, and the guy explodes. The date lasts about fifteen seconds! Time is money for a hooker, and she's got her dough. She doesn't want some three-hour marathon love encounter. They want you to hurry up and come! They aren't interested in getting to know you; they just want to know Andrew Jackson, Alexander

Hamilton, Abe Lincoln and, if they're lucky, Ben Franklin!

Then I relaxed a bit. I had never tried picking up hookers when I was in college. I didn't know anything about what it felt like to be one of these perverts, but after trying it for a while, I started walking the walk and talking the talk.

It was difficult to look over at somebody with a stubble beard and tell them how cute they look, how adorable they are, what nice long hair, or breasts, or goatee they have and still keep a straight face! So you have to play a role.

Way back then, a hundred prostitutes might be on the streets on a weekend night and maybe a dozen or so pimps, each with their own little territory. Crime was rampant, street drug use was common, and the residents and business owners were up in arms. Prostitutes were turning tricks in every dark corner, alley, vacant lot, and even on the street in broad daylight.

At the time, each of us worked alone. You wouldn't do that now for several reasons. One is that you need a backup during fights, an officer-safety issue. The other is that you need somebody to cover your ass. When you work drugs or prostitution, your suspects will often make up stories about your conduct to get out of the charge, or for revenge.

The Look of Love

Trolling for prostitutes was interesting. You could spot these prostitutes by just looking at them—a prostitute would give you what I called the unmistakable "look of love." If you drove around the block you'd miss her because somebody else would quickly pick them up. It was like the Daytona 500. If you see something out there, you better stop right now. If the girl comes running up to the car, you know pretty well she's a prostitute. I always worried that I would pull over and a normal person would come over to the car, but it seldom happened.

The typical sequence of events is that I would pull over, the girl would look around, then run over, hop in the car, and we'd go to a vacant lot under an interstate freeway nearby. She asked what I wanted. "Head," I told her. Usually that was all there was to it, but I remember one girl who wanted more. She was kind of homely. She said, "What's the matter with you guys, anyway? Doesn't anybody like to fuck anymore? Why do you always want your dick sucked? Let's climb in the back seat!" I said, "Okay." We discussed the price and settled on $25, and then I identified myself as a police officer and arrested her, and she started crying. I must have arrested at least a thousand street prostitutes, and I went to court on them *twice!*

Car Dates

Our undercover cars were really bad. Some still had the lights and sirens left over, and you'd have to try to explain that. Sometimes you'd get in a big brawl with a prostitute; she'd get in the car and want to open up the glove box. You couldn't let that happen because that's where you kept your police radio. The girls were wise to all of this and would look around the car for any evidence it had been used as an undercover car, like the place where the magnetic light was normally stored.

The girls were good at checking out both you and the car to make sure you weren't a cop. Sometimes you'd be in the middle of a date, and the gal would reach around under the seat and pull out a watch bulletin or a wanted sheet! Our guys were pigs! One time I got in the car and some dummy from the night before left a *gun* in the glovebox! We booked it into evidence, and he was pissed off! He had to go to the property room to get it back, and he had to let the sergeant know, the dumb shit left his gun in the glove box! Well, I'm not going to put a gun in there. A girl might get to it and somebody could get injured!

So you never knew for sure what you'd find in your assigned car, and the first thing you do before hitting the street is to make sure the car is set up right without anything in it to give you away.

You also add things to the car to support the identity you're portraying; a little beer splashed on the floor mats and an open can of beer, for example. Cops don't drink beer on the job, so that fit the image. They don't have traffic tickets, either, or booking sheets with their names on them, so having those things around helped, too.

Let's say you're working undercover alone; you see a suspected prostitute and pick her up. You get her in your car, and you agree on "head," or oral sex, for $20. "Fine," she says, "drive over here."

At that point, any forthright cop would identify himself, as we used to do, and bust her. It wasn't the best idea, safetywise, but I would identify myself as a police officer, say "You're under arrest," get my radio, and have her step out of the car. I would do a preliminary pat-down search, cuff her up, and then take her down to the prostitute center for booking.

But we don't work that way anymore. Now, a prostitute would call up Internal Affairs and tell them you got a little something "on the house," or accuse you of robbing her, or some other form of misconduct. If you're working alone, there's nobody to protect you from those charges. It's your word against hers, and in the department I work for they'll take her charges seriously! Even though they can't prove you did something, that charge will stick with you. If enough charges like that accumulate—false charges from crooks trying to get revenge—it will affect your career in this city's police force. A real proactive police officer who generates charges like that will get transferred to someplace boring—or out of the department!

As an example of how things work in this department, we had an undercover officer working a vice assignment alone a few years ago. He picked up a young black man turning tricks downtown. They negotiated a deal for sex and drove to a nearby school. When it came time to make the arrest, the kid pulled a knife on the cop. The two of them fought for the knife, during which the officer shot the guy, who later died.

There was a huge uproar in the black community, and the politicians and police administration went after the cop instead of defending him. He was kicked off the force, went through several civil trials, and basically had his life trashed even though he was acquitted. The only good to come from the case was that we don't get sent out to do these things alone anymore. We always have a backup for officer safety, physical and professional.

The Street-Crimes Sweepstakes

We certainly did some *stupid* things! We used to have contests to see who could pick up the most girls in a shift. I used to go for "doubles" and "triples" sometimes, two or three girls at a time. I'd have one hop in beside me and one or two in the back seat. The problem with that, besides the fact that I was on my own and without a recorder or backup, was that one girl would be hot to trot and the other would sometimes change her mind. That would really screw up a good bust. And if any of them had had a knife or gun and things had gone wrong, we would have been dead meat!

Sometimes when I pulled up to a corner and tried to set up a "prostitution by committee" situation, I might not be able to get a date. One girl would be ready to hop in my pants while the other would say, "I don't know about this guy. . . . I think I've seen this car someplace. Maybe he's a narc."

When that happens, I say to the other girl, "Hey, get in the car—you're mine! Forget the doubles. You're fine, baby. *You can rock my world. I didn't want to screw her anyway.*"

Stab and Shoot Bars

The bars in the zone, the ones frequented by the hookers and the johns—Shannon's Place, the Three Star, and others—were what we called "stab-and-shoot" places. They catered to pimps and prostitutes (male, female, and "other"), drug addicts, robbers, felons, crooks, parolees. The patrons and staff were all quite willing to fight it out with the police. As a cop, you couldn't walk into one of these places without coming back out with a body—you always arrested somebody in these places.

Many of the prostitutes were dangerous people. You'd walk in a bar and the girls would come up to you. You had to be careful or they'd pick your pockets or rob you. Often, they'd say, "Come upstairs with me," and then they'd rob you. We got a lot of robbery reports and a lot of assault reports about these prostitutes. A lot would carry knives and some of the he-shes would carry guns. The black gals, back in the early 1980s, carried what we called "cake-cutter" combs with real long teeth. They'd use those or a box cutter or ice pick, anything like that, as a weapon. They were dangerous!

The Tunnel of Love

One of the things I had to do while working undercover vice was visit adult theaters. You'd walk into one of these places, and it would be real dark and usually everybody in the audience would be male. Sometimes, though, you'd find a couple together, and when that happened I always sat near them because they'd draw the action. All the guys would gather around them. Pretty soon somebody would bring out "Big Willie" to breathe. All these guys would be whipping their dicks out and masturbating. You had to be *real* careful where you stepped and where you sat in those places! Those places were just cesspools with "spunk" all over the seats and floor.

There was a little place off the Alameda we called "the Tunnel of Love." It was part of a medical office building with a little tunnel to the parking area that dropped below street level. At night a lot of the "gay blades" would cruise in the area, and we'd make a lot of "lewd act" pinches in that neighborhood. We'd stand there on the street like we were looking for some action, and guys would drive by waving their dicks at us! They'd stop and offer to suck you off, or worse, and we'd arrest them.

We walked down to the Tunnel of Love one night and a guy solicited my partner, the legendary Hard Luck Fred. The guy was beating off and spraying splooges all over himself. Fred grabs him and arrests him for indecent exposure and lewd acts.

At that time we arrested people like that but didn't book them. There were a lot of professional people who liked anonymous sex with guys. But we ran the guy through the computer; Fred wrote up his citation, hands it to him, and the guy signs the "promise to appear."

We get back in the car and are driving around. Fred is on the passenger side, and he has the damn pen in his mouth! He's chewing on the end of the thing while he's putting the finishing touches on the citation for this guy we just arrested for jerking off.

"Nice pinch," I told him. He was new to vice at the

time, and I was training him. "Okay, what did you cite him for?" Fred told me.

"Did he *sign* the citation?" I asked him.

"Yeah, he did," Fred said. Fred was still writing a mile a minute.

"And what did he sign it *with?*"

Suddenly a light went on. The window went down, the pen flew outside, and I said, "You dumb shit, remember where that pen has been. If you want to have a pen strictly for spunkers, fine, but don't put it in your mouth!" So he finally got the point.

Hard Luck Fred was always getting in trouble. We used to tell him that we were going to preprint the forms used for officer injuries with his name at the top so all we'd have to do would be to fill in the date and location.

Once, I responded to a call involving an undercover officer in a fight with a prostitute out on the street. The two were wrestling on the sidewalk as I rolled up; then somebody jumped in on top of the officer. It was Fred, in a wig and wearing a stick-on goatee, playing undercover cop! He almost got his ass whipped by the other officers before we recognized him. The wig and goatee flew off. He was the kind of guy who meant well and did okay ninety percent of the time; the other ten percent of the time he was Nick at Nite, out in the ozone.

Looking for Love

The girls were pretty good about insisting that the customer wear protection; the gay-hustler guys *never* did! I only saw a couple of condoms on the guys, and it shouldn't surprise you about the spread of AIDS. The guys seem to love the thrill of anonymous sex, whether it is in a theater, a bathroom, a car, a bar.

The gay community had places called "tea rooms," places like bathrooms where homosexual men had anonymous sex. These places are advertised and rated in the gay newspapers. You go into one of these places, and there's a wall with a hole in it—that's called a "glory hole." They put a little tissue in there, we called them "spunk cushions," to keep your dick from getting abraded as it is sliding into somebody's mouth or ass. We had to tell the new guys, "Look, don't put your eye up to that hole."

There was even one guy, nicknamed "Squeaky," who took along a can of spray paint to these places, and when the guy stuck his dick through the hole, Squeaky painted it with a blast of spray. He said he was just "marking the evidence," and it sure made it difficult for the suspect to claim that he hadn't done anything!

Making the Case

In the old days, you had to have two elements to make a case, an offer of a sex act plus an amount of money for the service. Sometimes you'd pick up a girl, drive around, and agree on what you were supposed to be buying. Now you're waiting to find out how much money is involved. Then she says, "Okay, turn in here," and she'd lead you into a motel room, her house, or some similar place. In the old days, you'd do that because we knew we had only half a case. A lot of times, then, she'd start to undress, and she still hadn't named a price.

I remember one gal—man, she must have had size sixty-six boobs, a real tough gal. She lived up on Twelfth Street, and we sat down on her sofa, and she got undressed. Then she got around to the price, and I went to "buzz" her—but I had left my damn badge out in the car because she was so careful! I told her I was a cop, and she must have thought I was some kind of freak. She started resisting, and I tried to cuff her. We start fighting, and then we spill out onto the porch. She starts screaming for help from her friends, and her pimp friends started running down the street. I thought, *Aw, shit.* I pulled out my gun, then thought, *Well, I can't shoot her,* and put it away.

Her friends showed up, and we started playing tug-of-war with her. Then I let go, walked over to my car, got my radio, and called for backup. The boys showed up, and I finally arrested her for prostitution plus a few extras.

When something like that happens—and it does—with a hooker who happens to be high on PCP, you've really got your hands full! And when it's a "he-she," some big old thing, and he's all stoned—the fight is on! Some guys got hurt in those fights.

I remember applying a carotid restraint and rendering one guy unconscious three times in one arrest. He'd wake right back up, fighting! I got in a fight with a woman on PCP. My handcuffs jammed, my keys were in the car. I finally had to call a roofer down from the roof next door. I told him I was a cop, and he pitched in to help. He got my keys, I unjammed the cuffs, and the two of us subdued this gal. If it wasn't for him, I could have been seriously hurt.

The Rock

Anyway, I got to know some of these people quite well—too well, actually. There was one guy we called "The Rock"—Richie Hebner, who must have weighed at least three hundred pounds, six feet three inches tall—a guy who trolled the streets in drag. Richie is now deceased from AIDS, but he was once quite a sight. He wore a blond wig, but that still didn't really offset the shaving bumps on his face or his massive size. You'd think that nobody would be fooled by the wig and the dresses he wore, but you'd be surprised at what Richie pulled in! We'd pull a car over, and Richie would pop out. The driver would say, "This is my wife. . . ."

Snaggletooth

Another hooker I got to know pretty well we named "Snaggletooth." She was a heavy heroin user, real tall and skinny, and had a big silver tooth. Maybe in her younger years she might have looked pretty good, but the heroin took its toll. I arrested her four different times—that's how dumb she was!

One of the times I had an Asian officer along with me. Snaggletooth didn't recognize me because she was high on heroin at the time. The officer in the back seat started speaking Chinese.

"Can you tell me what this Chink is saying?" she demanded.

"Yeah, he says he's looking for a good time," I told her.

"Oh, okay," she said, and she dived over the seat, went to work on my officer's lap, attempting to have oral sex with him. A big fight resulted, and all of us rolled out of the car. We arrested her right in the middle of the street with her screaming, *Entrapment! I didn't understand what he said!*

Deaf and Dumb

We got a new sergeant who was a little tentative about making cases, so we helped him make up a story that worked really well. He became, for the evening, deaf and dumb. He had a little card and a pencil. The girl would climb in the car, tell him to start driving, and say, "Hi, sweetheart, what can I do for you?"

He'd say, "Urrrannugh! Naaahrhgh!" and hand her the card and pencil.

So she'd take the card and write on it, *"Do you want to fuck?"*

"URRRANNUGH! NAAAHRHGH!" the sergeant said, grinning and nodding his head vigorously.

"How much money do you have?" she wrote.

"Thirty dollars," he wrote, smiling and gesturing.

Well, usually this was just fine at making the case, but the problem was that the sergeant lost me and another officer, his cover unit in traffic; so, he had no cover! He starts looking around, and he gives all the signals for us to come in and bust her but nothing happens. He looks like a damn cheerleader giving all the signals. Fifteen minutes later we roll up on them in our marked car, and she starts tossing needles out the window. "Where were you guys?" he said. We didn't have the heart to tell him. But he sure was proud of that little card with *"Do you want to fuck?"* on it, and *"How much money do you have?"*

Do You Know the Way to San Jose?

Back in the glory days of prostitution in San Jose, girls would show up on the bus, fresh from the "circuit." The circuit was the series of cities that these women worked in rotation—Bakersfield, Fresno, Modesto, Sacramento, Oakland, San Jose. One of the things we did was to hang out at the bus station. These girls would hop off the bus, flag us down, and we'd be their first date—*"Welcome to San Jose, miss. You're under arrest!"*

For a Good Time, Call . . .

Besides working street crimes and prostitution, I also worked escort services. Those were fun! Your typical street date is going to cost around $20 for oral sex, $50 if you get laid. Your escort date for the same thing will cost you $120 to $300 or more!

When I started working escorts, I worked through the phone book calling every single escort agency with a 408 prefix. I closed down every single escort agency in the city of San Jose. Then I started to close them all down in the county. That took care of all the escort agencies in the 408 area code; so, I started going after the agencies in the 415 and 510 regions who would send their girls down here to me. As long as I could prove to the DA's office that an agency was sending enough girls down to Santa Clara County to sustain our jurisdiction, I could bust them. I was getting excellent cooperation from the prosecutors, and we were shutting down places seventy miles away and sending people to prison and jail.

Generally, these girls are a lot classier—very good looking, very attractive. I remember one who was a certified "11" on a ten scale. Some, on the other hand, were real "toads" that you'd never want to spend $300 for the chance to bed down.

Basically, you pay for an hour of the girl's services, normally $200 to $300. Out of that hour, you spend about ten minutes talking with her, then you get fifty minutes to complete your sex act. If the girl could get away with just talking to you for the hour, she would, but that's rare.

The girls get excellent money, tax free, because they don't declare the income. Most were getting $200 to $300 per date, and did four to six dates a night, and worked four nights a week. That's up to $6,000 gross per week, $24,000 per month, or more than a quarter-million dollars a year! Now, the escort service takes a big cut, up to $100 per date, but still the girl is raking in the money.

The girls get intoxicated on the money. They have a nice car, nice clothes, send their kid to private school; they become addicted to a lifestyle. She isn't a street whore, she isn't visible as a prostitute. And despite what most people think, these girls are not drug addicts—the agencies stay away from them since they are so unreliable in every way.

The escort agency is raking in the money, too. A typical agency fee is $50 to $100 per date, a kickback paid by the girl for the referral. If the agency is sending out twenty girls and have thirty-five completed dates a night, they're taking in a huge amount of money, too.

Now, the girls and the agencies keep very good records. We found that their clients included politicians, sports heroes, law enforcement officials, teachers, judges, doctors, professional people of all kinds. You name it, we've arrested it.

But we didn't go after the johns very often; we wanted the head people in the escort agencies. The DA's office isn't going to prosecute fifteen thousand johns on misdemeanors, but it will take their chances on the madams and the pimps if they can send them to prison. That's all we cared about.

Although prostitution is often called a "victimless crime," that really isn't true. For one thing, these people get addicted to money, but there is a real danger to the girls. They go out to some address and have no idea who is going to answer the door. It could be Ted Bundy, the ax murderer, or Jeffrey Dahmer, who wants to eat them for dinner. The call could be from some pervert wanting to do a "snuff" film, wanting to kill them. We busted a high school teacher who ran a gay escort service. He had recruited a lot of his former students into prostitution. We took him down and sent him to prison. That really sent some shock waves through the school system!

I arrested one Silicon Valley executive during one of these things. It turned out the guy had a huge coke habit, and when we got a look at the records of the escort service he was calling, he was dropping another $4,000 per week on girls. He was married and didn't want to get laid, but he liked getting head. He'd get high and pay the girls for oral sex.

I'm Pam—Fly Me

Anyway, you pay your money and do your deed. The policy is "one come to a customer," though, and if you blow off in three minutes and want more, you pay for another hour.

Working the escort services starts with getting your identity worked out from the beginning. You have to assume a role that you can convincingly play; then you get an apartment, a house, or a motel room. You check into this place with a bust crew and cover team, call up the gal, and make an appointment.

The girl will typically be about an hour late. You'll have ten or fifteen minutes of conversation. "Why are you calling me?" she'll ask. "Are you married?"

"This is the first time I've tried this," I might say. "My wife left me."

"Well, then, let's get comfortable," she says, taking off her clothes. "I'm Pam—fly me!"

Of course, we didn't engage in any actual sex, but when she takes her clothes off, that shows actual criminal intent. At that point the bust crew would come in the room and we arrest her. Photos are taken for the prosecutor that show she's not there just to provide company, as the escort services try to claim.

The girls function as independent contractors, and when you bust them, the pimps claim, "I didn't know my girl was doing that! If I had known I would have fired her!" Our big challenge is to get the agency, and we do that through interviews with the girls. If the girl says, "Sure, I told them about bad dates and other problems," then you have something to hang them up with. And that's a significant charge: pimping and pandering carry a mandatory state-prison sentence in California.

I took down over fifty escort agencies and debriefed hundreds of gals in the escort business. Typically, they performed only straight sex and avoided anything kinky. They did well financially. But they often didn't date men socially, weren't really into men romantically—a lot liked other women, actually—and sex wasn't fun anymore but was only a vehicle for making money. All they cared about was the money.

The escort business is like a big family, or industry, and everybody knows everybody else. If a girl rips a madam off by doing dates outside the agency, the madam discovers this right away. She notices that a steady customer suddenly isn't calling anymore, right after he has a date with, say, "Ginger." She figures the girl has given the man her card and said, "Don't call the escort agency any more. Call me!" A lot of the girls do that.

When that happens, the madam will call all the other services in town, saying "Don't hire Ginger. She's ripping me off and I'm firing her." If Ginger's only game is escort prostitute, she can only start her own agency, or she can become a street whore, or she can apologize, kiss, and make up. No girl wants to go out on the street. There are more freaks on the street, you're more visible to cops, there is a much lower class of clientele, and the price for your service is about ten or twenty percent of what you get for the same thing as a call girl. Most of the time, you're dealing with clean, professional men in a nice, clean bed—not in the crummy back seat of a 1982 Ford Fairlane with some guy who's a 3.0 drunk. Joe Businessman at the Holiday Inn is a better deal for a girl all the way around.

The madam has complete control of the girl's income, and if she turns off the business or cuts it way back, suddenly you're getting one date a night and $1,200 a week. When that happens, you're eating dog food, the bills pile up, and you're desperate. You've got no education, no training, nothing else to fall back on. That's how the pimps and madams keep control of the girls.

The Gift That Keeps On Giving

Talk about the gift that keeps on giving, that's the IRS! You take down an escort agency and are sitting there interviewing the madam, "Heidi, how long has the service been in business?" you ask her.

"Five years," she says.

"Okay, how many girls in the agency?"

"Twenty-five," she says.

"And how many dates did you have a night?"

"Ten to fifteen completed dates a night, average," she would typically say.

Then somebody from the IRS Criminal Investigation Division would pull out a calculator, wade through the records, do the math, and say, "You owe the federal government $675,389.22, and if you want to dispute that, bring in your receipts and tax returns and we'll talk." I watched the IRS drive cars out of garages, take rings off fingers, and destroy lives. Did I care? No, not really. These escort people are crooks, so a lot of times we had more luck going after these agencies with the IRS than with conventional prosecution.

The IRS was actually quite useful in that way. When you take a prostitution agency down, a lot of times the witnesses will disappear and the prostitutes will move away. Even with a "killer interview" with them, unless you have her there in court to testify, the statement is useless. (If you can't find the witness, you haven't got a case.) Sometimes there would be witness intimidation, too. These factors made it difficult to get convictions, but the IRS was always reliable.

A Common
Son of a Bitch

Don Newcomer worked some of the most difficult, challenging, and dangerous undercover assignments tasked to any officer, murder for hire and undercover in jail. His story, though, describes some of the conflicts and ethical and emotional dilemmas facing an undercover officer when "right" and "wrong" don't seem to exist, and when the crime seems like no crime at all.

The local police had been working on the disappearance of a man for more than two years. They had executed search warrants on his place out in western Maryland, trying to come up with leads, but found nothing. The man they were looking for, Bill Stinson, was a unique character. He was one of a handful of people in America who knew how to do a particular kind of natural gas well drilling. He also knew how to repair well-casing deep in the ground. Both skills made him a valuable commodity and rare individual.

He was employed by a company in Pennsylvania. They called Stinson's residence numerous times. Every time his wife, Jennie, reported that he was out of the country, but she didn't know exactly where or what he was doing.

Shortly before Bill's disappearance, it was known by the local cops that the two of them had had some kind of altercation. He had given her some shit, and she creased his head with a frying pan. The police were called, and she was charged with some kind of spousal abuse.

As I learned later, this was very ironic. The two had been married almost thirty years. During this time, the wife had been very submissive, and the husband very abusive. Bill constantly told Jennie that he was going to leave her and marry somebody else. He was a pretty nasty person, and she seemed to have reconciled herself to his behavior. Besides, Bill was a huge man, over six-feet tall and about two hundred fifty pounds, and she was a tiny thing, only about five feet one inch tall.

Their marriage produced five children, three boys and two girls, and had been rocky for years. Bill sometimes threw Jennie out of the house, and she'd have to sleep in a truck overnight; he sometimes poured scalding water on her until the skin dropped off her body; and on occasion Bill chased her and the children out onto a second-floor balcony in their nightclothes in freezing weather and kept them out there for hours before he allowed them back inside. So he was kind of a mean bastard, but this was all well known, and when Bill disappeared, everybody was suspicious that she had something to do with the disappearance.

When the court date for the assault charge came up, Jennie appeared with a typewritten letter purportedly from Bill in South Africa. The letter said that he was out of the country, that he wished to drop all charges against his wife, and that he didn't know when he'd return to the United States. There was no envelope. The local court dropped the charges, but the State Attorney got very suspicious and felt there was something wrong.

Normally, Jennie had access to Bill's bank account. There was over $200,000 in it when he disappeared, and she was living off that money. The State Attorney froze their assets until Bill showed up, and suddenly Jennie had no income.

But she was very ingenious and resourceful. She won money at bingo, and that helped. She was good at repairing things and made money fixing resort homes around Deep Creek Lake, and that helped, too.

The local police suspected foul play but didn't have any further way of developing the case, so they called the headquarters of the Maryland State Police and asked for somebody to come in and work on it undercover. I was called in and met with them.

"How do you propose to introduce me to her?" I asked them.

"Why don't you go out there and pretend to know something about the gas-well business?" the barracks commander suggested.

"Look," I said, "this woman's been in the business for thirty years; she's forgotten more about it than I'll ever know. That would be the quickest way to trip me up. I don't want to pretend that I know anything about their business at all."

Instead, I assumed the identity of a guy who ran a group of whores. My story for Jennie was that Bill had hired me to supply women, food, and a motel to entertain a group of oilmen in an effort to get their business, and Bill skipped out without paying for the party. He owed me $7,500. That was the story.

I drove up to their farm in a big Lincoln Continental, looking like Mr. Pimp, got out and introduced myself. "Hello, I'm Don Parker," I said, "and I'm looking for Bill Stinson."

She explained that he wasn't around. I told her my story.

"That doesn't sound like him at all," she said. "He always pays his bills. But he is in South Africa right now, and I don't know when he'll be back."

"Listen, I don't give a shit where he is. All I want is my money!" I leaned on her a bit, then left.

Shortly after that, the local police served another

search warrant on the place. They were looking for the typewriter used to write that letter shown to the court, so she clearly knew she was under suspicion.

I called her the next day. "Listen, the cops just left; they're bugging the shit out of me," I told her. "They came in here with a search warrant last night, looking for a typewriter! They turned my office upside down!" Suddenly, the two of us had an alliance; we were both getting the same treatment from the cops. I hoped this would build a bond of trust between us, and it did.

I mentioned to Jennie that some of my girls were working at a local resort where a convention of States' Attorneys were having a convention. I said one of the girls told me that the State's Attorney for her county said Jennie Stinson was going to be charged with Bill's murder.

"I don't know how they could do that," Jennie said. "They don't have any information about him or where he is."

"That's just what the girl told me," I said.

I just couldn't break through Jennie's shell. She was quite shrewd about the whole thing and didn't really tell me anything at all. She also avoided talking on her own phone since she was convinced, correctly, that there was a trap on the line.

But we figured out her pattern. She went to the local hospital to call me. There were four public pay phones in the lobby, and we managed to put wiretaps on each of these four phones. When she called her son, who was in the local jail, to talk to him about things, we were able to overhear some useful conversations.

Tapping a public phone booth is a problem, though, and to do it we had to send in an undercover trooper behind her. He'd call into the tap office and report, "Okay, she's using number four," and then we could activate that tap. It was complicated.

She went through a long period of difficulty with the police—searches, threats, interviews. After each one, I told her similar things were happening to me. We might not talk for as much as two months before I'd call to check in. Each time I'd say, "Have you heard from Bill yet? I need my money!" Finally, after about eighteen months of dealing with me, and three years after Bill's disappearance, she warmed up a bit.

She told me that her money was tied up by the State's Attorney and that she couldn't pay the bill herself. "Why don't we find a way to get around the State's Attorney?" I asked her.

I came up with a brainstorm. The State's Attorney, I told her, had been "entertained" by one of my girls. He had talked quite a lot about the case to the prostitute, and the State's Attorney for this county had gotten my girl pregnant!

As luck would have it, we had a female trooper in my office who had become pregnant about the time of the actual Maryland State's Attorney's convention several months earlier. She was now starting to look pregnant, and I recruited her to the operation.

I went to Jennie and said, "I think we have the State's Attorney right where we want him. We might be able to get that money released!"

"How are you going to do that?" she wanted to know.

"He's got one of my girls knocked up. I think we've got him locked up tight. We can threaten to expose his extramarital affair and his bastard kid. Instead of that nice, comfortable retirement he's got planned, his wife will toss him out on his ear."

She thought that was great. We arranged a meeting at a local motel, and I put Jennie in a room adjacent to mine. I brought in the pregnant trooper and an investigator from the State's Attorney's office. With Jennie listening through the door, I accused the "acting" State's Attorney of getting my girl pregnant, and I tore into him pretty hard. "Listen, you little bastard," I yelled, "I come up here to get my money. That's all I want! You've got this woman's money all tied up. If you don't release it, if you don't let this money float, I am going to expose you to everybody up here, and I am going to have this girl walking down Main Street telling everybody, 'This is what your State's Attorney did to me!' And that nice little house of yours with the roses out front, you can forget that because your old lady is going to kick you out!" Of course, Jennie is listening to all this. Then it got physical. I threw the man right out of the room, and she could hear it happen.

After he disappeared, I went and brought Jennie into the room with the trooper and me. She hugged the trooper. "You poor thing," she said. "How could you possibly have anything to do with such an ugly bastard!" She was very emotional about the whole thing, and it was very touching. I had my arms around both of them, trying to be comforting, but I was thinking to myself, *What a prick I am!*

We were ready to give up on the case. If nothing came from this, we were prepared to drop the investigation the next day.

But the incident succeeded in finally gaining her full trust. I met with her, away from the house, the next day and said, "Listen, we've *got* to get this thing worked out! I have got to get my money! The State's Attorney is so frightened of us, he'll do anything for us. Look, if you know where Bill is, let me know. We'll produce the body—out of state! As long as it doesn't happen in his county, he doesn't give a shit! If we can find his body somewhere, that's all we need to release your money and get me paid off. Then I'm out of your life!"

That still didn't do it. She said, "I wish I could help you, but I don't know where he is."

So in desperation I said, "Look, I'm in trouble with the State's Attorney, too. I can't even drive through this county without getting my ass locked up. I'm fighting for you. You can't even trust me enough to tell me what's going on?"

She hesitated a moment. Then she said, "I know where he is, but they'll never find him."

At last! I was wearing a wire, and suddenly I felt that the case was about to be solved. "Well, where is the son of a bitch?" I said.

"I can't tell you, but I can show you."

"Let's go!"

"No, not now," she told me. "I'm afraid to do it during the day."

I tried to convince her that we should do it right away. The backup team, of course, missed that little bit of conversation over the transmitter, but I was also carrying a tiny tape recorder; so, the conversation was captured.

"Come out to the house, then," she said, "but be careful you're not being followed."

I drove out and she walked me out to an adjacent pasture about a quarter mile from the house. "You see that log out in the field?" she asked. "He's under that."

"Tell me how this happened," I said.

She told me the story. "I came in and found my youngest grandchild, my youngest son's little boy, in the house, sick. He had a fever. I picked him up and was holding him. Bill came over in a rage. He grabbed the child out of my arms. He said to my son, 'Don't let this bitch touch the child. I think she has AIDS!' We were married twenty-seven years, and I never cheated on him one time! He had a different woman every night! When that bastard accused me of having AIDS, it really pissed me off!"

She didn't kill him right away while the son and grandson were there, but the next morning she went into Bill's bedroom, a garage converted to sleeping quarters next to the kitchen. "I took his mini-M14 and shot him through the legs. He squealed like a pig!" He'd been lying flat on his back with his knees elevated, and she shot him through the back of the legs. "I got so angry that I walked to the foot of the bed with that rifle and told him, 'You know, you've had all these women over the years, and then you accuse *me* of having AIDS?'" Then she shot him right in the balls. He sat up holding his balls and his legs in agony. Then she shot him again, right in the heart. "It was such a violent thing," she told me. "I was still shaking after it was over. Then I didn't know what to do with him; he was so big."

I was listening very intently. "Then I backed the pickup truck to the door. It had a trailer hitchball on the back. I ran a rope from the ball to Bill's feet, through the house, through the kitchen, and down into his bedroom. I had just waxed the floor the morning before, and when I started pulling with that pickup truck, *his ass came sliding across that floor slick as a whistle!*" I was laughing at this, she was a good storyteller. She dragged his body across the yard, over to a shed, then covered his body with tarps. Then the rain began, and an intense downpour followed for several days.

She told me about spending several days working out a plan to hide the body. While listening to this, I was admiring how she had done it all. She didn't involve anyone except herself. Finally, she went to one of the shop buildings, found an ax and shovel, and then started cutting the body up into manageable pieces. The arms came off first, at the shoulders; they went in garbage bags. She put the torso in another bag, with the head attached. The legs each went in a garbage bag, too.

Bill had taught her sometime before that bleach works well to stop deterioration of dead animals, so she went out and bought seven gallons and bleached all his body parts. This, she figured, would help keep animals from digging up the body.

With all the parts bagged and bleached, she found a burial site out in the pasture. She cut the bottom three strands of the fence, just enough to get her wheelbarrow through, and left the top two intact. She later showed me where she repaired the fence.

Then, she explained that she cut the sod with the shovel, rolled it back, and started digging. She dug just about all night. It was hard soil and tough going. She dug a deep hole. Then she dumped Bill in the hole, filled it in, and rolled the sod back in place. Finally, she rolled a large log over the spot to help further discourage animals from investigating. Then she boiled all the tools she'd used in boiling water, then rubbed each with oil so there wouldn't be any trace of blood on them, then put all the tools right back where they'd been. She didn't tell anybody anything.

Well, the police came out, of course, and searched everywhere. They dug up a patio Jennie had poured not long after the disappearance, thinking he was under that, but of course they found nothing. The police brought dogs in, and the dogs alerted on the spot by the shed where there had been blood from the dismemberment. But the dogs couldn't find a trail away from the spot, they went crazy at that spot but couldn't find anything. While it confirmed their suspicions, it didn't do more than that.

She told me that investigators came out many times to question her. They looked for evidence of foul play but couldn't find anything. Once, while one of them was questioning Jennie outside on the patio, she noticed one of the bullets lying on the concrete, in plain sight! She placed her foot over the slug, then scooped it up as soon as he walked away, then put it in her pocket. It was a masterful job in every way. If she hadn't told me, we would never have found him!

Now, during the course of the investigation, I really came to admire this little lady. She was inventive, resourceful, and had been treated very badly. I sympathized with her.

All this was going on the recorder. I knew we had our case made; then, she started telling me too much! She told me about putting a rubber sheet down on the bed to keep the blood from getting on the mattress; that indicated premeditation, and that means a first-degree murder charge and a possible death penalty. I really didn't want to hang her up on a first-degree charge, so

I started coughing and trying to keep this stuff from getting on tape or on the transmitter.

But she said more than that. She started talking about the State's Attorney, and said, "You know, that son of a bitch walks all around town with his fly open, his dick hanging out, thinking he's going to pick up a girl . . ."

Well, these tapes were going right to the State's Attorney's office. He called me and said, "Look, you guys are going too far with this State's Attorney business!"

"Hey, I can't tell her what to say," I told him. It was amusing for me but not for him. He really wasn't that kind of guy, despite the impression I had created in Jennie's mind. Even so, it wasn't something the State's Attorney wanted coming out in court.

After she told me all this, she decided that the only way to resolve the matter would be for the State's Attorney to sign an agreement with her. She was very businesslike and was used to making contracts; she thought she could do so with the State's Attorney, too. That, of course, wasn't actually possible. He couldn't agree to something illegal, but I didn't tell her that. She wanted something in writing that said he would release her money and not prosecute her, and that if he did that, he was bound by it.

I left and came back the next day. "He's so scared that he's ready to sign an agreement," I told her. Now that she had divulged the true story of Bill's disappearance to me, Jennie felt very close to me. I picked her up and drove her into town. She expected to meet the State's Attorney and sign the agreement, get her money, and get on with her life. "This is the best day of my life," she said.

We drove the five miles into town and pulled up to the State's Attorney's office. I had an undercover trooper waiting on the curb for us. I pulled over and took her hand in mine. "Jennie," I said, "I want you to listen to me. My name is not Don Parker. It's Don Newcomer. And I don't run a bunch of whorehouses. I am an undercover police officer. And I am here to arrest you for Bill's homicide."

She looked like the life drained right out of her. She looked at the floor. "That's a trooper out there waiting for you. I want you to go with him."

She stepped out of the car, then turned, and looked back in. "You are a common son of a bitch," she said. Her eyes were cold and black. She turned and the trooper took her into custody.

My body wire and tape recorder were still running. I said into the recorder, "You know, she's right. I am a common son of a bitch."

If ever there was a case of justifiable homicide, this was it. I felt badly about the whole thing. The State's Attorney wanted to plea-bargain her case very quickly. He really didn't want any of those allegations about him accidentally coming out in court, even if they were false, and you couldn't blame him.

The agreement they came up with specified a term in prison of eight years. Shortly after she went to prison, the governor suddenly became sensitive to spousal abuse. Jennie was granted clemency just with time served, three or four months. Once it became known that she'd killed him, the whole business was resolved. She went back to the farm, and people treated her pretty much as they had before.

I've seen her several times in the years since. I don't know if she's forgiven me or not, but I still admire her.

My sergeant, Tommy Moore, one of the greatest guys I ever worked with, sat with me after the arrest and assured me I had done the right thing. He told me to take some time off and try not to think about Jennie Stinson's fate but to leave it in the hands of the Almighty. I took his advice, and it seemed the Almighty did intervene.

Cybersmugglers
Snagged in the Net

Don Daufenbach, a special agent for the U.S. Customs Service, works many kinds of cases. His unusual specialty, though, is computer crime, particularly the distribution of child pornography on the Internet. The rapid development of the Internet as a device to communicate and transfer information has produced new opportunities for criminal conduct and for imaginative ways to detect it.

Nobody seems to know much about the U.S. Customs Service except that we're the guys at the airport who look inside your luggage. In fact, Customs is one of the biggest and most effective law enforcement agencies in the country. We are one big vice unit. We enforce over four hundred laws and have incredible authority and jurisdiction. We can search vehicles, mail, cargo, and people without a warrant! We have authority over everything that comes into or goes out of the country. We are involved in counter-drug operations and seize more drugs than all other U.S. law enforcement agencies combined, but we also go after all kinds of other prohibited materials, including my specialty, child pornography. The FBI also has jurisdiction over child pornography, and they are a much larger agency than we are, but we've made about five times as many arrests in that area over the past few years.

Pornographic materials featuring children specifically became illegal in the early 1970s, under 18 USC 2252, although it was prohibited even before that under broader laws governing obscenity. Even a first conviction can get the offender up to ten years in prison. Because of these laws, child pornography is unavailable even at your corner adult bookstore. You can't purchase the stuff in any conventional way.

Child pornography is a curious kind of problem. Not only is the material formally illegal, it is socially unacceptable to almost everybody. It is viewed as being so taboo that people who are interested in it become very secretive, and the distribution of it is a very clandestine enterprise. While drugs are obviously also illegal, their use is not nearly as unacceptable to society as is child pornography.

The result is a secret underworld of people who produce and distribute kiddy porn, and it takes a lot of work to penetrate that world. Drugs are a conventional commercial enterprise in which you have to get your piggies to market, and even the smartest drug distributor can be infiltrated by working up through the street-level dealer and middleman. The whole nature of the drug business is a desire to make money; child pornography is essentially a different game with a secretive and mysterious underworld community that is not usually in it for financial gain.

Because these materials are not readily available in the United States, people have tried to bring them in from Thailand, Scandinavia, or Mexico, places where child pornography is much more acceptable. That's when the Customs Service gets involved because that is a prohibited importation. Now, in the old precomputer days, people interested in this stuff would communicate through letters, bulletin boards, and newsletters, often published overseas. Customs officers searched for this kind of thing before the mail was released to the Postal Service. When the stuff turned up, we used to do "controlled deliveries" to the addressee—somebody would dress up as a letter carrier and deliver the goods, then arrest them, and search the house. Typically there would be more of the same kind of material.

Now, it is important to understand that it isn't just dirty pictures that are illegal. The pictures are evidence of a crime. The child in the picture is being molested. You might not know who the child is, where or when the photograph was taken, but that kid is exploited and molested every time the picture is shown. When it happens on the Internet, the exploitation is extensive.

Second, we know many molesters use these materials to "normalize" this aberrant behavior to their intended victims. "Look at this!" they say. "Other kids like to do this, too!" This is an even darker side to the materials, and when they are used to make more victims, they are even more evil.

Over the past few years, Customs noticed a drop-off in volume of printed material entering the United States as the Internet began being used instead of the mails. The Internet started serving as a conduit for all kinds of prohibited material in the early 1990s, and I conducted the first Internet drug case in 1992. That case opened my eyes to the Internet as a system for importing stuff— it is essentially free, allows people to conspire, to hatch their criminal schemes, and to transfer contraband material like child pornography fairly secretly. Now I realize the importance of the Internet as a device used by people in criminal activity, and I have been actively involved in these types of cases for more than three years now.

Undercover work on the Internet uses many of the same skills as in conventional undercover cases. I've worked many drug cases, stolen-car rings, and art theft cases. In the process I've learned not to be scared and to act convincingly in a role. This attitude applies to computer crime. The more cases you do, the more you learn about the behavior of criminals, how they think, how they act, how they communicate.

There is, in fact, a whole language associated with kiddie porn, just as there is with the drug culture, and you have to learn it. For example, you'll hear somebody say "LL," meaning "Little Lolita," a reference to underage girls. And when somebody says "I'm into BL," he's referring to "boy love" and a preference for underage males.

Another thing you learn when you start working these cases is that people interested in kiddie porn are the most paranoid, kinky people in the world, even more kinky than any drug dealer or smuggler I have ever dealt with. First, they know that they can go to jail for possessing this stuff. They also know that the material is so disgusting to most normal people that those who are fascinated with it need to keep it secret. They know that society universally loathes the pedophile, so there are all sorts of reasons for them to keep their interest secret. That is one of the reasons the Internet is the perfect match for the pedophile.

The computer and Internet allow you to communicate with people all over the world in an anonymous way and to avoid the risk of ordering books, videos, and magazines through the mail. Now you just log on and sign up in a chat room, web site, news room, or FTP site where you can download these materials. You can try to hide this stuff on your computer with encryption, or hidden directories and files to avoid detection. We know from long study that the pedophile keeps his materials near at hand and carefully hidden. It used to be locked boxes full of magazines and videos. Now it is hundreds or thousands of JPG and GIF files often sorted into dozens of hidden directories dedicated to a particular, illegal sex act. As, I think it was, Bill Gates once said, "The Internet will bring like-minded people together," and that's as true for pornography as anything else. The computer and Internet allow you to run a business distributing almost anything, legitimate or otherwise, from home. The computer has changed the way people communicate with each other, do business, and commit crime.

The Customs Service gets into pornographic crime from several angles. For one thing, the Internet is international by definition. You can be talking to a guy in the next state, but your internet network connection might be through a server located in Canada or in Europe. Furthermore, most commercially available child pornography was originally produced in Thailand, Mexico, Sweden, or Denmark, and since virtually every computer used in the United States is manufactured with components from outside the United States, this also gives us jurisdiction. The criminal wave of the future is computer network crime, and that's the kind of case I expect to work in the future.

Working Internet crime requires an agent to play a believable role, just as in a normal drug case. If I know how to talk the talk and walk the walk, these criminals will believe me. Working these Internet cases scares a lot of agents because you have to really think fast. When kiddie porn was done through the mails, you could spend all day writing a letter to a suspect, having lawyers review it, making changes, getting it just right. With the Internet Relay Chat (IRC) function, it all happens in real time, just like conversation, and you have to think on your feet. You have to respond to the suspect in character but still stay "clean" and creditable with a jury.

You also have to be able to discriminate between the person who is casually interested and the hardcore child molesters. The producers, the commercial distributors— those are the people we're looking for. Of the thousands of people who are interested in the stuff, we focus only on the key players and take them to jail.

Amateur Action

One important case started in 1993 with a citizen complaint. A casual Internet user logged on to a local service called Amateur Action, based in Milpitas, California. He called us up and said, "I don't mind computer pornography, but I signed on to this board; their stuff goes beyond the pale. It's disgusting."

"How so?" I asked him.

"Well, they have people having sex with animals, people urinating on each other, defecating on each other, and they have pictures of *very* young girls!"

This is the sort of thing we look into, so I started to document what this person had told us. I got undercover accounts and started downloading these materials. Then we showed the material to pediatricians and asked for their opinions on the ages of the boys and girls in the pictures. During the investigation, we also started getting complaints from law enforcement agencies in foreign nations. I noticed that people were logging on to this Internet site from Israel, Canada, England, Italy, and from all over the world, so we knew these materials were being distributed worldwide.

We took the owners of the service, a Mr. and Mrs. Thomas, to trial, and both were convicted under the child pornography laws. They were making a lot of money from the service; it was a very lucrative business. After efforts to get around the charges, Mr. Thomas decided to plead guilty to one count of distribution of child pornography, covered under 18 USC 2252.

Although we didn't know it at the time, the U.S. Postal Service inspectors were also charging the same couple with adult obscenity for some of the videotapes they were sending through the mail. They went after the postal element of the crime; my office went after the computer and Internet parts of the crime, both successfully. The news services all made it sound like a Postal Service case, of course, while it was actually two separate and successful investigations. That was one of the first important Internet cyberporn prosecutions.

Casting the Net

While the Amateur Action case started with a citizen complaint, other complaints result from "trolling." I may go to an IRC site and log on undercover for a while and participate in a discussion. Sometimes I also log on to a Usenet site and employ sophisticated tracking skills to track postings of child pornography back to the person who posted them. A lot of my cases come from busting small-scale distributors and asking them to identify their sources.

I had a case that started with a local child pornography collector in Utah. I arrested him and started dealing with his other associates located around the country. That first arrest rolled into numerous cases, including one pornographer in Ohio who sent me two, large data tapes with over 4,000 images of child pornography produced in foreign commerce. He, in turn, coughed up his sources. That's the way it usually works, and this makes it very risky for the people involved in distributing these materials over the Internet. The person to whom a pornographer sends stuff in a chat room might very well be an undercover agent. The suspect might think he or she is talking to somebody known, when in fact that person's computer is sitting in my office, humming away, and I am checking his or her e-mail to see who's offering child pornography.

One of the nice things about this work I'm doing is that about half the criminals we pick up turn out to be actual child molesters—not just closet perverts, but people actively involved in hurting kids. We get those people off the street.

I've Got a Secret

I worked a case that started out with a local police officer in Florida. He had been dinking around on the Internet and began writing to a guy here in Utah who believed the officer to be a young boy. The guy started sending child pornography. He also sent underwear and asked that the undercover officer masturbate into the underwear, then return it . . . weird stuff like that.

We went over and arrested the guy. He had been working in a clothing store for eighteen years and was immediately fired. He was also new to computers and didn't have a lot to offer in exchange for lighter treatment. "You're taking my computer anyway," he said, "so why don't I give you my accounts and the names of some of the people I write to?" So he gave me this information and sure enough, after about a month, I got some e-mail from a guy down in Louisiana. Along with the message, he attached a couple of images of child pornography.

I then assumed the personality of the man I had just arrested. I struck up a correspondence with the guy in Louisiana. We exchange information about the kind of stuff we're trying to get, and he sent me a few more pictures. He asked me to do some live-time discussion on the IRC. A lot of agents are reluctant to do that, but I took the plunge. He told me about the different kinds of young boys he liked, and the kinds of sex acts he liked to perform with them.

During these discussions, I try to be very nonjudgmental and to say as little as possible. The idea is to let these guys hang themselves, which is more difficult with kiddie-porn collectors than with most other criminals.

Anyway, he's been hiding behind a screen name. I quickly discovered the actual identity of this man—something I do pretty well—and then start to move him away from the Internet. That's a big step in this kind of investigation. He's been warm and happy corresponding anonymously over the computer, thinking that I don't actually know who he is. So now I lure him out onto the telephone. We talk about all kinds of things, and in many respects he's a regular guy. He has a business and is interested in sports and many normal things.

But it turns out he has a deep, dark secret. He is fascinated with young boys, and previously he has been convicted of crimes with them. I have taken him from Internet correspondence to IRC, to telephone conversation with real names (although mine was invented). At this point I have enough to charge the guy, but I decide to take it one step further, and I dangle a carrot in front of him. I told him that I was involved in a function involving young boys, and he decided that he would come out to visit. He flew out to Utah to have access to these young boys.

He got off the airplane and we met. We chatted for a few minutes, collected his bags, and walked out to the parking lot. "You know, I've got to tell you something," I said to him.

"What's that?" he asked.

"Well—I'm a cop."

"No shit?" he said, laughing. He thought it was really cool that he had a pedophile friend who was also a cop.

"Yeah," I said, "and I've got to arrest you." His eyes got as big as dinner plates. He was in shock. He dropped his bags. We placed him under arrest and took him away.

That case is a good example of how an undercover officer can work the Internet, and how the same old tricks we use to work conventional cases work with computer crime, too.

Another interesting case involved a Hollywood connection. I was investigating a pedophile who maintained a somewhat arrogant attitude in our first contacts on the Internet. He was working in Hollywood and had a lot of entertainment connections. Eventually, though, we got together and he sent me a bunch of diskettes through the mail, each loaded with child pornography. I dropped by his home to pay him a social visit and arrested him.

When he realized how serious the consequences of the arrest were, he offered to cooperate. He offered a name of somebody very well known in Hollywood. This man distributed nudist and naturist films (which are legal) but was also involved in illegal videos of young boys.

I contacted him and told him I was a film producer, working as coproducer with the first guy, who has rolled over for us and is now functioning as a snitch. I let him know that I was planning to shoot a video featuring young boys, and the guy's interest was immediately and enormously piqued. But at the same time, he was very nervous. He worked as the CEO of a company that was under investigation by the Feds for over a decade and he was very smart. "We need to meet and talk about this," I tell him, but he always evades me.

Agencies had been trying to catch him for all this time, but he had always been too smart for us. This time, though, we snagged him. He is interested in the project and wants to participate. I convinced him that if he really wants into the game, he has to put something on the table. So finally he ships me some videotapes produced in Mexico featuring young boys engaged in sex acts. The package came from a fictitious address, as is typical with these deliveries.

While I think I know what the real identity of this guy is, I am not sure. He is extremely careful. So I take the tapes to the crime lab. The crime lab dusts for prints and uses all their magic tricks. The crime-lab technician calls up and says, "Hey, Don, you've got to come over here and look at this!" He showed me how somebody had taken a spray bottle of cleaner and a rag and removed all traces of fingerprints from the tapes. Now, is that a cautious person or not?

Okay, now it's time for the next step. I tell him that we'll be shooting out in the desert and he agrees to join us. He flies in and gets off the plane with his camping gear and sleeping bag. He waits for me at the airport while I scurry around getting an arrest warrant, then I meet him. We go out for dinner, and he tells me a bit about himself. He has a degree in cinematography; he is very sharp, intelligent, and articulate. After a very nice dinner, we walk out to the parking lot and I place him under arrest. "Oh, shit!" he said. He was mortified!

It turned out that he'd served time previously for the same kind of offense. He'd been under surveillance all this time and had always managed to avoid arrest by being very careful. He was interested in bargaining with us and could have gotten a better deal, but his attorneys played hardball and he went to federal prison for a few years.

This was a case that couldn't have been made without the magic of the Internet and with careful, conventional undercover police skills.

Undercover cyberporn investigations are quite challenging, and you never know who you'll end up with. For example, I arrested a police officer who was also a pedophile and sent him to jail. I recently arrested another man who earned a huge income, had a secret clearance, and worked on government computer contracts. He was running an FTP site distributing large volumes of kiddie porn, and we seized a lot of material from him, including over nine hundred diskettes of child pornography.

Not all the cases I work involve the Internet. Some require conventional undercover techniques. For example, a book publisher in Texas recently received a letter from a man asking for pictures of young people having sex. They interpreted this as a red-flag warning and contacted the local police who called us. "We know you've done a lot of undercover child-pornography work. Can you help us out with this?"

So I created a fictitious publishing company and wrote the guy back, telling him that I had a referral from the original publisher to whom he had written. "We do carry these kinds of materials," I wrote.

He wrote back right away, very anxious to get the material. He said he was specifically interested in young boys engaged in hardcore sex. Well, at that point we had almost everything we needed for a case. All it would have taken was a controlled delivery of these materials, to ship him what he wanted, then arrest him on the spot. Instead of that, though, I wanted to find out more about him. What he was actively doing, perhaps with kids, as a result of his interest?

So I strung him along a little more, and he started sending me information about orphanages in Mexico, then he sent me children's underwear. He sent me two books, one about Catholic priests who had assaulted their alter boys. He had highlighted all the passages in the books describing sexual activity. The other book was about Wesley Allen Dodd, a man who had abducted and murdered a large number of children, and again all the passages describing murder and molestation were highlighted with a yellow marker.

With the help of the postal inspector down in Texas, a controlled delivery of materials were made to him, and he was arrested. We quickly learned he had been molesting children in his neighborhood. The walls of his room were papered with posters for missing and exploited children. We apparently got this guy off the street before he acted out some of his more extreme fantasies, but it was probably a close call.

Canadian Sunset

One thing about working undercover on the Internet, if you sell yourself convincingly to one guy, pretty soon you can be referred to somebody else, and the next thing you know you've got friends all over the place. Thanks to computers, it is a very small world.

I started getting messages from a guy in Canada who offered me a large volume of undeveloped film of children that he wanted to sell. Given the context, I thought he was suggesting that the pictures involved child pornography, although he didn't say so explicitly. He told me to call him and provided a number with a 604 area code and a password to identify myself. The 604 area code is for the city of Vancouver, and I had worked previously with the police there. I called and they told me the guy had been convicted for some sexual contact with a very young girl aged 2 or 3.

Well, what to do? He was talking about coming down to the States and selling these pictures. What was actually in them? He was telling me a bit about his sexual interests and activities. In the course of the discussion, he told me that he would be baby-sitting the following week, and that would give him a chance to make even better photographs.

I'm a law enforcement officer first and foremost, and one of the things we try to do is protect kids wherever they are. I was not about to wait for this guy to come here to bust him when there was a possibility he would molest children in Canada. We had to move, and national boundaries can't get in the way. So I called my friends in the Vancouver Police Department and said, "Listen, I think this guy is for real, and he's going to do the evil deed again. What can we do?"

I gave them all the stuff that I had here, and they obtained their warrant the following day. The day after that the Vancouver police went out to his house and busted him.

Inside his place they find over sixty rolls of undeveloped film on which were images of many neighborhood children he had been molesting. It turned out that he'd been offering free day care to the neighborhood. As memorialized on film, he had been having sex with children as well as with family pets. When I got off the witness stand, a veterinarian took my place, if that gives you any notion of how bizarre these cases can become.

You might think such cases would corrode your faith in mankind, but instead they've been very rewarding. We actually are protecting children. These have been the best cases I have ever worked. I have more sense of accomplishment when I take these guys off the street than any dope dealer or smuggler. The materials are disgusting, but you only have to look at them for a nanosecond. What's fun about these cases is the chase! You have to use all your undercover skills to find these people, to ferret them out, and build your case.

I've worked a lot of dope cases, and when you take a dope dealer off the street, somebody else takes his place almost immediately. You can always buy dope, and Customs is arresting somebody every minute for importing the stuff! But with these people, who aren't involved in a commercial enterprise, you have to find them, go into their little dens and lairs, convince them that you're one of them, gain their confidence, develop evidence against them, then put the "habeas grabbus" on them and take them to jail.

Shots Fired, Officer Down

Steve Blanusa was a Stanislaus County, California, deputy sheriff working undercover on a monumental drug case when he was shot three times by another officer, his best friend. Steve has recovered from his near-fatal wounds and can laugh about the incident now, in a wry sort of way, and he's still good friends with the other officer. The incident, and the tape recording made as it happened, are used around the country to help train officers and agents to avoid a recurrence.

This happened on March 21, 1988. I was working a detail called STIC (Special Team Investigating Crimes) and sitting in my office. The phone rang and a patrolman called to say, "I just picked up a Mexican guy for beating his wife. Enroute to the jail he starts telling me about a big drug dealer for whom he's been hauling cocaine. Would you be interested in debriefing him?"

The man was hauled into my office and the interview began. He readily told me that he had just taken seven kilos of coke up to Oregon and delivered it to a rich realtor. He also told me about his connection up there, a man named Jose Lopez, and that we could find a ton of cocaine in the back of a small bar in the town of

Crow's Landing. He claimed that he and a number of other "mules" were responsible for distributing this coke from the bar all over the western United States.

While we were talking, he says to me, "You know, you look exactly like the guy I just delivered to in Oregon. You could pass for his twin brother!"

That was provocative. "Well," I said, "do you think you could introduce me to Jose? Maybe I could buy some coke from him."

"I don't know why not. I'll try to set it up."

We set up a dummy booking sheet for him. He was booked for assault on his wife and released on bail. Then I told him, "You need to contact Jose. Tell him that the realtor's brother wants to buy some cocaine. See if you can set it up."

Sure enough, he calls me the next day and says, "I talked to him and he said for you to come down here to Modesto, and he'll make a deal with you for three kilos."

My unit was normally dealing with nickel and dime street-level dealers, and we didn't have the funds on hand to cover this deal. I went to my commander who told me to work with the county drug task force on the case. I called the commander of that unit, and we put together $50,000 to buy the three kilos of coke.

The informant set the deal up for a Monday delivery. He said we were to meet at the Chalet, a cheap motel in Modesto. The dealer expected me to be traveling down from Oregon. Jose was supposed to bring the three kilos to the motel, I would flash the $50,000 cash, and the deal would be done. "Be careful," he said, "these guys are gangsters; they carry guns. Be careful of a rip-off!"

The guys on the task force and I put our plan together. Once they produced the coke and I tested it, they would be arrested, a "buy-bust" in the trade. If they actually came up with three kilos of real cocaine, we were about to make the biggest "hand-to-hand" drug bust in the history of the county.

We set up in a seedy motel with the surveillance and five-man arrest team in one room and the informant and me in the one next door. The whole motel is surrounded by undercover officers waiting for the deal to go down. About 4:30 on Monday afternoon, two Hispanic males arrive, but instead of Jose, the big dealer, one of them is his nephew.

They had the dope in a zippered bag. We unzipped it, and instead of three kilos they bring just one. I flash the $50,000. I tested the kilo, and it seems to be good stuff.

"Is there more than that?" I asked them.

"No, just one kilo," he says.

"It was supposed to be *three* kilos," I told him. "Where are the other ones?"

"We gotta go get them."

"Well, I have to catch a plane at 9:30 from Sacramento," I said. "It's 7:30 now. How long is it going to take you?"

"Fifteen minutes!"

They start to take off, still holding my cash. The single kilo is on the table.

"No, leave the money, and you can take the kilo and go get the other two. If you guys want the money, go get the other two. I came a long way for three kilos, and I don't want to go all the way back up to Oregon with just one! Either you want to make the deal or not!"

"Yeah, we want to deal"

"Well, I brought the money. Here it is, you can see I got it. If you don't want to deal, just tell me. I'm getting tired. I got to catch a plane back to Oregon. I'm not going to fuck with just one kilo. Hurry up!"

"We'll be back in three minutes!" one says, and then they are gone.

As soon as they are safely away, I report into the surveillance audio system, "I got one kilo sitting here in the room. They've gone back to get the other two, so DO NOT BUST, DO NOT BUST, DO NOT BUST! They are going to come back with the other two. Let them go! Can you guys hear me? I have one kilo sitting here in the bedroom; they've gone to get the other two. They *have not*, repeat, *have not* taken any money with them. I have the money."

After a few minutes, the phone rings. It is one of the surveillance team reporting that the pair have returned. "They're here," I tell the informant. We get ready.

But they don't have the dope. They want the money for the first kilo, apparently to buy the other two. "Let me tell you again," I say, "I'm not going to take a chance getting back on the plane with just one kilo. It's just not worth it! So I'm going to take my money, and I am leaving! If you don't want to make the deal, fine. I'll go elsewhere! I don't know you; you don't know me, but you know I have the money. You've seen it."

"Okay, okay," one says, "we'll go get it."

As soon as the pair left, I went next door to talk to the arrest team about ripping them off. We already have a case because they have, in essence, sold me the single kilo. "Why don't we just burn these guys," I said, "and keep the dope? The informant can stay here and tell them I burned them for the coke."

"No, these guys will come back with two more kilos. When they do, that will make it the biggest buy in the history of the county. Let's wait it out."

Two hours later the two guys come back, but they don't have any more dope. Now they want the money for the first kilo, they say they can't get any more.

"Three kilos or nothing," I tell them.

"We'll be right back," they say, and they take off again.

While they are gone, we all rehearse the bust. The signal for the arrest team to come charging in will be when I say, "Looks like good coke to me." As soon as I give the signal, I am supposed to lie on the floor by the bed. That way, if there is any shooting when the team came in, I will be out of the line of fire. Just before the pair comes back, one of the team says to me, "You're doing good, brother!" In spite of the difficulties with the dealers, we seem to have the operation under control.

Within a short time the pair returns, with two more kilos of cocaine. While I am testing it, one of them comes around to watch what I am doing. He stands right where I am supposed to lie on the floor. If I follow the plan, I will crash into this guy at the knees. Instead, I decide to back away from him.

The coke tests okay. "Seems like good coke to me," I say, giving the signal. I started backing away and notice that the guy next to me seems to be going for a concealed gun. Acting on reflexes, I go for my own gun just as the arrest team enters the room through a door on my left.

"Freeze! Police! Freeze!"

The first officer through the door sees, through the dim light, somebody holding a gun, and it is pointed at the spot where I am supposed to be! He starts shooting, and the guy behind him starts to fire, too. They fire eight rounds, three of which hit me, one in the left wrist, one in the back, and one in the groin.

You hear stories about such experiences, and how things start to move in slow motion. That's the way it worked for me. I remember having my gun on this guy, then feeling a sharp pain, and looking over at my left wrist. All I could see of it was white bone and tendon.

Almost immediately I got hit in the back, and I remember thinking, *Why are you guys still shooting? You've already hit me twice!* I was thinking about dropping to the ground to avoid getting hit again when I got shot in the groin. It was all recorded on tape, and I have listened to it many times. The whole thing was over in two seconds. The events seemed to happen in slow motion, but my mind was racing!

The shot in the groin was the worst pain I can imagine anybody experiencing. It felt like somebody reached inside and ripped me open from left to right. I thought they shot my dick off.

All eight shots were fired within about one second. On the surveillance tape you hear a short burst of overlapping pops followed by the sound of me gasping.

I started screaming and swearing. "GOD DAMN, YOU FUCKERS! YOU SHOT ME, YOU FUCKERS!"

The motel room erupts in confusion. Somebody yells, "Get an ambulance!"

I was so angry! My buddies, Raul DeLeon and Gary Deckard, who served with me on the SWAT team, had shot me. On the tape you can Raul wail in grief, "I'm sorry!"

I yelled and swore at them all at the top of my voice for several minutes.

"Just tell me where you're shot," Dave Yonan asks, holding me in his arms as I lay on the floor.

"I'm shot in the back, I'm shot in the leg, I'm shot in the arm, Dave!" I said. "They blew my dick off!"

"You're going to be all right," he says.

"I'm *not*, man. You guys shot me in the nuts," I said. "I think you got me in an artery. *You better get me the fuck out of here!*"

"Blue," he said, "don't worry about your dick! You've got two holes in your back!" He thought both were entrance wounds.

At this point, police humor starts to take over. My sergeant, Myron Larson, showed up. "Myron," I told him, "you've gotta check and see if it's still there!"

They started stripping my clothes away, and Myron smiles and says, "Blue, I think it's still there!" I knew I was all right then because I had been thinking, *If it is gone, just go ahead and put me out of my misery!*

Dave told me later, "When you were cussing and screaming, I was sure you were going to make it. Your color was good, but as soon as you started to calm down, you turned white and went into shock, and I got really worried."

I was worried too. I kept thinking I was about to die in this cheap, sleazy motel room.

The aftermath in the room was very chaotic. The arrest team went essentially crazy. "If he dies, you're dead, you fucking assholes!" Dave screams at the two bewildered Mexican dealers, still thinking that they had been the shooters.

We were just two minutes from the hospital, and some of the guys were screaming that they should load me up into a patrol car and transport me that way. Others insisted we wait for the paramedics, and that's what they did. The ambulance was there within five minutes.

I was very fortunate. All the shots were fired from my left side toward my right, and none penetrated the chest cavity. The first bullet went cleanly through my wrist. The second shot to the back entered just below the shoulder blade and exited by my spine. The third entered in front of my left hip socket, went across the lower abdomen, then into my right leg. If I had been facing them, those shots would have fatal.

Another thing that saved me was that my department had changed over from three-fifty-seven Magnum pistols to nine-millimeters just a month before, and the nine-millimeter is notorious for doing far less damage. Had we still been using the Magnum, I would have been gone almost immediately. The exit wound on my back was right on the spine, and the Magnum would have blown my spine out. Both the shooters, Raul and Gary, and I had all been on the SWAT team and had trained to make head shots in such a situation, but both aimed for "center-of-mass" this time, another lucky break.

There were a lot of lessons learned. Raul had previously been trained that the undercover officer *never* pulls a gun, but in my unit it was common for the undercover officer to help with the arrest, often by holding the suspect at gunpoint. We also discovered that none of the suspects had guns or weapons.

The residual physical damage to me has been minor. The emotional damage has been more serious and long-lasting, and although I recovered from the physical wounds, I resigned from the sheriff's department and am no longer in law enforcement.

Raul and I are still the best of friends. He took it harder than anybody and has had a lot of problems with guilt over the incident. He named his son after me, and when I was awarded the Medal of Valor for the shooting last year, he presented it to me. It was a very emotional presentation, and there wasn't a dry eye in the house.

The tape of the incident is played around the country in officer-survival training sessions.

Afterword

Law enforcement, particularly undercover law enforcement, can sometimes be a funny business. It is probably the most dangerous, most difficult, and most challenging role for any cop in any department or agency. It is the kind of job where you can make a lot of arrests or get shot by your best friend. It is a job where you can take tons of marijuana off the street, put a dealer in child pornography in prison, or stop a money-laundering operation handling millions of dollars and operating in many countries. Sometimes you can win your case and still feel like a failure.

It really does take a special kind of officer or agent to work successfully undercover—someone who can play a role, act a part, and still retain a high level of integrity. As Don Newcomer's story reveals, it is easy to get sucked into close personal relationships with people for whom you may have strong sympathy, but who you must arrest and charge nonetheless.

Undercover work is not something most people can do for a whole career. The experience is abrasive, personally and professionally, physically and emotionally. Most of the officers and agents whose stories appear in this book have moved on to other assignments or have retired, some with happy memories, others disillusioned and disappointed.

Some, like Ron Martinelli and Special Agent Anonymous, are full-time trainers of law enforcement officers and agents. Some are retired after long careers. A couple quit law enforcement as a result of the undercover assignment's aftermath.

Anthony Tait is still being pursued by the Hells Angels. He and Tim McKinley managed to evade an apparent assassination attempt recently as both emerged from court after testifying in a Hells Angels murder case.

Others, like Bonni Tischler, use their own experience to refine and adjust the art form, directing their agency's undercover operations and training a new crop of eager young agents.

Covert law enforcement operations have grown, evolved, and been improved during the past fifteen years or so, and these stories represent the full spectrum of that time and experience. Thanks to these officers and agents, anyone engaged in any kind of criminal activity, from prostitution to money laundering to drug manufacture and distribution, can never be entirely sure who they're dealing with. Criminals now know that law enforcement officers can pop out of the woodwork to make an arrest any time, anywhere, coming out from under cover.

Then she shot him right in the head, to be on the safe side.